Indigenous Discourses on Knowledge and Development in Africa

African social development is often explained from outsider perspectives that are mainly European and Euro-American, leaving African indigenous discourses and ways of knowing and doing absent from discussions and debates on knowledge and development. This book is intended to present Africanist indigenous voices in current debates on economic, educational, political and social development in Africa. The authors and contributors to the volume present bold and timely ideas and scholarship for defining Africa through its challenges, possible policy formations, planning and implementation at the local, regional, and national levels. The book also reveals insightful examinations of the hype, the myths and the realities of many topics of concern with respect to dominant development discourses, and challenges the misconceptions and misrepresentations of indigenous perspectives on knowledge productions and overall social well-being or lack thereof. The volume brings together researchers who are concerned with comparative education, international development, and African development, research and practice in particular. Policy makers, institutional planners, education specialists, governmental and non-governmental managers and the wider public should all benefit from the contents and analyses of this book.

Edward Shizha is Associate Professor in Contemporary Studies at Wilfrid Laurier University (Brantford) in Canada.

Ali A. Abdi is Professor and Co-director, Centre for Global Citizenship Education and Research (CGCER) in the Department of Educational Policy Studies at the University of Alberta.

Routledge African Studies

1 **Facts, Fiction, and African Creative Imaginations**
Edited by Toyin Falola and Fallou Ngom

2 **The Darfur Conflict**
Geography or Institutions?
Osman Suliman

3 **Music, Performance and African Identities**
Edited by Toyin Falola and Tyler Fleming

4 **Environment and Economics in Nigeria**
Edited by Toyin Falola and Adam Paddock

5 **Close to the Sources**
Essays on Contemporary African Culture, Politics and Academy
Abebe Zegeye and Maurice Vambe

6 **Landscape and Environment in Colonial and Postcolonial Africa**
Edited by Toyin Falola and Emily Brownell

7 **Development, Modernism and Modernity in Africa**
Edited by Augustine Agwuele

8 **Natural Resources, Conflict, and Sustainable Development**
Lessons from the Niger Delta
Edited by Okechukwu Ukaga, Ukoha O. Ukiwo and Ibaba Samuel Ibaba

9 **Regime Change and Succession Politics in Africa**
Five Decades of Misrule
Edited by Maurice Nyamanga Amutabi and Shadrack Wanjala Nasong'o

10 **The Political Economy of Development and Underdevelopment in Africa**
Edited by Toyin Falola and Jessica Achberger

11 **Pan-Africanism, and the Politics of African Citizenship and Identity**
Edited by Toyin Falola and Kwame Essien

12 **Securing Africa**
Local Crises and Foreign Interventions
Edited by Toyin Falola and Charles Thomas

13 **African Youth in Contemporary Literature and Popular Culture**
Identity Quest
Edited by Vivian Yenika-Agbaw and Lindah Mhando

14 **Indigenous Discourses on Knowledge and Development in Africa**
Edited by Edward Shizha and Ali A. Abdi

Indigenous Discourses on Knowledge and Development in Africa

Edited by Edward Shizha and Ali A. Abdi

Routledge
Taylor & Francis Group
New York London

First published 2014
by Routledge
711 Third Avenue, New York, NY 10017

and by Routledge
2 Park Square, Milton Park, Abingdon, Oxon OX14 4RN

First issued in paperback 2017

Routledge is an imprint of the Taylor & Francis Group, an informa business

Library of Congress Cataloging-in-Publication Data

Indigenous discourses on knowledge and development in Africa / edited by Edward Shizha and Ali A. Abdi.
pages cm. — (Routledge African studies ; 14)
Includes bibliographical references and index.
1. Ethnoscience—Africa. 2. Indigenous peoples—Education—Africa. 3. Economic development—Effect of education on—Africa. 4. Economic development—Social aspects—Africa. 5. Social planning—Africa. 6. Africa—Social policy. 7. Africa—Politics and government. I. Shizha, Edward. II. Abdi, Ali A., 1955–
GN645.I524 2014
338.96—dc23
2013024021

ISBN 13: 978-1-138-09263-1 (pbk)
ISBN 13: 978-0-415-70336-9 (hbk)

Typeset in Sabon
by IBT Global.

Contents

Tables

Acknowledgments

As any book, this volume has been a result of the involvement of many people. We are grateful to all those colleagues, students and others who have, in one way or another and over the years, encouraged or even inspired us through their work and friendship. They have motivated us to advance, as much as we can, the timeliness and expanding importance of African knowledge contexts and the anti-hegemonic or liberating discursive formations that inform them. Beyond this wide recognition, we are, of course, grateful to the contributors who, despite the heavy pressures on their times, accepted our invitation to submit chapters, and it is with their contributions that the physicality of this work is now with us. For our families, our consistent gratitude is always present for their support and understanding. Finally, we would like to thank the Routledge team of Max Novick and Jennifer Morrow as well as Edward Perella and Michael Watters of Integrated Book Techonology for their patience and support.

Introduction

Indigenous Discourses on Knowledge and Development in Africa

Edward Shizha and Ali A. Abdi

This book focuses on different possibilities and analyses that emanate from and are, with different emphasis, attached to indigenous discourses on knowledge and development in Africa. Discourses are conceptualized as multidimensional and interactive processes where the boundaries between social life, social events and language are less relevant (Dyck, 2005). By indigenous discourses in this book, we mean a way of telling the African narrative about knowledge, education and development in diverse African cultural voices in ways that decolonize our minds. As such, all ideas, perspectives and epistemic connections that are about Africa and especially constructed by Africans qualify, in our understanding and observations, as indigenous knowledge. The reason for this expansive generalist assumption should be clear. Indigenous knowledge defines and is a response to the way people live in a given socio-cultural context over a period of time. And it is via this experience that people construct the way they explain, control and manage their lives, and as well as how they relate to their attendant social and physical environments. That should include all aspects of family context and relations, ways of learning and attaching meaning to learning systems and aspects of political, economic and technological management.

With respect to the term discourses, we use it pluralistically for we are cognizant of the fact that there are different forms and structures of discourses as well as diverse ways in which African communities construct actual and emergent discursive formations that speak and can act upon their lives. Undeniably, we could unreservedly use the term 'discourse' in the Foucauldian notion that includes not only communicative practices, but also "systems of social and political practice more generally, as well as the ideological systems that animate these wide fields of practice" (Beier, Michael & Sherzer, 2002, p. 121). This, therefore, implies that our application of indigenous discourses is both socio-cultural and political. Discourses are patterns of life that are more than the linguistic element, therefore in this book, language components are not the intended primary platforms that are analytically referenced. We knowingly focus on the social, ideological, political, even selectively, the economic, elements of the debate. Whereas the discursive patterns of African ethnic/social groups remain highly specified and distinct, the recognition of a shared social space as the basis for a shared discursive space where relevant knowledge is shared (Greymorning, 2000) creates more room for previously alienated voices within academic and development discourses (Dyck, 2005). The experience of colonialism and imported knowledges creates a common bond between the formerly colonized African countries. This common bond has important epistemic and learning signposts that continue to serve as reference points as well as practices of resistance to Africa's onto-epistemological and educational deformations where colonialism deliberately attempted to extinguish all elements of African traditional knowledge systems that were established to actively respond to the continent's progress and general well-being. Hence, the situatedness of the concerned discourses in ongoing (even if selectively weakened) indigenous worldviews are anchored in "belief systems, decision making, assumptions and modes of problem solving" (Hart, 2010, p. 1). Certainly, the connections and the interactive nature of all these is what assures the survivabilities of indigenous ways of seeing, doing and responding to the world.

It was not only during the colonial era that African indigenous epistemic systems were problematically deconstructed, but even after political independence in most African countries, indigenous discourses were and continue to be marginalized by the indigenous post-colonial elite who did/do not challenge much of the colonizers' projects in this domain. It is only in recent years when this critical strand of thought has been recognized as an important critical opposition to the *modernity/coloniality* perspective. Modernity and coloniality are inseparable when applied in the context of formerly colonized African nations. Coloniality was a form of hegemonic modernity that was targeted at harvesting, expropriating and appropriating African resources. Indeed, in the way modernity's academic luminaries including Huntington (1971) and Rostow (1990) taught it, its depictions of Africa and other colonized spaces of the world were both theoretically and practically exclusionist. These non-European or non-Euro-American locations of the world were stuck in de-rationalized tempo-spatial conjectures that rendered their peoples primitive, backward and in need of modernist salvation. It was then, through this Eurocentric reading of the world, where knowledge superiority assumptions were made and colonialism itself was partially justified. Certainly, the academic writing about the dichotomy between modern and traditional was started long before the professional reign of Huntington, Rostow and others like them, and was actually advanced by some of the so-called luminaries of European philosophy, history and politics (Abdi, 2008).

Therefore, coloniality/modernity refers to the fact that the relationship between colonialism and coloniality is structural and persisting, and that colonialism, as a large parcel of the enlightenment driven project is not yet over (Suárez-Krabbe, 2009) but being re-enacted through neo-liberal globalization and development paradigms. Central to both colonialism and coloniality, is that the global ethnoracial hierarchy that was constructed by hegemonic and colonizing modernist paradigms remains the main organizing principle of social relations on a world scale (Quijano, 2000). Anchoring African knowledge and development in indigenous discourses is a way of disrupting the global ethnoracial hierarchy, hence in turn presenting African ideas of development on the global scale on equal terms to other paradigms, and from there challenging the Eurocentric perspective that tends to perceive indigenous Africans as incapable of achieving their own forms of development. This counter-colonial indigenous perspective also challenges and deconstructs what we term 'coloniality of knowledge' that has clouded our mental capacities, our indigenous epistemologies and our ontologies.

The continuing coloniality of knowledge involves Eurocentric practices that marginalize local discourses and dictate that the only discourse for articulating ideas and development is a Euro-American one. Anibal Quijano (2000) argues that the coloniality of knowledge keeps us from accepting the idea of being knowing subjects outside the confines of 'modern' epistemic rationality, whereas Enrique Dussel (1995) and Walter Mignolo (2000) note that, within Western intellectual practice, the coloniality of knowledge is a process of translating and rewriting other cultures, other knowledges, other ways of being and presuming commensurability through Western rationality. In this book, we argue that Africa does not need to be lectured on what is desirable and worthwhile knowledge for social, educational, political and socio-economic development. Africa possessed and still possesses adequate local knowledges and practices that have driven the engine for Africa's development. Without such indigenous notions and practices of development, Africans would not have thrived over millennia in the historiographical points and platforms of explaining, doing and achieving. The epistemic coloniality and counter-cultural modernity want us to believe that Africans were devoid of such primary realities of life, which not only tragically but also totally irrationally announces their benighted ideas (only ideas), invasion and conquest of other people's lands and livelihoods.

Our pointed criticisms of the global hegemonic world in ideas and knowledges do not negate the fact that we now live in a globalized world, but in such context a change has to happen, and such change should lead to a situation where African indigenous knowledge systems and discourses of development can be equally considered when policies and programs that affect the African people are being debated and implemented within or outside Africa. African indigenous knowledges and discourses of development should be recognized and acknowledged for their value outside what Sandra Hoagland (forthcoming) describes as a discursive enactment of colonial relations. African knowledge and development require decolonization and freedom from being perceived as colonized practices "in the context of today's global [presumptively] polycentric capitalism" (Suárez-Krabbe, 2009, p. 7). Africa continues to lag behind other continents, such as Asia, because African nations have fallen into the capitalist trap that has encouraged a form of 'counterfeit development' rather than genuine development. Counterfeit development is false and fake development that results from blindly following imitative paradigms postulated by Western agents. A reinvention of Western modernity has proved to be a futile project for Africa. Therefore, Africa has to re-think and re-engage development partners on its own terms. Indeed, one way that African knowledges and development platforms have been continuously negated in the past 60 or so years has been the way African development was designed and decided outside Africa (Ake, 1996), complemented by the draconian imposition of neoliberal globalization's structural adjustment programs (SAPs) which have not only suppressed the continent's knowledge and social development, but have also suppressed the presence as well as the advancement of African indigenous debates and inventive capacities (Abdi, 2013).

In this book, the decolonization of African indigenous discourses and ways of doing are presented in an anti-colonial, anti-racist and anti-Western perspective. The purpose of the indigenous discourses, particularly African propositions, is to highlight the capabilities and philosophical thinking inherent in the people of Africa. More often than not, Africa has tended to follow blindly knowledge and development discourses that are imported from Western regimes and paradigms. These development discourses include everything from public management contexts to general epistemologies of education and related analyses of continental and global issues that affect the lives of Africans. Through indigenous discourses, we as African people should be able to define who we are, and define and determine our destiny without having to make reference to Western definitions that misrepresent our socio-economic needs and social development interests. Here we give credit to Taiaiake Alfred and Jeff Corntassel who propose the following about indigenous self-representation and determination:

> It is still true that the first part of self-determination is the self. In our minds and in our souls, we need to reject the colonists' control and authority, their definition of who we are and what our rights are, their definition of what is worthwhile and how one should live, their hypocritical and pacifying moralities. We need to rebel against what they want us to become, start remembering the qualities of our ancestors and act on those remembrances. This is the kind of spiritual revolution that will ensure our survival. (2005, p. 598)

Recently, the realization and acknowledgment of indigenous perspectives have begun to bear fruits. The new ways of not only reconstructing colonially deformed epistemic and discursive locations of life, but also of achieving a comprehensive scheme of cultural and mental decolonizations (wa Thiong'o, 1986; Achebe, 2000) are important and timely. Surely, there is a growing desire and determination by Africans and others around the world to redeem for themselves and future generations reconstructed knowledge and knowing clusters that re-affirm their histories and contemporary needs as they are situated within local communities and meaningful living relationships. These emerging realities are not, as we said earlier, an attempt to delink Africa and Africans from the rest of the world (in post-facto, that is basically impossible), but more than in any time in recent history, to accord us a sense of viable attachment to present beings and futures. To achieve this, indigenous discourses and indigenous knowledges are being applied in different disciplines, such as education, sustainable development, environmental studies, agriculture, rural development, aqua-culture, animal husbandry, social sciences, health science, cultural studies, language and linguistics and many other branches of social sciences (Islam, 2012). The application of the discourses arises from a consciousness that they can no longer be ignored in the well-being and welfare of indigenous and non-indigenous people.

In Africa, about 60% of its population lives in rural areas where they depend largely on their indigenous worldviews to solve problems that affect their well-being and social development. As such, their lives and development rely on their ontological, epistemological, methodological and axiological frameworks. Relating indigenous propositions to social development in Asia/Pacific and Africa, Kapoor and Shizha (2010) contend that indigenous discourses and worldviews are about "engaging indigenous post-mortems/critical appreciations and expositions of the colonial project of modernity and its tentacular manifestations" (p. 1). Colonial modernity that has appeared in the form of present global economic and political configurations has the danger and unwarranted possibility of re-imposing outsider (Euro-Americentric) paradigms to the African human–ecology relations. Indigenous worldviews provide a counterhegemonic perspective to knowledge production and the use of that knowledge in education and health systems, as well as in the general development discourse.

In our attempts to explain our social reality therefore, our worldviews are likely to be shaped and affected by the discourses we utilize. The concept of worldviews has been described by Olsen, Lodwick and Dunlap in Hart (2010, p. 2) as "mental lenses that are entrenched ways of perceiving the world". They are cognitive, perceptual and affective maps that people continuously use to make sense of their social world. They are also used to define goals and means of achieving those goals. McKenzie and Morrissette (2003) explained that indigenous worldviews emerged as a result of the people's close relationship with the environment. Consequently, they influence knowledge production and affect how development projects are designed, planned and carried out. This implies that indigenous knowledge systems are a combination of knowledge systems that encompass technology, social, economic, philosophical learning/educational, legal and governance systems. Indigenous discourses and perspectives have a high potential for embedding knowledge and development in the worldview of the affected. Therefore, African indigenous perspectives are vital for social development in Africa.

Indeed, if Africa is to have a viable chance to developmentally move faster, and relatively speaking, catch up with the world, African researchers and policymakers have to design heavy situationally-effective schemes that reconstruct the ways we create and conduct our educational, political, economic and socio-cultural programs, which should all be designed for the primary well-being of *dadka Afrikaanka ah* (African people).

Surveys have shown that indigenous perspectives perform well in risk avoidance and management, ecosystem maintenance and human health (Eyong, 2007). The perspectives provide guidelines for social equity, relationships with non-human beings, ecological responsibility and respect for the supernatural. Every society has a history behind its knowledge resources, which guides its development process. Time passage and contact with others affect knowledge systems as well as a society's development. Subsequently, some development theorists propose a hybridization of indigenous discourses and modernist perspectives. However, when hybridization is preferred, caution should be taken to guard against colonial representations (Kapoor & Shizha, 2010) and "colonial assimilation projects, neglect, diminishment and racism" (Battiste, 2008, p. 85). Generally, what some proponents of hybridization may not pay enough attention to are the realities of differential power relations where the interchangeability of power and knowledge (as Foucault, among others, advised us to consider) would technically and surely socio-politically advantage currently more established epistemes than marginalized ones, thus continually sidelining indigenous knoweldges, but this time with an added danger of falsely masquerading as representing diverse clusters of learning and knowing.

Indigenous discourses are accepted worldwide as important in social and sustainable development. Africa's survival depends on reinvigorating Africanized discourses on knowledge and development. Western models of development have not been successful in pushing forward Africa's agenda for development. Since colonial times, Africa's development has been defined as the subject that is approached only in terms of the concept of rationality constructed by modern Western epistemology. Western scientific practice thus positions the Western 'agent', 'researchers', 'intellectuals' and 'advisors' as the judges of credibility in defining African development. Much of the violation of our humanity and self-confidence as instigators of our own development as African societies has originated from the rejection or misunderstanding of our African indigenous discursive structures. As long as we allow ourselves and our modes of development to be judged by the criteria selected by outsiders, we run the risk of indulging in "the politics of *development as dispossession* and *development as violence*" (Kapoor, 2010, p. 25, emphasis in original) as it pertains to claims of knowledge and technology by the West.

Whether, as African scholars, we engage in debates that question and critique African leadership, governance, education systems, knowledge constructions or development, these debates should be anchored in indigenous discourses. We should be conscious of our self and cultural identities, sensibilities, consciousness and positionalities in a world in which Africa continues to be stigmatized. As Kapoor and Shizha (2010) astutely observe and encourage, as we engage in our struggles and aspirations, we should appeal to our history, origins, priorities, culture, culturally-embedded political economies and common struggles with modernist hegemony. Self-identification is definitely at the heart of African indigenous discourses/post-colonialism, which is the dominant approach utilized by contributors to this volume. What we propose in this book is an African indigenous discourse-centered approach to expanded notations of knowledge, education, political governance, social development and overall prospects of meaning making and acting on those meanings in ways that can finally benefit the extensively marginalized African public.

ORGANIZATION OF THE BOOK

This book is organized in three interrelated parts, each focusing on a specific theme. Part 1, "Indigenous Knowledge and Development", has three chapters that focus on the relationship between indigenous knowledges and sustainable economic development in Africa. In Chapter 1, "Reflections on 'African Development': Situating Indigeneity and Indigenous Knowledges", George Sefa Dei [Nana Sefa Atweneboah I] provides insights into African development that is situated in indigeneity and indigenous knowledges. The chapter discusses five discursive positions: the coloniality of 'Western-style' development, African intellectual and academic responsibility, the power of African local culture resource knowledge for 'development', re-thinking of science, technology and culture in 'development' and possibilities for creating African 'Centres of Excellence on Indigenous Knowledges and Languages'. His discursive critique of 'development' is intended to bring home the possibilities of 'something different' in development pursuits, one that is remarkably different from the current Euro-American discourse that is currently applied to African 'problems'. In Chapter 2, "Intersections Between Indigenous Knowledge and Economic Development in Africa", Gloria Emeagwali explores the intersections between indigenous knowledge and economic development in Africa, and reflects on Africa's indigenous technology and development strategy in light of current technologization of developments. Emeagwali argues that countries in Africa have been afflicted by two external economic models namely, 'the colonial model of exploitation' between the 16th and 20th centuries and 'the neo-colonial economic model' between the 1960s and today. She also discusses the extent to which Africa's indigenous knowledge systems should be important variables in Africa's quest to develop. Indigenization is a concept that forms the foundation of Ngoni Makuvaza's Chapter 3, "Indigenization and Sustainable Development for Zimbabwe: A Post-Colonial Philosophical Perspective".

Makuvaza contributes to the indigenization–development debate, with particular reference to Zimbabwe's '*upfumi kuvanhu*' (empowerment) philosophy. According to Makuvaza, his thesis is to develop an indigenous discourse of development that is not 'mimetic', but rather genuine, holistic and beneficial to the majority of Zimbabweans.

The five chapters in Part 2, "Indigenous Knowledge, Culture and Education", focus on the intersections between indigenous knowledge, culture and education. In Chapter 4, "Re-Culturing De-Cultured Education for Inclusive Social Development in Africa", Ali Abdi proposes a reconceptualization of African education to endorse inclusive social development in Africa. Abdi argues that in Africa, we cannot afford to ignore the extensity and centrality of the cultural dimension in education and any analytical discussion of social development. Edward Shizha's Chapter 5, "Counter-Visioning Contemporary African Education: Indigenous Science as a Tool for African Development", echoes Abdi's sentiments. Shizha advocates the use of indigenous sciences in education, and argues that indigenous sciences are fundamental to socio-economic development in Africa. His conclusion is that education for social development in contemporary post-colonial Africa should be founded on the principle of heterogeneity of knowledges in creating a vision for socio-economic development through inclusive science. In Chapter 6, "Reclaiming the Education for All Agenda in Africa: Prospects for Inclusive Policy Spaces", Musembi Nungu, remonstrates the failure of education for all (EFA) policies and proposes reclaiming the EFA agenda in Africa through implementing inclusive policy spaces. Nungu's chapter highlights the limitations of externally driven policy agendas, and eventually, suggests possibilities for locally-driven and inclusive policy spaces that are guided by an Afrocentric discourse or philosophy of education.

In Chapter 7, "Education Inequality and Economic Development in Eastern and Southern Africa", Oliver Masakure examines educational inequalities in Eastern and Southern Africa and their consequences on economic development. According to Masakure, economic development in Sub-Saharan Africa has trailed most other world regions over the past four decades and education inequality explains part of the story. His chapter provides a brief overview of studies on the relationship between economic development and inequality (wealth and education) and further describes the research methodology and empirical results derived from applying the education Gini index. Grace Rwiza's Chapter 8, "Learning by Doing: Julius Nyerere's Education Policy for Self-Reliance in Tanzania", unveils Tanzania's struggle with Julius Nyerere's education policy for self-reliance in Tanzania. The chapter focuses on the influence of the 'learning by doing' principle, a philosophy that was articulated in Tanzania's education and training policies and practices. Rwiza's chapter analyzes philosophical foundations of education for self-reliance (ESR) policy and the principle of learning by doing and their influence on teaching and learning. Touorouzou

Some's Chapter 9, "A Diploma for a Debt: Students' Perception of Their Student Loan Program in Burkina Faso", analyzes students' perception of their student loan program in Burkina Faso. This chapter is based on a study that was conducted to elicit the meanings that students at the University of Ouagadougou in Burkina Faso make about the student loan in the framework of cost sharing, through ethnographic interviews.

Part 3, "Politics and Development", has five chapters that deal with questions of politics and political development, governance and leadership. In Chapter 10, "International Corporate Politics and the Hubris of Development Discourses", Desmond Odugu discusses international corporate politics and the hubris of development discourses. This chapter outlines a convergence of ideas among mainstream historiography of international organization's legitimacy and critiques the assumption that a purely materialist conception of development is the primacy of the state as a viable agent of positive social change. In Chapter 11, "The Dual Sources of Political Development in Ethiopia and the Emergence of Ethnic Federalism", Berhanu Demeke analyzes the dual sources of political development in Ethiopia and the emergence of ethnic federalism. Demeke provides a historical analysis of Ethiopia's current political development. From a methodological point of view, the chapter argues for a balanced approach, one that takes both external and internal factors into account to provide an accurate picture of the country's current state of political development. Leadership and governance in Sub-Saharan Africa are issues that Lamine Diallo and Ginette Lafrenière deal with in Chapter 12, "Leadership and Governance in Sub-Saharan Africa: Conceptual and Historical Perspectives". The chapter integrates an analysis of leadership and governance in Africa using a multidisciplinary perspective and demonstrates how in current leadership and governance discourses leadership is becoming a central variable of governance practice and evaluation, and a key variable of governance strategies in the international development agenda.

In Chapter 13, "Revisiting the African Revolutionary Praxis in the Global Era", Siendou Konate reminds us that globalism and globalization have ruined cultural differences and identities. According to Siendou, culture remains a tool of resistance *par excellence* in a globalized world/village. The author concludes that Africans should revisit their revolutionary praxis in order to re-appropriate the potentialities of their people's culture so as to counter the ever-growing force of globalism. To conclude the book, in the final chapter, "The Shifting Boundaries of the African State in Agricultural Institutions and Policies in an Era of Globalization", Korbla Puplampu examines theoretical and policy contexts that have specific implications for the state's role in national development. He analyzes the similarities and differences in the historical and contemporary role of the African state in the agricultural policy and institutional framework. Drawing on the ensuing analysis, the chapter reconceptualizes the role of the state in African agricultural development in an era of globalization.

REFERENCES

Abdi, A.A. (2008). Europe and African thought systems and philosophies of education: 'Re-culturing' the trans-temporal discourses. *Cultural Studies*, 22(2), 309–327.

Abdi, A.A. (2013). Intensive globalizations of African education: Re-interrogating the relevance of Structural Adjustment Programs (SAPs). In Y. Hebert & A. Abdi (Eds.), *Critical perspectives on international education* (pp. 349–362). Rotterdam, Netherlands: Sense Publishers.

Achebe, C. (2000). *Home and exile*. New York: Oxford University Press.

Ake, C. (1996). *Democracy and Development in Africa*. Washington, D.C.: The Brookings Institution.

Alfred T. & Corntassel, J. (2005). Being indigenous: Resurgences against contemporary colonialism. *Government and Opposition*, 40(4), 597–614.

Battiste, M. (2008). The struggle and renaissance of indigenous knowledge in Eurocentric education". In M. Villegas, S.R. Neugebauer & K.R. Venegas (Eds.), *Indigenous knowledge and education: Site of struggle, strength, and survivance*. Cambridge: Harvard Education Review.

Beier, C., Michael, L. & Sherzer, J. (2002). Discourse forms and processes in indigenous lowland South America: An areal-typological perspective. *Annual Review of Anthropology*, 31, 121–145.

Dussel, E. (1995). *The invention of the Americas: Eclipse of "the other" and the myth of modernity*. (Trans. Michael D. Barber). New York: The Continuum Publishing Co.

Dyck, L.-R. (2005). *Redefined rhetorics: Academic discourse and Aboriginal students*. Paper presented at the First Nations, First Thoughts Conference Canadian Studies Centre, University of Edinburgh, May 5–6.

Eyong, C.T. (2007). Indigenous knowledge and sustainable development in Africa: Case study on Central Africa. In E.K. Boon & L. Hens (Eds.), *Indigenous knowledge systems and sustainable development: Relevance for Africa* (pp. 121–139). Dzlhi, India: Kamla-Raj Enterprises.

Greymorning, S. (2000). Observations on response towards Indigenous cultural perspectives as paradigms in the classroom. In J. Reyhner, J. Martin, L. Lockard & W. Sakiestewa Gilbert (Eds.), *Learn in beauty: Indigenous education for a new century* (pp. 71–84). Flagstaff, AZ: Northern Arizona University.

Hart, M.A. (2010). Indigenous worldviews, knowledge, and research: The development of an indigenous research paradigm. *Journal of Indigenous Voices in Social Work*, 1(1), 1–16.

Hoagland, S.L. (forthcoming). Epistemic shifts: Feminist advocacy research and the coloniality of knowledge. In H. Grasswick (Ed.), *Feminist epistemology and philosophy of science: Power in knowledge*. New York: Springer.

Huntington, S. (1971). The change to change: Modernization, development and politics. *Comparative Politics*, 3(3), 283–322.

Islam, M.R. (2012). Indigenous or global knowledge for development: Experiences from two NGOS in Bangladesh. *International NGO Journal*, 7(1), 9–18.

Kapoor, D. (2010). Learning from Adivasi (original dweller) political-ecological expositions of development: Claims on forests, land, and place in India. In D. Kapoor & E. Shizha (Eds.), *Indigenous knowledge and learning in Asia/Pacific and Africa: Perspectives on development, education, and culture* (pp. 17–33). New York: Palgave Macmillan.

Kapoor, D. & Shizha, E. (2010). Introduction. In D. Kapoor & E. Shizha (Eds.), *Indigenous knowledge and learning in Asia/Pacific and Africa: Perspectives on development, education, and culture* (pp. 1–13). New York: Palgave Macmillan.

McKenzie, B. & Morrissette, V. (2003). Social work practice with Canadians of Aboriginal background: Guidelines for respectful social work. In A. Al-Krenawi & J.R. Graham (Eds.), *Multicultural social work in Canada: Working with diverse ethno-racial communities* (pp. 251–282). Don Mills, ON, Canada: Oxford University Press.

Mignolo, W. (2000). The many faces of cosmo-polis: Border thinking and critical cosmopolitanism. *Public Culture,* 12(3), 721–748.Quijano, A. (2000). Coloniality of power, Eurocentrism, and Latin America. *Neplanta: Views from South,* 1(3), 533–580.

Rostow, W.W. (1990). *The stages of economic growth: A non-communist manifesto.* Cambridge: Cambridge University Press.

Suárez-Krabbe, J. (2009). Introduction: Coloniality of knowledge and epistemologies of transformation. *Kult—Postkolonial Temaserie: Epistemologies of Transformation: The Latin American Decolonial Option and its Ramifications,* 6(Special Issues), 1–9.

wa Thiong'o, N. (1986). *Decolonising the mind: The politics of language in African literature.* London: James Curry.

Part I

Indigenous Knowledge and Development

1 Reflections on "African Development" Situating Indigeneity and Indigenous Knowledges[1]

George J. Sefa Dei [Nana Sefa Atweneboah I]

INTRODUCTION

I am writing this chapter in perhaps 'not a fully conventional style'. I am exercising a right and a responsibility to do just that. As a traditional Chief [and one who asserts an African indigeneity], I begin by acknowledging the socio-historical contexts from which we speak and the power of ancestors and the ancestral knowledge that guard and guide all what we do. I come to engage the critical reader from a grounded and situated position as someone working in the area of indigenous philosophies and anti-colonial thought, and the search for African-centered development options. I was born and educated in Ghana and am now teaching at a Canadian university. My scholarship and research has always sought to intertwine North America and Africa. In fact, in recent years, I have been working closely with faculty colleagues and students at Ghanaian and other African universities as we share knowledge about the way forward for the continent. The question of African development has always been a primary concern.

I want to share a story with apologies if sensibilities are breached or offended. In the summer of 2011, I spent some time in Lagos doing research on African indigenous proverbs. While there, I learned a story. It is about a Pastor who joined a passenger bus on a road trip. After a very short while, a man smelling heavily of alcohol came on board the bus and sat next seat to the Pastor. The new passenger had in his hand a local newspaper and he started to read upon sitting down. Moments later, this man asked the Pastor, "Father, why do people get diabetes?" The Pastor in consternation about the man's drunk condition replied, "Oh, my son it is people who resort to heavy drinking daily, never taking good care of themselves and, in fact, are not worthy of the company of the decent and law abiding citizens who get such a dreadful disease". The presumed drunkard simply went back to his reading. After a little while, the Pastor felt bad about being too harsh on this poor soul. So the Pastor said, "Young man, I am sorry for what I said moments ago and I will pray to God to cure you on your diabetes". The man looked to the Pastor and said with a smirk on his face: "Oh no, Father I was just reading here, the Pope has diabetes. I don't have diabetes!"

Well isn't it funny how we easily judge? Africans are said to be sick and needing treatment and the prescribed medicine is the development wheel. Maybe the so-called developed communities need that medicine! Africa needs no one's medicine. Africa cannot be made in the image of Europe or some other place else! Africa has to find solutions to its own problems and we must accept the responsibility and challenge. This does not mean there is no room for allies, assistance and partnerships. But the partnerships and forms of assistance must be on Africa's own terms not the dictates and interpretations of the capitalists and global powerful.

As I begin sharing my thoughts, let me borrow a question recently posed by one of my doctoral students: How do we offer indigenous African critiques of the conventional Western discourse on 'African development' and not feel a need "to box oneself into one of (usually two) analogue categories and how do we carve a space of critique that does not assume our membership in one camp or another, but rather complicates the very existence and limitation of these camps?" (Sium, 2012, p. 25). This question can be taken up differently, but for me, it presents a challenge when positing oppositional and counter narratives to dominant discourses. In coming to a critique of Western discursive approach to African development, I maintain that we must always pursue an anti-colonial and anti-racist intellectuality so as to reclaim and recover our indigenous knowledges, but not simply as counter, oppositional or alternative knowings (Abraham, 2011). We must see an indigenous anti-colonial discursive practice as resistance to the historic and continuing spiritual, emotional, psychological, physical, economic and material wounding or damage that dominant [Western-informed] narratives and practice of development have and continue to foster on the African human condition. We need to develop and promote our own "home grown indigenous perspectives steeped in culture-specific paradigms" (Yankah, 2004, p. 26).

The indigenous anti-colonial intellectuality helps us carve a critical path to a genuinely African-centered development. There is no single story of Africa and as such we must challenge the development logic that sees the singularity of Africa. Africa is multidimensional and makes for a far more complex and fascinating reading. Africa does not render itself so simply to Westocentric solutions, quick fixes and understandings. True, Africa is not all about success cases, but Africa is not all failures either. We cannot let Africa become synonymous with narratives of 'crisis', 'chaos', 'collapse', 'destruction and human suffering', 'failure', 'disease' and 'corruption'. We must speak of local creativity and resourcefulness, the indigenous desire to beat the odds, as well as the power of the African human-hood, agency and resistance.

Borrowing from Steyerl (2008), therefore, I maintain that I have no craving to present Africa and the African voice and knowledge about development to be the object of a voyeuristic gaze that is interested in 'authenticity' but not in change. My discursive critique of 'development' is intended to bring home the possibilities of 'something different' in development pursuits, one that is remarkably different than we are currently used to. To achieve this, we have to re-think 'development' and we must also concretely engage in political work to bring about meaningful change.

THE INFANTILIZING OF AFRICA

By infantilizing, I gesture to the paternalism that has undergird discussions about the African 'plight' and 'crisis', Africa as a 'basket case' that needs a Western imperial savior. Many may argue that Africa registers very low on the global landscape and contemporary geo-politics and that the image of Africa as 'coming apart'. This is evoked to justify a paternalistic defense of Western imperialist aggression on Africa. Those of us who criticize Africa's geo-politics are supposed to be grateful for Western 'development' interventions. Sometimes, we are told to bring the gaze back to our 'suffering' communities and our 'corrupt' leaders. But, we need to interrupt the imperial project of development that is duly informed by a sense of Western moralism and superiority. The encroachment on Africa in defense of 'human rights' or for the altruistic concerns of 'humanitarianism' has simply offered fertile grounds for the pursuit and promotion of Western imperialism (Sium, 2012).

There is a disturbing arrogance of a particular dominant knowledge in purporting to understand Africa's problems. Such colonizing knowledge promulgates solutions to Africa's problems and challenges informed by a Eurocentric lens. What is so disturbing is the failure and outright refusal to admit to the enduring Western complicity in the so-called African malaise. Many African scholars have spoken about the insulting idea that others know us better (as Africans) more than we know ourselves (Prah, 1997; Zeleza, 1997). Lauer (2007) has noted that even today degrading stereotypes about African governments persist in the idea that Africa needs foreign direction to manage her own affairs! In the infantilizing of Africa the discursive power, intellectual agencies and resistance of local peoples have been denied or devalued. The African indomitable spirit for a capacity for resuscitation, that is, to (a)rise from its challenges and the imposed misery is discounted. Africa is perceived as a hopeless case!

Very recently, in the global public sphere, we have had the spectacle of 'Invisible Children', a non-profit organization with their so-called 'Kony 2012 Video'. For me, the fact of 'Invisible Children' as cultural storytellers, social activists and community workers using the power of the social media to raise collective awareness is not the issue. In order to bring attention to Joseph Kony's Lord's Resistance Army reign of terror in some parts of Africa (not just Uganda), we must also insist that there are other ways to inspire the world youth to take action against global atrocities other than infantilizing Africa. And by the way, why is this global awareness only being created now and for whose consumption? These events and developments are often decontextualized and the complicity of the powerful is often a diminished voice. In other words, the Kony 2012 video simplifies a long-standing human rights tragedy and in so doing makes Africans and Africa look helpless and hapless. It brings an imperial view and mandate to 'save Africa' from itself. We are not made to understand the local resistance struggles and the intellectual and political agencies of African peoples themselves. These are the 'missing voices' in dialogues of global fights for equity and social justice.

Infantilization of Africa is also scripted in Canadian youth projects such as 'Toonies for Africa' or 'Books for Africa' to solicit assistance for Africa. Well-intentioned as they may seem, when I hear about them I cringe a bit. These causes leave unasked some fundamental questions: Who and what defines the parameters of African development and assistance? Where are the boundaries drawn, who is in and who is out, and simultaneously, who is policing the boundaries? Why is the idea of 'saving Africa' so seductive and appealing to our humanistic instincts? How does Africa connect to the global? How is the "global mobilized and global engagements framed" (Charania, 2011, p. 354) in the current prevailing discourses of global justice and development? How do we come to understand the specific historical, material relations, social networks and political contexts for global engagements in Africa? How does the West's engagement in Africa teach us about the violence of colonialism, imperialism, racism, patriarchy and development? What are our relative complicities in the hegemonic sway of the global development and our matching responsibilities to uncover and subvert the power hierarchies of the global through an anti-colonial perspective? (Dei, 2012a; Charania, 2011)

THE FALSITY OF THE 'TRADITION/MODERNITY' DICHOTOMY

A great extent of the 'problem of Africa' is bestowed on outmoded traditions and customary practices and beyond. History is evoked not so much as a tool of colonization, but how African history is its own doing. Those who speak of colonial legacies are deemed stuck in the past. In fact, there is a perverted sense that Africa is forever stuck in its own traditions. Sure no tradition is immune from criticism, but we often hear that the problem with Africa is that it needs to modernize! There is a resurrection of modernization theory today that argues that Africa needs a 'culture adjustment program' where our social values and cultural norms are in tune with a global capitalist competitive market. In such discourse, there is the conflation of modernity and the modernist project. The 'traditional/modern' split is presented as an attractive allegory that is however a 'ridiculous imagery' (Lauer, 2007). Such dualism, it has rightly been argued, serves to "disassociate the social realities of Africa from social reality in general" (Appiah, 1992, p. 136). Africa is about the past, present and the future. Africa is like every other continent struggling with tensions and the dynamics of change.

Disturbingly, there is an over-simplification of African cultural realities, and sadly, the colonized mind is still also a factor in African development (Lauer, 2007). In the views of Westernized theorists, tradition is often condemned and equated with pre-modernity, barbarism and evil. Rather than the binary of tradition/modernity, I assert a critical engagement of 'tradition/traditional' in contemporary Africa for the purpose of serving solution-oriented approaches to current Africa's challenges (Kanu, 2006).

THE COLONIALITY AND VIOLENCE OF ON-GOING (GLOBAL) DEVELOPMENT

The coloniality of development discourse has been discussed elsewhere at length (Escobar, 1995; Munck, 1999; Munck & O'Hearn, 1999). Sachs' (1992) pioneering work alludes to a degree of the violence of development for the South. The current era of neo-liberalism and global capitalist modernity has not only implicated us in terms of how we think of our identities and subjectivities, but fundamentally, what collective meanings we produce and bring to the sense and purpose of development. It is important for us to have a critical gaze that allows us to trouble the conceptual and dominant meanings of global development, one that allows us to focus on resistance to development and, perhaps, abandon development all together, if at all possible. We must re-imagine current processes and practices of development and its roots in a neo-liberal/globalization agenda. We need to ask: Does the concept of globalization have any redemptive qualities, a transformative potential, or is it simply a form of evil? Global relations are exploitative and make some of us see the 'terror of the Global'. Given the ills of contemporary society that can be connected so much to the forces of globalization, what makes us so sure of some transformative qualities in the pursuit of global development?

By virtue of asking such questions, we can claim and redeem the transformative potentials and possibilities of the global while challenging its coloniality. As an educator in the academy of higher learning, I see that institutionalization of 'development' has become a race to international markets. In the process, we seem to be losing our souls as to what development and the search for social existence is all about (Abdi, 2006; Dei, 2012b; Portelli & Solomon, 2001; Peters, Britton & Blee, 2008; Grosfuguel, 2007; Golmohamad, 2008—in the varying context of education).

Conventional development has been about external control and the colonizing or re-colonizing of African communities into the wider "global cultures of globalization, trade liberalization spreading democracy" (Lauer, 2007, p. 290). Neo-colonial ideologies have ratified global trade practices that perpetuate the conditions of Africa's "dependency on foreign aid and its economic incapacity" (Abudu, 1996, as cited in Lauer, 2007, p. 296). Re-colonialization is produced and reproduced by forces of globalization and contemporary geo-politics of global power structures. 'Anti-development' advocates are often criticized as romanticizing poverty, tradition and indigenous cultures. But, we need a critique of cultural and material imperialism of development, which says we have this development that is often heralded and talked about and we don't want it! Why? This is because global trade and finance policies of international financial community and institutions constitute the untold violence in Africa.

Externally imposed economic austerity measures of structural adjustment programs (SAPs), post-SAPs, heavily indebted poor countries (HIPC) and post-HIPC policies are wreaking untold havoc in Africa. In fact, there is an excessive dependence on the World Bank/IMF advice, a form of 'charity' that is aimed at the integration of African economies into a global finance community. Through HIPC and post-HIPC initiatives, for example, we are presented with 'solutions' to Africa's problems and the possibility of hope. But frankly, HIPC policy is still situated within a neo-modernization paradigm of development long touted through SAPs. These policies are attempts to promote 'development' to meet the interests of global capital. They offer a techno-fix approach to solving human problems.

NEW SOUTH-SOUTH DYNAMIC: NEW QUESTIONS AND ALTERNATIVES TO CURRENT DEVELOPMENT

Besides the colonial legacies and contemporary North–South arrangements, we must also ask: How is the colonial legacy being perpetuated in dominant discourses of the new 'South–South' relations? As we seek new South–South relations (e.g., the BRICS—China, Russia, Brazil, India and South Africa—as emerging Southern economic powers) has China, in particular become the new imperial order in the context of Africa? What shapes/is shaping such discourses of South–South alliances? I will point the reader to some of the writings on the 'New South–South' dynamic and international geo-politics (such as Aguilar, 2010; Alden & Vieira, 2005; Jiabao, 2011). For example, the old dictates still prevail in the way these partnerships are defined by a need for oil and gas, unfettered access to trade investments and opening up Southern markets to the Northern powers, concerns about debt servicing and the perpetual indebtedness, continuing environment use and degradation; human rights abuses, governance and immigration, the problem of brain drain and Africa being at the short end of the so-called 'brain circulation'. So I ask: Could the South–South partnership be a viable transformative alternative to the current global economic power structure? How can we genuinely create a 'New International Economic Order'? What are the possibilities and limitations of the BRICS partnerships and leadership in helping to design futures for the South or for Africa? Are we theoretically prepared to capture the promises and the perils of these emerging global power dynamics? Furthermore, internal colonialism(s) has/have been a constant variable in global geo-politics, so how do we envision global change and transformation given this dynamic? If the new South–South dynamic is in part about creating 'a world community', how do we work with differences and develop a shared and collective consciousness and social action for the South? How do we situate the North in this? What would be the best avenue for further opening up and creating an 'authentic dialogue' among Southern partners? Are there lessons for the North?

The African Union and the New Economic Partnership for African Development (NEPAD)

The NEPAD initiative of 2000 has sought to encourage good governance and regional co-operation and co-ordination. But these expectations have primarily been to make African development so appealing that it could attract international partnerships. What is the inspiration behind these ideas and how are they truly anti-colonial and Pan-Africanist? Whose interests are fundamentally protected? I dare say it is those of Western international finance capital. In fact, the need for cultural solidarity, trade/investments, political alliances, regional aid/assistance, as well as attention to African governance and democracy, human rights—accountability/transparency—have all been recognized as rhetorical. For example, discussions and concerns about democracy are pursued without recourse to African indigenous democratic institutions and systems of governance that sustained local peoples over years before the advent of Western colonialism and Western style democracies. What is the responsibility of local initiatives spearheaded by African intellectuals, policymakers and politicians working with local knowings and understandings (see also Dei, Hall & Rosenberg, 2000; Dei, 2011b)?

DISCURSIVE POSITIONS

I will take five discursive claims/positions to support my case to reframe 'development' via situated indigeneity and indigenous knowledges. First, there is a coloniality of 'Western-style' development. Modernity is *not* solely a European concept. As Escobar (1995) points out we must challenge the location of modernity within European enlightenment and instead root its phase within the colonization of indigenous populations that began even well before Europeans got lost in the Americas over many centuries ago. Today, such coloniality of development can be seen in the professionalization of development (with a whole cadre of 'experts', 'specialists' and scholars let loose on Africa). Development has proceeded unabated with a technologization of the development agenda. Such coloniality of development works with the privileged notion of the individual actor free from community bondage and acting as a rational economistic subject.

Second, we must be clear about the intellectual and academic responsibility of African scholars. As Africans we are not innocent in the development quagmire. We are implicated with our silence. As African scholars, it is particularly our responsibility to articulate indigeneity and indigenous knowledge as a necessary exercise in our own decolonization. Our theories and paradigms cannot be a mere extension of existing dominant Eurocentric paradigms. We must decolonize our theorization through the application of African indigenous discourses.

Third is the power of local African cultural resource knowledges, which have been the least analyzed for their contributions to the development process (see also Matowanyika, 1990). Such local knowledge emphasizes a physical and metaphysical interdependence. As a form of epistemology, the consciousness of indigenousness signals a society, culture and nature nexus (see Dei, 2011b). In effect, spiritual ontologies and epistemologies are central to a re-conceptualization of the African development in general. Ontology is the nature of social reality, what accounts for reality and the essence of being. A spiritual ontology and spiritual teachings shape culture and what is development for African people (Belay, 2011). Hence, development must take up and work with an indigenous spiritual ontology that asserts that: (a) the Universe is basically a spiritual universe; (b) there is a particular essence of the relationship of the individual to society/community and to nature; individuals exist in relation to a community that they are part of and there are rights and responsibilities to such group/community membership; and (c) as human subjects we do not stand apart from, and neither are we above, the natural world. We are part of the natural world/cosmos.

Fourth, there is an imperative to move towards a re-thinking of science, technology and culture in development. The link between science, technology and development is often assumed and not sufficiently theorized. When we claim science, technology and industry as critical to development, we must also ask: What knowledge forms regarding science and technology are we seeking to articulate this connection with development? What is the place of local culture in defining science and technology? And how does this understanding of science, technology and culture challenge dominant paradigms of development? We must seek to understand science as culture and vice versa, as well as the ways communities, through culture, articulate the links of poverty, democracy, environment and development. This prism of indigenous science and culture as interdependent of the development process must begin with re-conceptualizing 'development' and the role of local cultures and indigenous sciences. It is also a discursive lens that marries a 'cultural political economy' and culturally-sustainable development framework, placing spirituality as a knowledge base/bedrock for development (Belay, 2011).

Last, we identify the creation of African 'Centres of Excellence' on indigenous knowledges and languages as an important phase in indigenous discourses. African development cannot proceed without a rigorous study of what our indigenous knowledge systems have to offer. To this end, we must create 'Centres of Excellence' for the study, research and application of indigenous knowledges in the search of solutions to the more practical problems of everyday development. Such Centres will focus on indigenous science as it relates to local biological and physical sciences, as well as social sciences, including arts, literatures, culture, politics, economics, etc.

INTERROGATING THE 'INDIGENOUS' AND 'INDIGENEITY' AS KNOWLEDGE FOR DEVELOPMENT

As an African academic, I am calling for a reclamation, maintenance and sustenance of indigenous knowledge for 'education' about 'development'. Indigenous knowledge and sciences belong to indigenous peoples of a particular land and has been used over centuries of their existence for everyday living and survival. In contrast, local knowledge can be possessed by any group (not necessarily indigenous to the land) that has lived in a particular place/location for a period of time (Dei, 2000, 2011a; Purcell, 1998). Such knowledge resides in the body and cultural memory and has never been frozen in time and space. They are continually relied upon in everyday challenges of human survival. They are also demarcated by race/ethnicity, gender, class, religion and language.

Despite foreign influences and ever-changing trends of modernity and post-modernity, indigenous knowledges have remained dynamic and evolved with contemporary challenges. In indigenous communities, such knowledges are found in their stories, myths and mythologies, fables, tales and folklore. They can also be found in other forms of material culture, such as symbolic ornaments and body ware and the meanings encoded in cultural artifacts. They are also found in local resource knowledge and practices associated with traditional pharmacology/plant medicine, farming technologies and agricultural methods, environmental management, soils and vegetation classification, arts and crafts, cultural norms, belief systems, cultural festivals and social organization of families and kinship groups. Through the power of oral traditions, we witness the flourishing of a truly indigenous literary tradition with succeeding generations of indigenous communities.

Fundamental to indigenous cultural knowings and development is spirituality and spiritual knowing. Spirituality in development is about our relations with the Creator, Mother Earth and the Land, understanding the self and the collective. Everyday communal living is about living in relation to the Land, Earth and Nature, and how such relations inform the way we 'do' development. The spiritual space nurtures conversations that acknowledge the importance and implications of working with a knowledge base about the society, culture and nature nexus. Such spaces can only be created when we open our minds broadly to revision development as practice and opportunity to challenge dominant paradigms and reasoning (Dei, 2012a).

Indigenous knowledges uphold the philosophy of circularity and have implications for how we come to talk and practice development. Development can neither be seen nor pursued in a linear direction of progress such that Africa will follow the West/Europe to 'development'. Western values, ideas and technologies, the infusion of Western capital and the regulation of such capital, alongside the assumption that capital accumulation is a prerequisite for African development to take off are all inimical to African-centered and indigenously-informed development. Open market reforms, trade liberation and the role for the private sector in development are not innocent engagements. They have a bearing on the African human-hood. Cutting down on state expenditures and pursuing export-led development agendas have broader implications on what it means to be human. Therefore, development is more than economic and technological growth, but it is fundamental social, cultural and spiritual workings with interface of culture, society and nature.

To effectively practice development calls for investments in indigenous knowledges, research development, intellectual capacity building and protection of local sciences. We cannot trade our culture for someone else's (recall 'backwardness' of our culture, traditional perspectives and the tradition/modernity split). African indigenous sciences constitute (and therefore must be investigated) our cultural inheritance and they are a fund of knowledge as well as a process of knowledge construction (see also Prah, 2011). African science and technology can be pursued and studied through the instrumentality of African indigenous languages. Science and knowledge must be fully integrated in local knowledge systems. The pursuit of science and technology is grounded in African languages, ingenuity and indigenousness. For the African scholar and researcher this calls on us to pioneer new analytical systems for understanding Africa and search for solutions to our problems (Yankah, 2004).

In re-thinking this indigenously-informed development decolonized/anti-colonial education is critical. The anti-colonial prism raises question of what type of education, how and why? Africa needs an education that has local social relevance. African education must be conceived, planned and executed for African people's benefit, not in the service of neo-colonial agenda. Education must assist African peoples in a cultural rebirth that helps young learners attain cultural empowerment, reclaim their past history and provide lessons for the present and the future. Education should not promote alienation and entanglement. There is a role for local science and technology and a people's knowledge base which focuses on local knowledge capabilities and a people's humanness. It is a development approach that builds on what people know and what they have come to know through time.

MOVING FORWARD

In moving forward I am calling for a re-thinking of development in African contexts away from the overemphasis on a 'capital/resource-based' to a 'local culture and science knowledge-based' approach that nurtures indigenous creativity and resourcefulness.

Creation of Indigenous Knowledge and Language Research Centres and African Human Capacity Building

Our thinking of African development must shift from the unquestioned faith in the power and efficacy of intensive foreign capital investment/infusion to the examination of indigenous knowledge systems dealing with local science and technology. Development must proceed with innovations in indigenous science, technology and culture through the creation of 'Centres of Indigenous Knowledge Systems and Languages' devoted to African development. Such 'Centres' will stress appropriate-science education and technological innovations specifically devoted to the exploration of indigenous science, technology and culture for the purpose of contributing to the development process through 'African human cultural development' and 'indigenous resource applications'. The model of development being advocated will require a strong interaction among institutions of higher learning for human capacity building through sustained research and applied knowledge of indigenous science, technology and culture (Etzkowitz & Dzisah, 2007). State funding will be purposely directed to research innovations and excellence in indigenous systems of thought as catalysts for scientific, industrial and technological accomplishments in the coming years (Etzkowitz & Dzisah, 2008).

The Role of the African University

African universities should produce their own national 'experts' on development (not imported or foreign-trained) who are well-versed in indigenous knowledge systems for local science, culture and industrial development and for government policymaking in these areas. The university should engage in a conscious attempt to circulate such indigenous-informed 'experts' in university–industry–government partnerships (Etzkowitz & Dzisah, 2010). Local human capacity building and institutional development will involve universities as intensive research centers and incubators for the development and promotion of indigenous knowledge, science and technology. The work of such indigenous scholars will challenge existing dominant epistemological paradigms and re-conceptualize 'African development' from anti-colonial and locally-centered discourses.

A People-Centered and Culturally-Sustainable Development Framework

With indigenous science as a starting point, national policy must embark upon a new development approach that builds upon small-scale and home-grown industries using indigenous technologies in a culturally-sustainable development manner (Lebakeng, 2010; e.g., local artisans, vocational skills, traditional pharmacology, primary health care, rural development and adult education). This development framework is intended to counteract the prism of a market-oriented economics.

Development as Equity and Transparency

Uneven development is not development. Indigenous conceptions of wholeness/holistic and interdependence must be brought to bear in development practice. Meaningful development is about equity and is also transparent. Development should address sectorial and regional imbalances, as well as inequities perpetuated along lines of social difference (e.g., ethnicity, gender and class). There must be a national commitment to ensure that communities benefit from infrastructural development when resources are extracted from their environments. This issue may be more apparent in Ghana where the recent discovery of oil and gas highlights tensions that may result if the resource is equitably distributed. If Ghana is to avoid the ethnic clashes that have plagued oil rich countries, with the Niger Delta region in Nigeria as a case in mind, the oil and gas should benefit local communities by providing infrastructural development.

CONCLUSION

We hold indigenous possibilities of a global re-imagination of development that goes beyond an exploration of ways local cultures "interact with one another and engage in issues of poverty, democracy and environment" (MacNeill, 2011, p. 9). Such re-imaginings would offer deep insights into ways of re-conceptualizing 'development' and understanding the place and role of culture, local science and technology in the process. In light of the current push for indigenous scholars to challenge existing dominant and hegemonic epistemological paradigms and the coloniality of development, we must challenge any silence on questions of social difference. As argued in the chapter, conventional development has perpetuated regional, sectorial, ethnic, class and gender inequities within and among communities. Also, rather than being dismissive we need a critical 'cultural political economy' that acknowledges the place of spirituality as a significant knowledge base and bedrock for development. The study of local culture, science and technology and their place in development is significant (Warren, 1991). A key question is what does an understanding of culture mean when it is taken up in development work? As noted already, creating a traditional/modern split is part of the problem. Although I agree that it is important not to accord modernity to Europe or to imply that "it is simply a European phenomenon" (MacNeill, 2011, p. 111) in development work, it is also critical to make that distinction between 'modernity' and the 'modernist project' of development.

Let me not leave anyone with a feeling that there are no intellectual risks and challenges. In fact, we must scrutinize power and resistance to dominant development paradigms, models and initiatives that continually subjugate or marginalize local voices and intellectual agencies. In thinking through what development is, we have to find ways to make sense of the conceptual accounts of real politics, socio-material activity and institutional development that take place with or without conscious paradigms to articulate them. Today, the role and activities of (external) capitalist economic systems and imperialism in shaping possibilities for African development or imaginings still point to ways colonialism, neo-colonialism and re-colonialisms continue to produce damaging outcomes, including wasted lives in Africa. So, what is the nature of the political structures and organization around indigenous cultural knowledge for development? What knowledge systems undergirding traditional institutions are useful for imagining new development possibilities? Given the dominant structures and processes of social formations and, particularly, the unequal power relations in knowledge production, validation and dissemination currently in place in our communities, we must respond to how effectively (pragmatically) local culture, science and technology knowledge can be effectively be applied to engage multiple voices and counter-visions of society. I do believe asking these questions and attempting to offer some responses are important beginnings. It helps to offer us some sense of how local communities can truly and effectively engage and address the social, political, ethical and moral concerns in the praxis of development.

NOTES

1. This chapter was initially presented as a keynote address at the 2nd Africa Regional Conference on: 'Endogenous Development' at the University for Development Studies (UDS), Tamale, Ghana, August 18–19, 2011. A longer version is published by the University of Development Studies Monographs for the conference. I want to thank Dr. Agnes Apusigah and Pro-Vice Chancellor David Millar for the opportunity to share my ideas at the UDS conference. I also thank Yumiko Kawano of the Department of Sociology and Equity Studies of the Ontario Institute for Studies in Education of the

University of Toronto for her work to recover portions of my initial notes for this address that was lost on the computer.

REFERENCES

Abdi, A.A. (2006). Culture of education, social development, and globalization: Historical and current analyses of Africa. In A.A. Abdi, K.P. Puplampu & G.J.S. Dei (Eds.), *African education and globalization: Critical perspectives* (pp. 13–30). Lanham, MD: Rowman and Littlefield Publishers.

Abraham, A. (2011). *African and Western knowledge synthesis*. Unpublished course paper, SES 1924H, Modernization, Development and Education in African Context [Fall, 2011]. Toronto: Department of Sociology and Equity Studies, Ontario Institute for Studies in Education of the University of Toronto [OISE/UT].

Aguilar, C.G. (2010). South–South relations in the new international geopolitics. *Global Studies Review*, 22(80), 2–7.

Alden, C. & Vieira, M.A. (2005). The new diplomacy of the South: South Africa, Brazil, India and Trilateralism. *Third World Quarterly*, 26(7), 1077–1095.

Appiah, K.A. (1992). *In my father's house: Africa in the philosophy of culture*. New York: Oxford University Press.

Belay, S. (2011). *Recapturing spiritual and cultural values into science education: The case of Ethiopia*. Paper presented at CIDEC Seminar, OISE/UT, February 24.

Charania, G. (2011). Grounding the global: A call for more situated practices of pedagogical and political engagement. *ACME: An International E.Journal for Critical Geographies*, 10(3), 351–371.

Dei, G.J.S. (2000). Rethinking the role of indigenous knowledges in the academy. *International Journal of Inclusive Education*, 4(2), 111–132.

Dei, G.J.S. (2011a). *Democracy, good governance and education*. Keynote Address at the International Conference on Democracy, Good Governance and Education, First Annual International Conference, Faculty of Education, Lagos State University, Lagos, Nigeria, July 26–29.

Dei, G.J.S. (Ed.). (2011b). *Indigenous philosophies and critical education*. New York: Peter Lang.

Dei, G.J.S. (2012a). *Global education from an anti-colonial perspective*. Keynote Address at the Department of Education Graduate Symposium/Conference on Global Education, Towards New Frontiers, Concordia University, Montreal Quebec, May 4.

Dei, G.J.S. (2012b). *Interrogating global citizenship education from an indigenous knowledge perspective*. Paper presented on the panel session on Re-Imagining the Global Citizenship Discourse: A View from the contexts of Developing Countries at the Annual Meeting of the American Educational Research Association, Vancouver, BC, April 13–17.

Dei, G.J.S., Hall, B. & Rosenberg, D.G. (Eds.). (2000). *Indigenous knowledges in global contexts: Multiple readings of our world*. Toronto: University of Toronto Press.

Escobar, A. (1995). *Encountering development. The making and unmaking of the Third World*. Princeton, NJ: Princeton University Press.

Etzkowitz, H. & Dzisah, J. (2007). The triple helix of innovation: Towards a university-led development strategy for Africa. *Africa Technology Development Forum (AFDT) Journal*, 4(2), 3–10.

Etzkowitz, H. & Dzisah, J. (2008). Rethinking development: Circulation in the triple helix. *Technology Analysis and Strategic Management*, 20(6), 653–666.

Etzkowitz, H. & Dzisah, J. (2010). Who influences whom? The transformation of university–industry–government relations. *Critical Sociology*, 36(4), 491–501.
Golmohamad, M. (2008). Global citizenship: From theory to practice, unlocking hearts and minds. In M.A. Peters, A. Britton & H. Blee (Eds.), *Global citizenship education: Philosophy, theory and pedagogy* (pp. 519–533). Rotterdam: Sense Publishers.
Grosfuguel, R. (2007). The epistemic colonial turn: Beyond political economy paradigms. *Cultural Studies*, 21(2), 211–223.
Jiabao, W. (2011). *Building China–Africa strategic partnership*. Excerpts from Wen Jiabao, Premier of the State Council of the People's Republic of China's remarks at the opening of the 4th Ministerial Conference of the Forum on China-African Cooperation in Egypt (FOCAC). The African Executive, 1–4.
Kanu, Y. (2006). Reappropriating traditions in the postcolonial curriculum imagination. In. Y. Kanu (Ed.), *Curriculum and cultural practice: Postcolonial imaginations* (pp. 203–222). Toronto: University of Toronto Press.
Lauer, H. (2007). Depreciating African political culture. *Journal of Black Studies*, 38(2), 288–307.
Lebakeng, T.G. (2010). Discourse on indigenous knowledge systems, sustainable socio-economic development and the challenge of the academy in Africa. *CODESRIA Bulletin*, 1/2, 24–29.
MacNeill, T. (2011). *Culturally sustainable development: And the idea of development*. Unpublished Ph.D. dissertation, Graduate Program in Communication and Culture, York University, Toronto.
Matowanyika, J. (1990). *Cultural heritage as a resource towards sustaining rural Africa into the twenty-first century*. Paper read at the Annual Conference of the Canadian Association of African Studies, Dalhousie University, Halifax, NS, May 9–12.
Munck, R. (1999). Deconstructing development discourses: Of impasses, alternatives and politics. In. R. Munck & D. O'Hearn (Eds.), *Critical development theory: contributions to the new paradigm* (pp. 195–209). London: Zed Books.
Munck, R. & O'Hearn, D. (Eds.). (1999). *Critical development theory: Contributions to the new paradigm*. London: Zed Books.
Peters, M.A., Britton, A. & Blee, H. (Eds.). (2008). *Global citizenship education: Philosophy, theory and pedagogy*. Rotterdam: Sense Publishers.
Portelli, J.P. & Solomon, R.P. (2001). Introduction. In J.P. Portelli & R.P. Solomon (Eds.), *The erosion of democracy in education: From critique to possibilities* (pp. 15–28). Calgary: Detselig Enterprises Ltd.
Prah, K. (1997). Accusing the victims—In my father's house: A review of Kwame Anthony Appiah's 'In my father's house'. *CODESRIA Bulletin*, 1, 14–22.
Prah, K. (2011). *Betting on our strength: Endogenous development, research, education in higher education institutions in Africa: Prospects, challenges and the way forward*. Paper presented at the 2nd Africa Regional Conference on Endogenous Development, University for Development Studies (UDS), Tamale, Ghana, August 18–19.
Purcell, T.W. (1998). Indigenous knowledge and applied anthropology: Question of definition and direction. *Human Organization*, 57(3), 258–272.
Sachs, W. (Ed.). (1992). *The development dictionary: A guide to knowledge and power*. London: Zed Books.
Sium, A. (2012). *From starving child to rebel-pirate: The West's new imagery of a failed state*. Unpublished course paper, SES 1921Y, Principles of Anti-Racism Education, Department of Sociology and Equity Studies, [OISE/UT] University of Toronto.
Steyerl, H. (2008). *Can witnesses speak? On the philosophy of the interview*. European Institute for Progressive Cultural Policies (A Derieg Translation). Retrieved May 12, 2011 from http://eipcp.net/transversal/0408/steyerl/en

Warren, D.M (1991). *Using indigenous knowledge for agricultural development.* Washington: The World Bank.
Yankah, K. (2004). *Globalization and the African scholar.* Faculty of Arts, University of Ghana Monograph.
Zeleza, T. (1997). Fictions of the postcolonial: A review. CODESRIA Bulletin, 2, 15–19

2 Intersections Between Indigenous Knowledge and Economic Development in Africa

Gloria T. Emeagwali

INTRODUCTION

Countries in Africa have been afflicted by two externally influenced economic models to date, namely, 'the colonial model of exploitation' emerging between the 16th and 20th centuries, and 'the neo-colonial economic model' that took shape between the 1960s and the present time. We briefly reflect on these models, and then discuss Africa's Indigenous Knowledge Systems (AIK) and the extent to which they should be important variables in Africa's quest to develop. The questions that need answering are: Is AIK important for Africa's development? Why and how should AIK be utilized in Africa's quest for economic development? What are the threats to AIK in development in Africa? In the final section of the chapter we reflect on Africa's indigenous technology and development strategy in light of current technologization of developments. First of all, however, we make some comments about Africa's current resource base.

AFRICA'S CURRENT RESOURCES

The African continent consists of about 54 countries. It is about four times the size of the United States and the second largest continent both in land area and population (Khapoya, 2012). It is a continent rich in natural resources, having over half of the total world reserves in several important industrial minerals. Africa seems to be indispensable at the present time for the global soft drink, pharmaceutical, cell phone and computer industries. For example, Sudan is the world's largest producer of *acacia senegal*, also known as *gum arabic*, an indigenous resource resin used as an emulsifier in the soft drink industry and an indispensable ingredient for Pepsi and Coca-Cola (Milbank, 2007). *Acacia Senegal*, which is also an indigenous plant, is also used extensively in the pharmaceutical, beer making and textile industries as a binder, thickener, foam stabilizer and mordant. The gum is essential in the making of pills and tablets. It is also useful in the manufacture of cough syrups and lozenges. The resin is also a major ingredient in snack foods, cereals, gelatins, baked goods, soups, milk products and a wide variety of candy in the world's major confectionary and food industries. Its function as a thickener makes it valuable for wax polishes, water colors and various types of pigments. In the textile industry its major function is to give luster to materials such as silk and crepe, and to add permanence to color in its role as a mordant.

With a bottle of Coca-Cola in one hand and a microphone in the other, the Sudanese Ambassador to the United States, John Ukec Lueth Ukec, an abettor of genocide in Darfur, reminded the West: "I want you to know that the gum arabic which runs all the soft drinks all over the world, including the United States, mainly 80% is imported from my country" (Milbank, 2007, online). Ironically, Darfur in Western Sudan, is part of the so-called 'gum belt' and a major supplier of the resin along with the Sudanese regions of Kordofan and Kassala.

Southern Darfur hosts one of the world's largest reserves of uranium, indispensable for fuel in nuclear reactors and the trillion-dollar weapons industry (Sudan Watch, 2006). Surprisingly, Sudan's uranium deposits are not included in the recent International Atomic Energy Agency (IAEA) report that lists Niger, Namibia, South Africa, Tanzania, Gabon, the Congo and Nigeria as regions with sizable uranium deposits (IAEA, 2009). Meanwhile, Western companies have been lining up to sign deals with the rogue state. Darfur also has sizable reserves of copper, vital in the making of components in the electrical and electronic industries and various alloys, whereas the petroleum reserves of Northern Darfur may rival that of Saudi Arabia (Flounder, 2006).

Most computer systems, mobile phones, video cameras and camcorders, video game consoles, iPods, jet engines and automotive systems in the world make use of *columbite- tantalite*, popularly known as *coltan* (Nzongola-Ntalaja, 2002). When refined, coltan becomes tantalum. Northeast Congo is endowed with over 60% of the world reserves of this vital resource that has become indispensable for the operating systems of Nokia, Ericsson, Intel, Sony, Motorola and others, given its use in the capacitors and semiconductors of today's electronic devices (Essick, 2001).

Other mineral resources should also be noted. Nigeria, Mauritania, Cote d'Ivoire, Ghana, Equatorial Guinea, Gabon, Angola and Uganda are among the top 10 petroleum producers in the continent, whereas South Africa, Sierra Leone, Angola and Botswana continue to be major sources of diamonds. The United Nations *Survey of Economic Conditions in Africa* up to 1964 had this to say about the continent's natural resources:

> Actually, African potential is shown to be greater every day with new discoveries of mineral wealth. On the agricultural side, African soil is not as rich as the picture of tropical forests might lead one to believe; but there are other climatic advantages so that with proper irrigation crops can be grown all the year round in most parts of the continent. (Rodney, 1972, p. 29)

This observation is relevant today as it was then in 1964. Zimbabwe's mineral discovery is a case that works as a good example. Zimbabwe has one of the most exciting diamond discoveries in the world today and the country is now thought to be the third biggest producer of diamonds in the world. The recent large scale discoveries of diamonds in the Marange District have shown the potential for the sector. Diamonds are in great demand in the cutting and polishing of precision tools, for a wide range of industries. From medical scalpels used in complicated operations to kitchen grinders or industrial cranks, diamonds remain the best friend of the industrial tool making and engineering industries—no less than that of the jewelry industry.

COLONIAL AND NEO-COLONIAL DEVELOPMENT MODELS

In Africa, the colonial model of exploitation which was consolidated in the 20th century was in the context of various systems of occupation, characterized by authoritarianism, centralization of power, compulsory labor, high levels of taxation and militarization (Korten, 1999). The Belgian, Portuguese, German, Italian, French, British, Spanish and Dutch forced and violent occupation of Africa was a devastating blow to the indigenous development projects that were taking place on the continent. Built into the colonial model were unwholesome presuppositions about race, gender, discriminatory and segregationist colonial policies with respect to the allocation and appropriation of indigenous lands and resources, and the compulsory requisitioning of recruits and raw materials for the European civil wars of 1914 and 1939. The colonial and imperial rule and governance sought to assimilate indigenous people in some countries, whereas in others it sought to co-opt indigenous people as collaborators in their oppression. Policies of assimilation and association had several features in common. They were both aimed at the aggrandizement of the colonial power at the expense of local economies (Korten, 1999).

The post-colonial model of the 1960s and after has been, in effect, a neo-colonial one. A neo-colonial model is characterized by export-oriented growth, mono-culture and agricultural and mineral extraction, with minimal domestic processing, refining and manufacture, and varying levels of authoritarianism and democratization (Korten, 2001). Kwame Nkrumah (1965) described neo-colonialism as the so-called 'invisible trade' that endows the Western monopolies with yet another means of economic penetration. He also described it as the last stage of imperialism. As Rodney (1972, p. 29) noted about half a century ago:

> The situation is that Africa has not yet come anywhere close to making the most of its natural wealth and most of the wealth now being produced is not being retained within Africa for the benefit of Africans. Zambia and Congo produce vast quantities of copper, but that is

> for the benefit of Europe, North America and Japan. Even the goods and services which are produced inside of Africa and which remain in Africa nevertheless fall into the hands of non-Africans.

This largely externally derived model, which feeds the developed nations at the expense of less developed nations has been sustained in conjunction with segments of the domestic elite and local collaborators. Some of these domestic elite were a result of the colonial administrations in Sub-Saharan Africa who intentionally created and expeditiously groomed African elites as collaborators with the administration (Kees, 2007). In post-colonial Africa, these elites manifested themselves as the ruling class.

A major feature of the neo-colonial model in Africa is the emergence of a small affluent elite sustained by domestic clientelism and favoritism (Korten, 2001). The model is essentially a continuation of the earlier colonial model in terms of its export dependent structure and focus on primary products and extractive mining with little or no emphasis on agro-industrial processing and refining. The economic situation is characterized by a low savings rate and high inflation due to numerous imported inputs, and heavy reliance on imported manufactured goods. Zimbabwe provides a good example where, in recent years, clientelism and hyperinflation have caused an economic crisis in a country that used to be the bread basket and envy of Africa (Shizha & Kariwo, 2011).

Three decades ago, during the Reagan administration in the United States, the International Monetary Fund (IMF) and the World Bank (WB) introduced new variables called '*conditionalities*' into the economic model, ostensibly to enhance economic growth and bring about structural change through market forces. These *conditionalities* included the assumption that deregulation and non-interventionism by the government was essential for growth, and that privatized property ownership was superior to communal, communitarian or government ownership (Emeagwali, 1995; Stiglitz, 2012). Currency devaluation and the removal of subsidies on health, education and social services were touted as being indispensable. A rapid decline in purchasing power often took place along with recessions and negative growth rates (Emeagwali, 2006a). Ideologically, the *conditionalities* were guided by monetarist anti-Keynesian economic philosophy which called for stringent budgetary cuts rather than stimulus funds (Stiglitz, 2002). Monetarists generally associated their ideas with free market ideology that generally rejected government intervention and regulations (Stiglitz, 2010; Bello, 2003; Blustein, 2003).

Against the odds, however, vibrant indigenous informal sectors and parallel economies emerged, reflecting in some cases strong family ties and communal or kin-based support systems. Undocumented, and left out of official Gross Domestic Product (GDP) statistics, this sector was seen by some as a sign of weakening state control, whereas others viewed these informal sectors as exemplary forms of home-grown and endogenous economic activity. The informal segments were also viewed as the purveyors of the knowledge systems inherited from the past and potentially lifesavers in the quest for internal endogenous growth as opposed to growth that was externally generated. We shall revisit this issue in the course of discussion but, before that, let us reflect on the China factor.

THE CHINA FACTOR IN AFRICA'S DEVELOPMENT

Global powers, both new and old, are jostling for influence in Africa. This renewed 'scramble for Africa', to borrow a term from history, is largely to gain access to increasingly scarce natural resources such as oil and natural gas (Safdar, 2012). Sino–African relations took an interesting turn in 2005 with Beijing's hosting of the Forum on China–Africa Cooperation (FOCAC). China decided to wipe away debt worth about 10 billion RMB (about US$162 million). Mutually beneficial cooperation in a wide range of fields was agreed to by the 44 African countries invited to the forum. Projects in conservation, road construction, transportation, telecommunications, hydropower development, construction and oil-drilling were earmarked for cooperation. In West Africa, China has been involved in various projects that include the construction of a port in Gabon and the building of a football stadium, office blocks and an industrial complex in Sierra Leone. The Chinese have invested in gold and coal mining in South Africa, nickel mining in Burundi, and coffee growing and fishing in Uganda. In Zimbabwe, the government's 'Look East' policy (dubbed an alternative to the West, is supposed to be about fighting neo-colonialism and resisting Western hegemony over Zimbabwean sovereign affairs and welfare as a society) has attracted Chinese businesses in the construction industry, road construction and diamond mining (Youde, 2007). Projects in Sudan include the constructions of the Heglig oil pipeline and a major dam. Chinese-run vegetable farms have been set up in Zambia and joint ventures in mining, transportation and telecommunications have been identified in Ethiopia and Kenya. Some people argue that China is exploiting African resources for its own economic benefits.

China has taken the lead in fostering relations with African countries and over the last few years, Chinese influence in the continent has increased markedly and by 2006, 800 Chinese companies were active in 49 countries investing in the infrastructure, energy and banking sectors (Safdar, 2012). The country has emerged as Africa's largest trading partner. It has been estimated that between 2000 and 2005, trade between China and Africa grew by 500%. China–Africa trade rose 80% in 2009 and by 2010 this trade was worth over $100 billion (China Economic Review, 2010). The 45% takeover of a Nigerian oil and gas field by China National Offshore Oil Company (CNOOC) signaled China's entry into the West African petroleum sector. To date, China has interests in the oil holdings of

Nigeria, Sudan, Angola and more recently, Ghana. A $2.5 billion deal by CNOOC signaled a stake in Uganda's oil assets. Uganda's oil reserves are estimated to be worth more than a billion barrels. Recent estimates suggest that about 25% of China's petroleum requirements come from Africa (China Economic Review, 2010). A two-way trade between China and Africa has increased dramatically to an all-time high of $166.3 billion, triple the figure for 2006 (Safdar, 2012).

China's activity in Africa substantially increased the bargaining power of African countries. It triggered a new rush to the continent of countries such as India, South Korea, Japan and Brazil. Indeed, the former European colonial powers are in competition with several of their former protégés for access to Africa's resources. As a result of this, the terms of trade for commodities have improved substantially when compared to the late-1980s and early-1990s, not only in agrarian products such as cotton and cocoa, but also for industrial minerals such as coltan, cobalt and titanium, some of which we earlier cited in our discussion of African resources. China's voracious appetite for these minerals is reflected in the various kinds of lucrative contractual agreements that have emerged. Contrary to the Western tendency to obscure their economic gains from Africa in hypocritical self-serving language of development, humanitarianism and 'aid', Sino–African relations have generally evolved with dignity and respect and an open acknowledgement by China of anticipated economic benefits. However, there are still questions on whether China's activities in Africa are not another form of re/colonization of Africa. The increase in Chinese influence in Africa has been met with alarm in Western countries. According to Safdar (2012, online),

> Critics, both outside and within Africa, say that there is little or no long-term benefit of the increase in trade to the continent as exports to China comprise mostly primary commodities such as oil and agricultural produce. They also assert that the no strings-attached aid policy pursued by the Chinese leads to a reduction in the pressure on governments to improve on issues such as human rights.

China has challenged Western hegemonic discourse with a narrative that speaks more about partnership and interdependence than condescending paternalism. IMF financial 'terror' has been replaced by more favorable interest rates, with neither strings nor *conditionalities* attached (Emeagwali, 2011).

Chinese aid to Africa is unconditional and usually spent on infrastructural projects that have a greater impact on people's lives. A '*resource for infrastructure swap*' is one of the more intriguing examples of the agreements that have emerged between Africa and China. According to Howard French, for 11 million tons of copper, and 620,000 tons of cobalt, over a 25-year period, China would construct 1,800 railways, 2,000 miles of road, hundreds of schools and hospitals and two universities in the Democratic Republic of the Congo in a deal negotiated by the Joseph Kabila regime (French, 2010). Supporters of the '*resource for infrastructure swap*' argue that kleptocratic officials and corrupt government officials would have less opportunity to siphon out funds and engage in corrupt practices with this arrangement and that infrastructural development, elusive under the previous Mobutu and Kabila regimes, would now stand a chance of completion. China's Export-Import Bank would fund the massive projects to which dozens of Chinese construction companies have been assigned. Such an agreement would necessitate sophisticated accounting and evaluation procedures related to the evacuation of the ore, and efficient systems of measurement and accountability, to keep track of this massive exchange of resources. One expects that transparent modalities are being worked out to accomplish this goal.

China has become a new colonizing power in Africa through its capital investments and high-tech production. For example, one area of concern is the 25-year time range allocated to Chinese evacuation of Congo's copper and cobalt. Because copper and cobalt are non-renewable resources, what steps would be taken to avoid the excessive mining and depletion of the resource? Would extractive mining generate backward and forward linkages in the economy and the necessary multiplier effects that stimulate long term growth? With 5% of the world's natural gas, Trinidad and Tobago was able to develop nine ammonia plants, an iron and steel complex and two of the world's largest methanol plants (Romero, 2004). So what of the Congo with 50% of the world's cobalt? Shouldn't the Congo, at the least, be the world's leading exporter of batteries?

Critics of ongoing China–Africa relations, point to the Zambian protests of 2007 and 2008. Low wages, a ban on union activity and underemployment of Zambians triggered the massive protests centered in the mining region of Chambishi where 52 copper miners lost their lives in 2005. The discontent was fueled by Zambia's high unemployment rate and perceptions that Chinese firms were either under-employing Zambian nationals or ill-treating those that worked for them. In the words of one of the critics:

> They bring Chinese to come and push wheelbarrows, they bring Chinese bricklayers, they bring Chinese carpenters, Chinese plumbers—we have plenty of those in Zambia. Pushing a wheelbarrow is pushing a wheelbarrow. They're doing manual work. We don't need to import laborers from China—we need to import people with skill, with skills which we don't have in Zambia. But the Chinese are not going to train our people how to push wheelbarrows. (Ofeibea, 2008, online)

Making the situation worse were the job losses from the closure of 200 textile factories that could not compete with cheap Chinese textiles—a plight experienced also in Nigeria, Kenya and Lesotho (La Gamma, 2009). In

Nigeria alone, by 2005, there were at least 1.5 million job losses in the garment industry, whilst Lesotho witnessed the closure of 10 factories. Even so, those who joined the ranks of the unemployed had difficulty finding jobs with the Chinese firms given the Chinese general tendency to bring in Chinese workers from their country, China. This has caused some Western and African scholars to argue that China is involved in some form of neo-colonialism. This neo-colonialism embraces all aspects of classic colonialism except for occupying foreign lands, because all states in Africa remain technically independent (Junbo, 2007). In this neo-colonialism, the exploiting power (China) controls weaker states' economic resources and political systems and exploits their wealth under the name of partnerships.

So accompanying the previously stated benefits associated with China–Africa relations are grave matters for concern with respect to indigenous participation and the utilization of indigenous and endogenous skills and expertise. Indeed, a fundamental weakness of the current China–Africa model, whether in terms of 'resource for infrastructure swap' or infrastructural development, is that entire communities have been marginalized and left out of the projects with little opportunities for utilizing their accumulated skills, expertise and insights or acquiring new ones. Chinese infrastructural development is also plundering indigenous resources without giving back benefits to the immediate communities. We argue that the assumption that local communities were unwilling, incapable or uninterested in contributing to the development of their own communities is a false one given the achievements made in various parts of the continent in indigenous capacity building, historically, in spite of various constraints (Emeagwali 1992, 1993, 2006a; Akinwumi, Okpeh, Ogbogbo & Onoja, 2007). As earlier indicated, informal segments earlier identified were purveyors of the knowledge systems inherited from the past and a product of internal endogenous growth as opposed to growth that was externally generated. In the section that follows we elaborate on this issue.

AFRICA'S INDIGENOUS KNOWLEDGE SYSTEMS

In various parts of ancient and contemporary Africa, building constructions of various dimensions, shapes and types emerged, reflecting various concepts, techniques, raw material preferences and decorative principles. Builders integrated the concepts of the arch and the dome, and constructed columns and aisles underground vaults and passages, as well as rock-hewn churches and pyramids of various dimensions. Various kinds of local building materials were exploited. In the Sahelian region, adobe, or dried clay, was preferred for contours molded by hand and skillfully integrated into the overall structure. Elaborate walls and structures were constructed in city states such as Kano, Sokoto and other polities of Hausaland in West Africa. We have other testimonies to the local engineering activities of ancient Africans. About 20,000 miles of terraces were done in northeast Nigeria, whereas Patrick Darling, who is an archeologist, has estimated the Benin earthworks to be about 10,000 miles long (Emeagwali, 1992). Irrigation terraces and earthworks had several features in common. The people who constructed them wanted to make up for land scarcity and grow their food in a secure place so they created numerous layers each rising above the other, on the slopes of hills in the region as well as on the plains in terms of dry stone terraces and earth terraces (Emeagwali, 2006a).

Skill and expertise developed in many parts of the continent in terms of the making of yarn, weaving, and the dyeing of cloth involving various kinds of looms, beaters and shuttles and other technical devices for making cloth. Numerous kinds of vegetable dyes were used. Women played a major role in this area of activity, as in food processing. Generally, the raw materials used in textile included camel hair, wool, flax, raffia palm and cotton in various parts of West, Central and Southern Africa (La Gamma, 2009). Silk was produced in Western and Central Nigeria in small quantities. Some city-states and empires became famous for particular types of cloth and product design. Ideas, emotions, attitudes, beliefs and views about politics and individual leaders were represented in specific ways. Different types of symbols and motifs were embedded into the various kinds of cloth. Kente (Ashanti), Adinkra (Ivory Coast), Sanyan (silk made in Western Nigeria), Adire (starch resist also from the West), Aso Olona (title cloths of the Ijebu; Gillow, 2009) and kitenge/chitenge (Malawi) are some of the various names given to indigenous African cloth. The earliest surviving cloth of Mali dates back a thousand years.

Akinwumi et al. (2007) pointed out that African traditional medicine consisted of an accumulated body of knowledge, techniques and explanations about health. We also note that diagnosis involved observation of the patient, the questioning of family members and case history, clinical examination of body temperature and the observation of urine. Divination, water gazing and sand divination were not excluded from the process. There was a blending of various types of diagnostic systems, some of which were more useful than others. Patient feedback provided the practitioners a fair sense of what worked and what did not. Trial and error experimentation was central to the activity of not only food processors, engineers and cloth makers but also traditional practitioners. For example, Nigerian practitioners came to the conclusion that plants such as *bridelia ferruginea* and *piper guiniense* were effective in the treatment of diabetes and as sedatives (Sofowora, 1984). In Kenya, Wane (2010) found that *caesalpinia volkensii*, *strychnos henningsii*, *ajuga remota*, *waarbugia ugandensia* and *olea europaea* were identified as antimalarial herbal remedies. Numerous other conclusions were drawn on the basis of usage and proven effectiveness (Carlson et al., 2001; Mshigeni, 1991; Rodolfo, Simon & Ho, 2010). Plants, whether in terms of legumes, grain, vegetables, tubers, wild or cultivated fruits had medicinal implications for Africans. The plants were used as anesthetics or pain killers, analgesics for the control of fever, antidotes to counter poisons and antihelmintics aimed at de-worming and driving out worm parasites from the body. They were used also in treating heart problems, problems associated with indigestion as well as the treatment of skin problems (Sofowora, 1984; Konadu, 2009).

A variety of African plants now grown around the world were first domesticated in Africa, including finger millet, sorghum, coffee, the oil palm and African rice, *Oryza glabberima*. The domestication of these plants, as well as the transformation of their produce into edible flour and beverages, involved generalizations about soil texture, cross fertilization of seeds, weather patterns and a host of botanically-related matters (Lost Crops of Africa, 2008; Dirar, 1993). It also implied trial and error experimentation over time and space in the quest to understand and even control aspects of the environment. Techniques and methodologies were not static and there were numerous technical deficiencies over time but collectively the systems utilized were cost effective, appropriate and were locally managed. Africans utilized locally accessible raw materials, whether botanical or otherwise. Building materials were very often ecologically appropriate as was the case of adobe in the Sahelian zone. Before the epoch of colonial occupation, practitioners in various city states, kingdoms and empires, in various parts of the continent, shaped the agenda, and there were indicators of local empowerment, and participation in wide-ranging spheres such as health care, textiles, metallurgy and construction (Emeagwali, 2006b). Africans generally contributed to the development of their communities even during periods of stress and conflict.

IMPLICATIONS FOR DEVELOPMENT

For indigenous knowledge to occupy an important role in African economic development, several steps must be taken. In the first place, digital libraries comprising data bases of indigenous knowledge in various fields and diverse regions must be created along the lines set by the World Intellectual Property Organization (WIPO). By identifying and acknowledging the vast network of techniques and information utilized by various networks of traditional practitioners in selected fields, the groundwork for locally managed, cost effective and interactive systems would have been established. In the field of health care, for example, there is need to evaluate, rehabilitate, standardize and integrate traditional medical practice into the wider system of health care, where feasible, with a view to creating more holistic, integrated health care systems. At the core of this approach should be imaginative, creative and people-centered approaches that are aimed at empowering communities rather than marginalizing them.

Africa's dependency on the so-called developed nations creates unbalanced relations with imperial multinational corporations maintaining a balance of power on the continent. Economic ripples within these institutions are likely to be felt in Africa. For example, the United States' deficit spending, high energy costs and the $3 trillion Iraq war were among some of the variables associated, directly and indirectly, with the financial meltdown of September 2008 (Johnson & Kwak, 2010). These factors converged with other negative practices such as over-valued financial and housing loans and coordinated short selling. IndyMac, Fannie Mae, AIG, Merrill Lynch, AIG, Washington Mutual and Lehman Brothers were among the 80 public corporations in the United States declaring bankruptcy by September 2008 (Stiglitz, 2010, 2012). Repercussions were felt across the globe and continue to date. The possibility of a double dip recession still looms and the specter of global economic collapse is not completely out of the question given the rising debt levels of countries such as Portugal, Italy, Ireland and Greece (Moran & Roubini, 2012). The first lesson Africa learned from this economic meltdown relates to the phenomenon of export led growth and its pitfalls. Africa's role as a major exporter of minerals such as coltan, petroleum, cobalt and others is flattering and lucrative, but as China has discovered lately, over-reliance on external buyers for one's commodities is not without its dangers.

The global financial meltdown exposed the fragility of world trade, and highlighted the virtues of having a domestic consumer market with credible enough purchasing power. For China, the relentless purchase of U.S. treasury bonds as IOUs for Chinese goods imported into the United States is now a questionable strategy, given the decreasing credit worthiness of the super power. By implication, Africa must utilize its vast indigenous natural resources not in export- led trade but in capacity building and the development of its endogenous and indigenous human capital. The accumulation of huge debt obligations undermines the credibility and development options of countries, even superpowers such as the United States. China's debt forgiveness initiative to Africa gave a new lease of life to several African countries and care should be taken by African policymakers and financial managers to keep debt ratio to Gross National Product (GNP) at acceptable levels.

Secondly, the financial meltdown highlighted the significance of small-scale business enterprises rather than mega-industries and mega-banking systems that were 'too big to fail' and virtually indispensable. The virtue of supporting small indigenous enterprises, cooperatives and banks has been suggested by several researchers (Mander & Goldsmith, 1996). This point became clear after the collapse of Lehman Brothers and other well-established institutions. Americans, for example, have re-discovered small credit unions and local banks, ditching the long-standing monopolies in the process. Because African indigenous knowledge systems are community-based, local and self-sustaining, once upgraded, standardized and enhanced they could be priceless in periods before, during and after economic turbulence.

The third lesson to be derived from the 2008 financial crisis was the realization that globalization could be a double-edged sword and a recipe for economic disaster (Klein, 2007). The main characteristic of globalization is its tendency to integrate nations and people across political boundaries in order to facilitate the free flow of goods and services, capital, knowledge and skills, as well as people (Stiglitz, 2002). The earliest theoretical analyses of this new phase of globalization included the neo-Marxist world-systems and dependency theories formulated by Walllerstein (1974) and Frank (1980), respectively. Rather than focusing on nation-states Wallerstein provided a 'macro-level' model for a capitalist world-system instead, whereby an international division of labor has led to emergence of a hierarchy of various economic regions in the world, each with their specific processes of production, consumption and labor conditions. Available data also tend to support a global shift in the extent of labor mobility and movement of capital during the second phase of globalization (Chaichian, 2011). Countries such as Iceland plunged into economic crisis overnight with moments of boom turning almost magically into doom, for reasons that had more to do with financial mismanagement, thousands of miles away in Wall Street, than poor management at home (Roubini, 2010; Moran & Roubini, 2012).

For Africa the message is clear, namely, that extreme caution must accompany all policies and programs implemented in conjunction with external third parties. The 2008 financial meltdown occurred for several reasons, some of which were mentioned earlier. The most important cause may well be the removal of checks and balances on financial institutions and the banking sector, and deregulation of a system that could not regulate itself, contrary to the claims of neo-classical economists, anti-Keynesian monetarists and neo-conservatives (Stiglitz, 2012; Johnson & Kwak, 2010). The implications for African economies are clear. Shrewd and cautious regulation of the economy is necessary for economic development to take place.

Africa's involvement with China took place at an auspicious moment in history, a period of economic downturn, characterized by worsening terms of trade due to a glut of primary products. The IMF/WB Structural Adjustment Program had taken a toll on diversification and consumer spending. By engaging with China, African countries took appropriate action at a defining moment. China's role as the second-largest economy, the world's largest creditor nation and perhaps the most successful survivor of the financial meltdown made it a valuable ally in the global arena. However, self-sustained growth essentially must come from within, in the context of participatory action that rejects the marginalization and disempowerment of indigenous people. Partnerships should be built on existing knowledge bases in the context of informed interventionism. In the final analysis AIK should play a central role in Africa's development. Chinese activities in various African regions should therefore be viewed with customary caution and wisdom. Contracts should be shrewdly written, with serious considerations for the long term conservation of non-renewable resources and the resource needs of future generations. Lessons should be learned from China and India in terms of their attempts at integrating indigenous knowledges into their own development strategies.

REFERENCES

Akinwumi, O., Okpeh, O.O., Ogbogbo, C.B.N. & Onoja, A. (2007). *African indigenous science and knowledge systems—triumphs and tribulations—Essays in honour of Gloria Thomas Emeagwali*. Abuja: Roots.

Bello, W. (2003). *Deglobalization: Ideas for a new world economy*. London: Zed Books.

Blustein, P. (2003). *The chastening: Inside the crisis that rocked the global financial system and humbled the IMF*. New York: Public Affairs.

Carlson, T. et al. (2001). Case study of medicinal plant research in Guinea. *Econ Botany*, 55(4), 478–491.

Chaichian, M.A. (2011). The new phase of globalization and brain drain: Migration of educated and skilled Iranians to the United States. *International Journal of Social Economics*, 39(1), 18–38.

China Economic Review. (2010). *South Africa looks to boost investment from China*. Retrieved August 24, 2010 from http://www.busrep.co.za/index.php

Dirar, H. (1993). *The indigenous fermented foods of the Sudan: A study in African food and nutrition*. CAB International.

Emeagwali, G. (1992). *Science and technology in African history*. Lewiston, NY: Edwin Mellen.

Emeagwali, G. (Ed.). (1993). *Historical development of science and technology in Nigeria*. Lewiston, NY: Edwin Mellen.

Emeagwali, G. (1995). *Women pay the price*. Trenton, NJ: Africa World Press.

Emeagwali, G. (2006a). *Africa and the academy. Challenging hegemonic discourses on Africa*. Trenton, NJ: Africa World Press.

Emeagwali, G. (2006b). *The African experience: Past, present and future*. New York: Whittier.

Emeagwali, G. (2011). The neo-liberal agenda and the IMF/World Bank structural adjustment programs with reference to Africa. In D. Kapoor (Ed.), *Critical perspectives on neo-liberal globalization, development and education in Africa and Asia* (pp. 3–13). Rotterdam, The Netherlands: Sense Publishers.

Essick, K. (2001, June 11). Guns, money and cell phones. *The Industry Standard Magazine*. Retrieved January 21, 2012 from http://www.globalissues.org/article/442/guns-money-and-cell-phones

Flounder, S. (2006, June 6). The US role in Darfur Sudan. Oil Reserves rivaling those of Saudi Arabia. *Global Research*. Montreal, QC: Centre for Research and Globalization.

Frank, A.G. (1980). *Crisis in the world economy*. New York: Holmes and Meier.

French. H. (2010). The next empire. *The Atlantic.com Magazine*. Retrieved May 29, 2011 from http://www.theatlantic.com/magazine/archive/2010/05/the-next-empire/308018/

Gillow, J. (2009). *African textile—Color and creation across a continent*. London: Thames and Hudson.

International Atomic Energy Agency [IAEA]. (2009). *IAEA annual report 2009*. Retrieved April 13, 2011 from http://www.iaea.org/Publications/Reports/Anrep2009/anrep2009_full.pdf

Johnson, S. & Kwak, J. (2010). *13 bankers, the Wall Street takeover and the next financial meltdown.* New York: Pantheon Books.

Junbo, J. (2007, January 5). China in Africa: From capitalism to colonialism. *Asia Times Online* Retrieved May 13, 2012 from http://www.atimes.com/atimes/China/IA05Ad01.html

Kees, A. (2007). Living with ambiguity: Integrating an African elite in French and Portuguese Africa, 1930–61. Stuttgart: Franz Steiner Verlag Wiesbaden.

Khapoya, V. (2012). *The African experience. An introduction.* London: Longman.

Klein, N. (2007). *The shock doctrine: The rise of disaster capitalism.* New York: Picador.

Konadu, K. (2009). *Indigenous medicine and knowledge in African society.* New York: Routledge and Francis.

Korten, D. (1999). *The post-corporate world.* Hartford: Kumarian Press.

Korten, D. (2001). *When corporations rule the world.* Hartford: Kumarian Press.

La Gamma, A. (2009). *The essential art of African textile: Design without end.* Washington, DC: Metropolitan Museum of Art.

Lost Crops of Africa. (2008). Washington, DC: The National Academies Press.

Mander, J. & Goldsmith, E. (1996). *The case against the global economy and for a turn toward the local.* San Francisco: Sierra Club Books.

Milbank, D. (2007, May 31). Denying genocide in Darfur—Americans and their Coca-Cola. *The Washington Post.* Retrieved December 16, 2011 from http://www.washingtonpost.com/wp-yn/content/article/2007/05/30/AR200705300.html

Moran, M. & Roubini, N. (2012). *The reckoning: Debt, democracy and the future of American power.* New York: Palgrave Macmillan.

Mshigeni, K. (Ed.). (1991). *Traditional medicinal plants.* Dar-es-Salaam: University Press.

Nkrumah, K. (1965). Neo-colonialism, the last stage of imperialism. London: Thomas Nelson and Sons, Ltd.

Nzongola- Ntalaja, G. (2002). *The Congo: From Leopold to Kabila.* London: Zed Books.

Ofeibea, Q.-A. (2008, July 31). Chinese built Zambian smelter stirs controversy. *NPR.* Retrieved February 14, 2011 from http://www.npr.org/templates/story/story.php?storyId=930.html

Rodney, W. (1972). *How Europe underdeveloped Africa.* Dar-es-Salaam: Tanzanian Publishing House.

Rodolfo, J.H., Simon, J.E. & Ho, C.-T. (2010). *African natural products: New discoveries and challenges in chemistry and quality.* Oxford, UK: Oxford University Press.

Romero, S. (2004, October 13). Trinidad becomes a natural gas giant. *New York Times.* Retrieved May 8, 2006 from http://www.nytimes.com/2004/10/13/business/worldbusiness/gas.html

Roubini, N. (2010). *Crisis economics: A crash course in the future of finance.* New York: Penguin.

Safdar, T. (2012, August 30). China's growing influence in Africa. The Express Tribune. Retrieved November 29, 2012 from http://tribune.com.pk/story/428026/chinas-growing-influence-in-africa/

Shizha, E. & Kariwo, M. (2011). *Education and development in Zimbabwe: A social, political and economic analysis.* Rotterdam, The Netherlands: Sense Publishers.

Sofowora, A. (1984). *Medicinal plants and traditional medicine in Africa.* New York: John Wiley and Sons.

Stiglitz, J. (2002). *Globalization and its discontents.* London: Penguin.

Stiglitz, J. (2010). *Free fall—America, free markets and the sinking of the world economy*. New York: N.W. Norton and Co.
Stiglitz, J. (2012). *The price of inequality*. New York: W.W. Norton and Co.
Sudan Watch. (2006). Sudan: Uranium in Darfur? Retrieved April 25, 2006 from http://sudanwatch.com/
Wallerstein, I. (1974). *The modern world system: Capitalist agriculture and the origins of the European world economy in the sixteenth century*. New York: Academic Press.
Wane, N.N. (2010). Traditional healing practices: Conversations with herbalists in Kenya. In D. Kapoor & E. Shizha (Eds.), *Indigenous knowledge and learning in Asia/Pacific and Africa: Perspectives on development, education, and culture* (pp. 229–243). New York: Palgrave Macmillan.
Youde, J.R. (2007). Why look east? Zimbabwean foreign policy and China. *Africa Today*, 53(3), 3–19.

3 Indigenization and Sustainable Development for Zimbabwe

A Post-Colonial Philosophical Perspective

Ngoni Makuvaza

INTRODUCTION

Today's economic discourse in Zimbabwe is on indigenization or black empowerment (*upfumi kuvanhu*). This discourse, which was long overdue, is hopefully being undertaken in the context of sustainable development. It can thus be surmised that 32 years after independence, Zimbabweans have realized that the economy needs to be in indigenous hands. Indigenization, in this regard, becomes an attempt to return the economy of the country to its rightful owners—the indigenes of Zimbabwe. However, what is disturbing about the whole indigenization agenda is the absence of an articulated and explicit philosophy to inform the process, especially in view of the quasi-deterministic and quasi-dialectical relationship between and among philosophy, education and development (Nkrumah, 1970). Further, what is also disconcerting about the whole debate is the absence of any mention whatsoever to indigenize the education system as a prerequisite to indigenizing the economy. However, one of the issues related to indigenization which needs to be seriously addressed is the question of who are the indigenous people of Zimbabwe to whom economic power must be returned? It is this and other questions that are the concern of this chapter.

The preceding reservations notwithstanding, and as a gesture of both the government's and the people's seriousness over indigenization, several indigenous bodies have sprouted in Zimbabwe, notably, the Indigenous Business Development Centre (IBDC); the Affirmative Action Group (AAG); and Indigenous Business Women Organization (IBWO). At the national level, the government created the Ministry of Youth Development, Indigenization and Empowerment to specifically focus on indigenization, thus demonstrating the seriousness of government on implementing indigenization. In all this, probably the assumption is that both the government and people of Zimbabwe have realized that the attainment of political independence in 1980 was a necessary but not a sufficient prerequisite for genuine independence and liberation. Thus, in order to consolidate its independence and strive towards sustainable development, the economy needed to be indigenized.

Indeed, indigenization is a noble idea, although a belated one, especially if it is being done in the spirit of development and progress and in the context of post-colonial discourses (Chilisa & Preece, 2005). However, what is of great concern to us and which has prompted this chapter is the absence of a clear government policy on indigenization discourses on social development. The government does not seem to have a clear and convincing definition of 'indigenous people' and what indigenization entails and what it aims to achieve at both the individual and national levels. Further, what is particularly worrying to educationists is the apparent 'unmentioning' of the need to indigenize the education system. Our argument is that indigenizing the education system is a necessary precondition for promoting a meaningful indigenization program of the economy and a logical move towards sustainable development (cf. Shizha, 2009, 2010, 2011 on indigenous knowledges and sciences in education in Zimbabwe).

The contention of this chapter is that, any meaningful discourse on indigenization for sustainable development should be well-grounded in a sound philosophical theory and ideology that evolve from the people's way of life. Accordingly, the sound theory and philosophy provide the rationale, direction and goal of the indigenization process which should not be construed within the short-term goal of trying to 'make even' with our yesteryear enemies, but more importantly within the ultimate long-term goal of trying to achieve sustainable development. Consequently, in the absence of a sound philosophical theory to inform the indigenization discourse and agenda, Zimbabwe risks developing a haphazard and misdirected indigenization process. In addition, it risks undermining the very noble goal it had set up to achieve. It is also our contention, in view of the centrality of education in any development process, that if indigenization is to be successful and meaningful, then indeed the education system must of necessity be indigenized (See Shizha, 2011).

The purpose of this chapter is, therefore, twofold. Firstly, it is not intended to provide solutions to the questions raised earlier but to contribute to the indigenization debate and process through raising questions and thus opening other avenues of viewing the same debate. The hope is to develop an indigenous discourse of development that is not 'mimetic', but rather genuine, holistic and beneficial to the majority of Zimbabweans. Secondly, this chapter intends to situate the indigenization debate within the larger context of sustainable development enshrined in the United Nations Millennium Development Goals (MDGs) to give the development agenda an international character and focus. Moreover, more importantly, it will ensure the success of the long-term vision that is provided by the MDGs, so that indigenization ultimately achieves sustainable development. However, notwithstanding the preceding submissions, it needs to be reiterated that, if indigenization in the context of MDGs is to be authentic and relevant and not 'mimetic', it needs to be grounded in, and informed by a sound indigenous theory and an education system that articulates and addresses the indigenous people's historical and existential epistemologies.

RELEVANCE OF A 'THEORY' TO THE 'PRACTICE' OF INDIGENIZATION

A very close quasi-dialectical and quasi-deterministic relationship exists between theory and practice. The quasi-dialectical and quasi-deterministic approach contends that any practice is rooted in some theory, in which case the theory will be determining the practice (Nkrumah, 1970; Woods & Barrow, 1975; Rauche, 1985). However, it is also feasible that after a particular practice has been shaped by a particular theory, further reflection on the practice might require that the theory on which it is based be changed, modified or altered, in which case the practice will have altered the theory. Accordingly, human activities are based on some theory or philosophy of one form or another. Consequently, one is more likely to achieve something if one knows what one is trying to do and how one proposes to achieve it (Jefferey, 1968). Theory provides both the direction and goal of the intended practice and it is the rational aspect of practice. If we are to live and do things intelligently, we need at least some theory of life to guide our practical activities. Even though theory appears to be crucial to any practice, it needs to be further cautioned that "practice without thought is blind and thought without practice is empty" (Nkrumah, 1970, p. 79). It is, thus, inferred that theory and practice can be interdependent.

It needs to be pointed out that at times the theories or assumptions on which the practice is based upon maybe articulated consciously or unconsciously. This of course will be at a lesser level of theorizing and practising. At higher levels of theorizing, particularly, where other interested parties are involved, it is always necessary that the theory be identified and articulated. Even if articulated, it is quite possible that some of the theories could be grounded on "assumptions not generally accepted, often adopted 'unargued' and seldom based on systematic research" (Woods & Barrow, 1975, p. 81). It is instructive to note that the effect of such theories would be to distort reality and hence the need to be constantly revisited in view of new theories, knowledge and discoveries.

Our contention, in this regard, is that no "theory is conclusive or absolutely true, but is liable to modification through the discovery of new data" (Rauche, 1985, p. 8). In view of the interplay between theory and practice, and our discussion on indigenization, there is need for a theoretical discourse on implementing indigenization to be informed not by any theory but by a sound indigenous theory that draws from the people's historical, political and socio-cultural existential circumstances and philosophy of life. The theory must not be arrived at emotionally or arbitrarily but rationally through systematic research that should inform the policy and implementation of indigenization and the role of education in the whole process.

The point of departure in the preceding theory and practice interplay, in general, is on the indigenization issue in Zimbabwe, conceived as an activity or practice. If it is to be understood as such, then in line with the preceding logic, it needs to be informed by some philosophy for it to have a logical purpose, direction and goal. In the absence of an explicit and articulated philosophy, it risks being chaotic and unfortunately, counterproductive. In Zimbabwe, indigenization issues have not been either raised or have been raised but avoided because the discourse raises emotions which have been allowed 'to run over reason'. However, because that has happened, the whole noble idea of indigenization risks being hijacked, distorted and misrepresented by people who are indigenous by color (the main criterion being used by the political elite to characterize one as being indigenous) but are not indigenous at heart.

The whole idea, due to the absence of a policy anchored on sound reasoning and theorization, can be hijacked by the political elite, to mean 'making even' with certain segments of our society and not the system, thus resulting in positive discrimination, which is still discrimination. Yet, what needs to be indigenized should be the 'system' and not the people. To change the people without changing the system might be tantamount to confusing or mistaking symptoms of a disease with the causes of that particular disease and then proceed to treat the later not the former. To do that, which in fact is what has been happening in various sectors of the economy, in the name of black empowerment/indigenization, would affirm a very sarcastic comment made by one local prominent politician of the Rhodesian regime that: "If I had known that all what you (African-Zimbabweans) were fighting for all along was in order to change names of towns, streets/roads, rivers etc. into vernacular, I could have given you your country long ago". This prominent politician was raising a fundamental issue quite relevant to the current debate on indigenization. He was making a mockery in all the fuss about vernacularizing names of towns, rivers, streets, mountains and replacing white officers in government, public and private sectors with indigenous people, all in the name of black empowerment and indigenization, and failing to address the fundamental issues underpinning the system. In other words, what the veteran politician was implying was that what needs to be addressed and thus indigenized was/is the system, not the placeholders of that system.

In order to address the system, the indigenization process must be rooted in a sound theory or philosophy emanating from the indigenous people's philosophy of life. Precisely, because we do not seem to be able to identify any sustainable philosophy or theory on which the current indigenization process is rooted, yet one is required as a matter of logical necessity, this chapter is therefore arguing for Afrocentricism to inform the indigenization agenda in Zimbabwe. Afrocentricism is being adopted chiefly because of its liberative and emancipatory thrusts (Gibson, 1986; Dussel, 1985; Njobe, 1990). In other words, the indigenization process in this context is being perceived as a liberative and emancipatory quest, a process, if properly implemented, that would lead to genuine liberation and further consolidation of our political and economic independence, preconditions for sustainable development. Afrocentricism is also being posited because it is a critique of Western and dominant perceptions of reality in general, and development in particular, through its thrust on championing the African worldviews and values which are considered as vital for sustainable development. We are arguing that if indigenization is not to risk being 'mimetic' but bring about sustainable development to Zimbabwe, it should evolve from and seek to project and promote an African worldview.

For any human practice such as indigenization to be successful, it must be rooted in a sound theory and philosophy to give it direction and purpose. It is also our contention and assumption that indigenization is being forged in the spirit of development, development that must be constructed within the context of the indigenous culture and philosophy of life. We are, however, opposed to the conception of indigenization as development and progress which views it rather emotionally and narrowly as merely 'black empowerment'. We are opposed to this view firstly because it is racist and discriminatory—two evils we have been fighting against for the past 100 years and which we do not want to resuscitate and resurrect in a different disguise. Secondly, we are opposed to this view because of its emphasis on economic development as if economic development is all there is to development—a view that is narrow. Therefore, this view of indigenization and/or development is unacceptable to us because of its racial overtones and narrowness but more fundamentally because it is rooted in an alien theory and philosophy—a theory or philosophy which would result in placing the indigenes on the 'periphery' not being genuinely developed and liberated. Therefore, if we intend to attain genuine indigenization and thus sustainable development, we should be critical of such theories and paradigms of development especially from the 'North'—perceptions that regrettably seem to be uncritically adopted in most development agendas in post-colonial states, including Zimbabwe.

POPULAR PERCEPTIONS OF DEVELOPMENT —A POST-COLONIAL CRITIQUE

In the 'North' and internationally, there is a tendency to conceive development in strictly economic terms, as the path towards "the maximization of goods and services per head" (Mountjoy, 1978, p. 21). It is also understood as implying a state of underdevelopment and poverty of the poor countries as compared to the rich countries. Development in this context would be taken as a way of liberating oneself from underdevelopment while at the same time trying to catch up with the already developed nations. The implication being that the West has reached the 'zenith' of development and also that it is the author of any development and accordingly, any development should therefore be monitored and determined by the West.

Critiquing Western economic emphasis of development, Walter Rodney also admits that, "the term is generally used in exclusively economic terms, the rationale being that the economy is the axis on which other social factors revolve" (Rodney, 1972, p. 10). Guitirrez (1981) also concedes that in the West, development is regarded as purely economic, in which sense it becomes synonymous with economic growth. The degree of development of a country seems to be measured by "comparing its gross national product or per capital income with those of a country regarded as highly developed" (Guitirrez, 1981, p. 24). Implied in all the earlier definitions, is the view that development is the change by which poor countries become rich (Shaw & Heard, 1979). This perspective is founded on three assumptions and underlines the conventional wisdom that "development is primarily a measure of wealth, to develop is to become more like rich countries, and it is poor countries that require development" (Shaw & Heard, 1979, p. 73).

Historically, this is the meaning of development that appeared first in the early discourses of development and we must say it is still dominant in the 'North'. Unfortunately, it has split over into the 'periphery' through conquest, colonialism and capitalism. Emphasis is placed on economic growth and consumerism as a sign of development. In the West, it would appear as if *the person* has been made insignificant in the process. What matters are figures, and the amount of goods produced or the amount of profit made. According to the West, for any country from the periphery to be regarded as developed or developing, it must tow the Western line, otherwise it is not developing. Regrettably, it is this perspective our indigenous narrative is challenging. The modernist perspective is being rejected because of its apparent narrowness in scope and its tendency to peripherize and marginalize countries in the South, such as Zimbabwe. We are opposed, among other things, to the exclusive emphasis by the West on economic growth as the only indicator of growth. Whereas economic progress is a necessary and essential component of development—we are saying it is not a sufficient indicator.

Development should encompass more than the material and financial dimensions of people's lives. Mountjoy, like us, is opposed to the view of considering development simplistically in economic terms. He points out that,

> Development is no simple straight forward process of economies but it strikes at the very root of social and situational patterns. It means fundamental changes in society, in ways of life, in political and institutional patterns and the grasping of new concepts and new sets of ideas. (1978, p. 21)

Mountjoy introduces an important dimension in this analysis, namely that development should strike at the very roots of social and institutional patterns. In other words, development should be complete and should affect even the basic structures of society. This is the kind of development we are arguing for but then this is not all. We are also opposed to the view which treats development as Westernization or modernization models to be copied by the South. We reject this perspective for several reasons. For instance, we are aware of the implications of such a position with respect to our freedom and independence. In addition, such a position is incompatible with our specific conception of place-based, culturally-appropriate development. We hold the view that every nation strives after development of one form or another. The tendency to develop is inherent in people, and societies in the past are known to have developed on their own. This view is corroborated by Momjam who concedes that, "mankind's history is an ascent from less developed types of society to qualitatively new and higher types surpassing the earlier ones in all the major economic, social, political, cultural and moral criteria" (Momjam, 1978, p. 45).

It is also our view that development should try to respond to the needs and aspirations of a particular society. In other words, any development pattern should emanate from and respond to the needs of the particular people. By inference, it is essential to note that, the needs of societies cannot be identical. If this reasoning can be taken as cogent, then no country is justified in either imposing its concept on another or despising another's development model. In the same vein, no country should unnecessarily either copy, imitate or even adopt wholesale development patterns from other countries. We concede that, "each nation's path to development is to a certain degree unique. The individual characteristics of each country will determine what strategy of economy its leaders will adopt" (Alexander, 1976, p. 19). We hasten to point out that, in view of Alexander's contribution, we are taking economic development not in the narrow Western sense, where it stands for a quantitative measurement of Gross National Product. Rather we take it to mean:

> A multi-dimensional process involving changes in attitudes, structure and institutions in a given society. It is aimed at producing a more human life, concern being shown for the availability of the basic material requirements of all people for all. (Ogola, 1985, p. 1)

What we are expostulating is that the West has no right to try to 'force' the 'South' to adopt their models of development. The 'South' should be left to map out their specific paths. Where they need assistance they should seek it freely. Our position is that there is no conception or model of development necessarily and inherently better than the other. As long as the model of development directly articulates and seeks to address the needs of its people, it is just as good as any other. In other words, we do not find justification for the West to call our pattern of development inferior and then proceed to impose theirs on us. In fact we are at the same time querying not only the Western perspective of development but the criterion for judging it better than ours.

Westernization, the dominant view in the West, even in some countries in the 'South', is being challenged because its adoption by these countries means their further perpetration of domination, exploitation and underdevelopment. This is the case because it is the view of the present discussion that one who holds theory has power. We say this being aware of the colonial legacy of resources and skilled manpower shortage inherited by the 'peripheral' countries at independence and even after. Because of that, the 'periphery' inevitably turns to the West. True, the 'South' does not have enough financial resources and skilled manpower and has to import them, but where we have to import manpower the foreign manpower must be prepared to implement indigenous models which have relevance to the indigenous peoples.

On the whole, emphasis on the economic element of development does not take serious note of the social, cultural and political dimensions of the life of the people. We are therefore arguing for a notion of development which is total, whole and sustainable. We are calling for a holistic view of development one which views development as "a total social process, which includes economic, social, political and cultural aspects" (Guitierrez, 1981, p. 224). Our perspective on development is holistic, stressing interdependence of the different factors whereby advances in one area should imply advances in other areas as well; conversely, stagnation of one retards the growth of the rest. Emphasis on economic growth alone like in the Western school is unacceptable.

Pursuing indigenous paradigms leads us into a humanistic perspective of development, which in turn leads us into liberation discourse. A humanistic perspective views development "as a total social process which necessarily implies for some an ethical dimension, which presupposes a concern for human values" (Guitierrez, 1981, p. 4). This ethical dimension is missing in the Western perspectives. Because of its absence, human beings are superseded by products and profit. Goods and profits are given priority over people. We argue that people must be placed at the center of the development agenda. When people attain this stage of development they are not only fully developed, but they are also liberated from the constraints of existence. In other words:

> [A] humanistic approach attempts to place the notion of development in a wider context, a historical vision in which mankind assumes control of its own destiny . . . , this leads precisely to a change in perspective which after certain additions and corrections- we would prefer to call liberation. (Guiterrez, 1981, p. 24)

In further underlining our rejection of the Western tendency towards emphasizing economic growth as if that is all there is to development, we perceive development as "a multidimensional process, involving the reorganization and reorientation of entire economic and social systems" (Todaro,

1982, p. 87). Whilst it improves incomes and output, it should typically involve radical changes in institutional, social and administrative structures as well as in popular attitudes, customs and beliefs (Todaro, 1982). In light of this, it would be inadequate to treat development as purely economic growth, modernization or Westernization. The modification on the Western perspective of development implies the rejection of impositions of theories designed from and for the 'North'. We are saying, first, development should not be primarily a measure of wealth, or an increase in the income of individuals. Secondly, we argue that to develop is to satisfy certain human needs. In other words, for anything to be called development and to be meaningful and relevant, it should cater to "adequate and nutritious food, good health, sufficient and satisfactory employment, shelter and equality of wealth" (Shaw & Heard, 1979, p. 74). Finally, we argue that it is not only the South that needs to develop, but rather development is an ongoing open-ended process. Accordingly, in this chapter, development is being construed in the context of being—*becoming*, which should take as its point of departure a specific context notwithstanding the international context where it finds itself located.

Construing development as modernization or Westernization has serious epistemological and axiological implications for the 'South' or the post-colonial states in general. They will find themselves in a race where the 'winning point' is always being moved forward. In addition, they will find themselves in an 'unwinnable' race against the 'North' who consciously consider themselves as the 'pace setters' of Western development. Regrettably, post-colonial states and Zimbabwe included are engaged in this 'unwinnable', 'catch me if you can' or 'catch up' race, where post-colonial states are trying to catch up with the 'North'. Precisely, because post-colonial states are unconsciously engaged in this 'catch me if you can' development race, they end up engaging in 'mimetic' and unsustainable models and paradigms. For as long as post-colonial states see development in terms of trying to *be like them*, they will inevitably and regrettably find themselves in this unwinnable 'catch up' or 'catch me' race resulting in adopting development initiatives that are both irrelevant and unsustainable. This tendency by the South to ape the 'North' and their development paradigms and models has also serious political, epistemological and axiological implications for the South. Politically, it undermines the sovereignty of post-colonial states while they claim to be sovereign yet they still uncritically emulate the North. By adopting development paradigms and models from the 'North', post-colonial states are admitting that they are epistemologically inadequate in terms of coming up with their own indigenous models and paradigms. It is as a result of this feeling of inadequacy that development initiatives by the South are largely unsustainable. One major factor contributing to the unsustainability of such development initiatives is the lack of a relevant philosophy and ideology to inform, *root* and guide them. By a relevant philosophy in this discussion is meant an indigenous discourse that evolves from and seeks to articulate and interrogate an African people's historical and concrete existential circumstances and conditions.

PHILOSOPHY, EDUCATION AND INDIGENIZATION IN ZIMBABWE

The point of departure in this section is on philosophy and education as vehicles of not only indigenization but development in general. Thus, inasmuch as it has been submitted that "practice without thought is blind, thought without practice is empty" (Nkrumah, 1970, p. 79), similarly for indigenization as practice not to be blind and empty but to have 'eyes', it should necessarily be preceded by serious and critical 'thinking' or 'thoughtfulness'. Thought or thoughtfulness is a product of reflection or philosophizing. Accordingly, it is being surmised that for indigenization not to be 'blind' and 'empty', it should equally be preceded by thoughtfulness, philosophizing and not emotionalism or it risks being haphazard, mere 'activism' or reverse discrimination. In other words, if indigenization is to lead to development, it should be informed by a relevant and well-articulated indigenous philosophy. Subsequently, indigenization as sustainable development should have its roots, vision, direction and ethos in the indigenous Zimbabwean philosophy of life. Furthermore, it is also being argued that in view of the centrality of education to any development agenda, and if indigenization is to result in sustainable development, it should be preceded by the indigenization of the education system.

Sustainable development is being argued for precisely because current discourses on development focus on simplistic economic terms dubbed modernization or Westernization but not on sustainable development. By sustainable development, we refer to the World Commission on Environment and Development (1987) which states "development which meets the needs of the present without compromising the ability of future generations to meet their needs". This is the concept of development, which according to the MDGs should inform development initiatives internationally. In other words, for development to be sustainable it should not only be 'presentristic' but also 'futuristic' catering to the needs of the present without undermining the holistic needs of future generations. Therefore, for indigenization to be viewed in the context of development, it needs to be reconsidered and refocused on sustainable development.

For indigenization to succeed, the education system in Zimbabwe must be indigenized and be informed by a relevant African philosophy. However, it needs to be cautioned that whereas the education needs to be indigenized, it should have quality and not simply be 'more' of the 'same' type. In other words, a sustainable indigenization program must be rooted in a quality indigenous education system so that there is no discord between the implementers and the intended goals of the system or between theory and practice. What we anticipated from such a system, therefore, are people, who being products of an indigenized education system, do not only propagate and champion indigenization, but more importantly, are indeed indigenous themselves and are committed to indigenous discourses of development. Thus, we are suspicious about people who appear to champion the cause of indigenization yet they are not indigenous themselves 'spiritually' but are there to satisfy only their self-interests. Commitment needs to be emphasized in view of possible 'double talk' and 'double standards' by the political elite as well as in view of the magnitude of cultural uprootedness and cultural invasion of the mentalities of the African peoples due to several years of conquest and colonialism.

In view of the preceding, we are arguing that indigenization should be viewed and understood in the context of 'empowering' the present Zimbabweans without compromising the ability of future Zimbabweans to be empowered as well. However, unlike the present focus on economic empowerment (*upfumi kuvanhu*), we further suggest that indigenization should be viewed in the context of sustainable development. For indigenization and empowerment to be meaningful, relevant and sustainable, they need to be holistic and inclusive. This is precisely so, because the agenda of sustainable development itself should be informed by a holistic paradigm.

RECONSIDERING INDIGENIZATION IN THE CONTEXT OF TECHNOLOGY AND INCLUSIVE EDUCATION

The point of departure in this section of the discussion is on situating technology and inclusive education at the center of the present discourse on indigenization in Zimbabwe. We posit that for indigenization to bring about the so-called 'black empowerment' or *masimba kuvanhu,* it should not be informed by any education *per se*, but more importantly by inclusive education. Also, because we are living in a world which is technologically driven, inclusive education should be technologically driven. This view was aptly corroborated by the World Education Report which also submitted that:

> Information and communication technologies (ICTs) are a major factor in shaping the new global economy and producing rapid changes in society. Within the past decade, the new ICT tools have fundamentally changed the way people communicate and do business. They have produced significant transformations in industry, agriculture, medicine, business, engineering and other fields. (UNESCO, 1998, p. 16)

Thus, for the indigenization process to realize inclusive or comprehensive development for Zimbabwe, it should be inclusivist in outlook as well as being technologically driven. It should have a much broader outlook of focusing on all citizens lest it risks being viewed as reverse discrimination. Although there is no legal definition of inclusion or inclusive education, many organizations and advocacy groups have developed their own definitions. For instance, Halvorsen and Neary (2001, p. 37) submit that,

> Inclusive education, according to its most basic definition, means that students with disabilities are supported in chronologically age-appropriate general education classes in their home schools and receive the specialized instruction delineated by their individualized education programs (IEP's) within the context of the core curriculum and general class activities.

The National Committee of Special Needs in Education and Training (NCS-NET) of South Africa explained inclusive education as a learning environment that promotes the full personal, academic and professional development of all learners irrespective of gender, race, class, religion, culture, sexual preferences, learning styles and language (Department of Education, 2001). According to UNESCO (1998), inclusive education is seen as a process of addressing and responding to the diversity of needs of all learners through increasing participation in learning, cultures and communities, and reducing exclusion from education and from within education. The aim is that the whole education system will facilitate learning environments where teachers and learners embrace and welcome the challenge and benefits of diversity. Within an inclusive education approach, learning environments are fostered where individual needs are met and every student has an opportunity to succeed. Notwithstanding the absence of a binding definition of inclusion and inclusive education, it is, however, generally accepted that inclusive education is an educational intervention or strategy that seeks to ensure that disadvantaged students including those with disabilities go to school along with their friends and neighbors while also receiving specially designed instruction and support. Students with special needs should be assisted in their educational performance in order to achieve high academic standards and succeed as learners. In other words, the aim of inclusive education is to prepare, particularly disabled learners for an inclusive society, one in which they participate to the best of their abilities like any other learner.

Inclusive education also needs to be interrogated and appreciated against the context of a broad conventional paradigm of education which is inherently exclusivist. It is exclusivist not only because of the 75 million children for whom access to education is denied or those who drop out before school completion (UNESCO-IBE, 2010). Rather, it is largely viewed as such precisely because every day in schools, there are those who are segregated or discriminated against due to their social conditions, ethnic origins, cultural backgrounds, gender, sexual orientation or other individual characteristics or capacities. It is these students that inclusive education seeks to take aboard by advocating for policies, contents and pedagogies that adapt to the diversity of such students so that the students will have the conditions to learn effectively and acquire the skills that will allow them to be successful in work and life.

The present discussion proposes to adopt a rather broader *inclusive* view of inclusive education to include not only the disabled but also those who are segregated or discriminated against for various reasons, consciously or unconsciously, in their efforts to access education. We are also suggesting that, if indigenization is to succeed, the education system which informs it should be inclusive so that every child benefits from it. In other words, we are further arguing that an indigenized inclusive education system should empower all students. Empowerment of students should be serious considered if indigenization is to bring about genuine sustainable development to Zimbabwe.

POSSIBLE CHALLENGES

Notwithstanding the crucial roles technology and inclusive education have in any meaningful and sustainable indigenization initiative, it needs also to be submitted that much as this is desirable, there are some challenges particularly for post-colonial Zimbabwe. The major challenge is financial. Most post-colonial states do not have the financial resources to invest in meaningful technological development programs in their respective countries. They still depend on 'external' and foreign donor funding for most major development projects. Consequently, it is these donors who determine which project to fund depending on their 'interests' in those countries. Meaningful development for the post-colonial African states that has been discussed in this chapter is unlikely to be in the interests of most 'external' donors and therefore is unlikely to be funded. This means that the much needed financing of the required technology to bring about meaningful development through indigenization and inclusive education will not be realized.

The lack of adequate financial resources has implications for a meaningful implementation of a sound and broad-based inclusive education. This is because inclusive education calls for massive financial investment in infrastructure, support resources and manpower, which are regrettably, not readily available. Further, within those African states that have adopted indigenization as a development strategy, the whole initiative has been met with mixed responses due to the problem of definition and conceptualization. There have been problems regarding the articulation of who the indigenous people in these states are. In Zimbabwe for instance, indigenization is viewed as 'black empowerment' or 'wealth to the people'. Ironically, 'people' in this context seems not to include those who are not Africans by descent yet most of them can trace their 'indigeneity' to Africa and Zimbabwe. As a consequence, indigenization is being received with great suspicion because most critical minds view it as 'reverse discrimination'.

CONCLUSION

If indigenization in Africa and Zimbabwe, in particular, is being undertaken in the context of development, it therefore ought to be holistic, inclusive and sustainable. Properly defined, conceptualized and implemented policies have great potential of bringing about genuine sustainable development and independence to Africa. However, as a precondition, we suggested that indigenization and sustainable development should be informed by technology and an indigenized inclusive education. For indigenization to bring about sustainable holistic development, African states should consider investing in technology and inclusive indigenous education in their development agendas in order to realize the United Nations MDGs of sustainable development by 2015.

REFERENCES

Alexander, R.J. (1976). *A new development strategy*. New York: Orbis Books.

Chilisa, B. & Preece, P. (2005). *African perspectives on adult learning—Research methods for adult educators in Africa*. South Africa: David Langham.

Department of Education. (2001). *The national committee of special needs in education and training*. Pretoria: Government of the Republic of South Africa.

Dussel, E. (1985). *Philosophy of liberation*. New York: Orbis Books.

Gibson, R. (1986). *Critical theory and education*. London: Hodder and Stoughton.

Guitirrez, R. (1981). *Frontiers of liberation theology*. London: SCM Press Ltd.

Halvorsen, A.T. & Neary, T. (2001). *Building inclusive schools: Tools and strategies for success*. Needham Heights, MA: Allyn and Bacon.

Jeffrey, R.C. (1968). Probable knowledge. In I. Lakatos (Ed.), *The problem of inductive logic* (pp. 166–180). Amsterdam: North-Holland Publishing Company.

Momjam, K. (1978). *Landmarks in history—The Marxist doctrine of socio-economic formations*. Moscow: Progress Publishers.

Mountjoy, A. (Ed.). (1978). *The Third World: Problems and perspective*. Tokyo: Macmillan Press.

Njobe, M.W. (1990). *Education for liberation*. Cape Town: Skotaville Publishers.

Nkrumah, K. (1970). *Consciencism—Philosophy and ideology for decolonization*. London: Monthly Review Press.

Ogola, J.M. (1985). N*ational workshop on farm tools and equipment technology, basic needs and employment. East African Medical Journal*, 58(15), 593–600.

Rauche, G.A. (1985). *Theory and practice in philosophical argument*. Durban: The Institute of Social and Economic Research.

Rodney, W. (1972). *How Europe underdeveloped Africa*. Harare: Zimbabwe Publishing House.

Shaw, T.M. & Heard, R.A. (Eds.). (1979). *The politics of Africa: Dependence and development*. Hong Kong: Longman.

Shizha, E. (2009). Chara chimwe hachitswanyi inda: Indigenizing science education in Zimbabwe. In D. Kapoor & S. Jordan (Eds.), *Education, participatory action research, and social change: International perspectives* (pp. 139–154). New York: Palgrave Macmillan.

Shizha, E. (2010). Rethinking and reconstituting indigenous knowledge and voices in the academy in Zimbabwe: A decolonization process. In D. Kapoor & E.

Shizha (Eds.), *Indigenous knowledge and learning in Asia/Pacific and Africa: Perspectives on development, education and culture* (pp. 115–129). New York: Palgrave Macmillan.

Shizha, E. (2011). *Indigenous knowledge and science education in Zimbabwe: Perspectives of rural primary school teachers.* Saarbrűcken, Germany: Lambert Academic Publishing.

Todaro, M.P. (1982). *Economics for a developing world—An introduction to principles, problems and policies for development.* Essex: Longman.

UNESCO. (1998). *Teachers and teaching in a changing world.* Paris: UNESCO.

UNESCO-IBE. (2010). *World data on education*, 7th edition, 2010/11. Paris: UNESCO. Retrieved September 15, 2012 from http://www.ibe.unesco.org/fileadmin/user_upload /Publications/ WDE/2010/pdf-versions/Zimbabwe.pdf

Woods, R. & Barrow, R. (1975). *An introduction to philosophy of education.* New York: Methuen.

World Commission on Environment and Development. (1987). *Our common future.* London: Oxford University Press.

Part II

Indigenous Knowledge, Culture and Education

4 Re-Culturing De-Cultured Education for Inclusive Social Development in Africa

Ali A. Abdi

INTRODUCTION

In discussing African education and development, one can no longer afford to ignore the extensity as well as the centrality of the cultural dimension in any discussion that should have the analytical requisites to make sense of the situation. In critically interacting with this issue, and using the generic term Africa while actually talking about the situation of Sub-Saharan Africa, I happen not to reject the possible positive relationship learning programs could have with social development, defined for my purpose here, as the contextual well-being of individuals and groups in their concerned tempo-spatial locations and relationships. Surely the situation is not very easy to determine, and questions of how we define and implicate contextual well-being abound. But the hegemonic conceptual and quasi-practical constructions of development, has been achieved over the lives of Africans in the past 70 years or so. With some of the first officialization of international development contained in a speech by former American President Harry Truman in 1948, and with respect to the implementation of the post-war Marshall Plan for European reconstruction (Black, 2007), the idea of exporting development to foreign lands and peoples has been on course since that time. In Truman's talk, in fact, the prospect that one country can develop the other affirmed the presumptive superiority of Western ways of perceiving, relating to and doing the world. But there was more; this attitude of international development also initiated a new political sociology of depicting certain life contexts, indeed cultural contexts, as inferior and needy of intervention and aid.

The point of 'equating' cultural context with life context is deliberate in the sense that culture, as I want to use it in this discussion, defines and represents the way people live in specific geographical realities at identifiable temporal intersections and conjectures. Thus, as I have said few times before, in our lives, culture is everything, and that certainly includes educational platforms and modes of development or lack thereof. It is with this understanding that the inherent weaknesses of conventional development schemes and colonially constructed learning systems should be visible. Both are devoid of Africa's over millennia established cultural categories, and both have assumed problematic epistemological impositions that confuse the ontological locations of their subjects in Africa and elsewhere in colonized zones of our world. As such, the possible role of education as something that instigates meaningful social development (Fagerlind & Saha, 1989; Mandela, 1994; Abdi, 2006) could be untenable with respect to Africa's 'post-colonial' landscape (the point of qualification should not confuse anyone here; the promise of viable post-coloniality is still elusive). Indeed, in consulting the works of two brilliant Africanists on the topic, Julius Nyerere (1968, 1974) and Walter Rodney (1982), one should not find it complicated to realize how the destruction of African learning and development systems (also construable as the center of Africa's cultural systems) paved the way for the full colonization of both the minds and bodies of the people.

THE PRIMACY OF CULTURE (EDUCATIONAL CULTURE) AND THE PROBLEMATIC CONSTRUCTIONS OF THE STORY

With culture's intergenerational life-ways transmitter function, culture is learned through family socialization, ongoing informal learning realties, and where available, via organized formal educational platforms. In pre-colonial Africa, the former two were the dominant locations of cultural transfer, and for colonialism, that primal cultural capacity was to be first weakened and eventually rescinded. The reason for this calculated colonial intention is not also difficult to comprehend. Cultural constructions and the harnessing of these, accord people a psycho-social capacity that affirms their being and redeems them when they face onto-existential conflict and/or external threats to their personae and overall living realities. As such, with the arrival of colonialism, the first clash between the predatory European culture and the resident African culture was to be fought in the terrains of education and social life systems, which represented what we term today social development. Indeed, as I have relayed in few other writings and with the danger of repeating it too many times (even though that is justifiable due to the endurance of cultural colonialism), the trajectories of colonialism's entry into the African world was firstly cultural followed by the psycho-social, the educational (in formal terms) and the political and economic, all achieved through some aspect of superior technology (mostly in rationalized weaponry deployments).

By making the previous points, I am aware of the possibility that one may argue against my separation of culture and education, relative to what I have already said earlier. In fact, the primacy of the cultural point in the whole story should again affirm the precedence as well as enveloping nature of culture around everything. That is, with everything starting with culture, all the other categories *de facto* become select components of such culture. To even simplify it more, the educational, political and economic realities of the colonizing project are themselves clashes of the two cultures where one was intent on conquest and destruction, and the other, on humanist and co-existentialist notations and practices of life. I will not say a lot about the implicated philosophies of this clash; suffice it to note that as has been discussed by, among others, Demsond Tutu (1999), the African way of living was based on the radical humanist systems of *Ubuntu* that unqualifiably saw the humanity of each person through the humanity of everyone else. That is, all of us are human beings through every other human being, which in my analysis, minimally diminishes the whole-scale colonization and destruction of lands, peoples and lives. Surely, the invading group's worldview was not interested in such inter-human benevolence, but on rationalist and modernist driven economic calculations that saw other humans and everything else as useful resources that should be dominated and exploited. It is, indeed, this fact of the fateful clash that Nyerere's timeless analysis, in his celebrated essay "Education for Self-Reliance" in his book *Freedom and socialism* (1968) so cogently discussed and analyzed.

Nyerere's analysis highlighted the determined colonial project to rescind Africa's cultural realities via the long-term shelving of the educational and social perspectives created and maintained by Africans for contexts that justified their establishment for needs and analysis conceived through the multiperspective localities of people's lives. With this taking place, the location of the family and the community as important sites of informal education and socialization were weakened, and with the dominance of formal colonial schooling, the de-culturing of African education began in earnest. Indeed, as Africa's celebrated socio-historical and cultural-linguistic writers Chinua Achebe (2000, 2009) and Ngugi wa Thiong'o (1986, 2009) reminded us, the deconstruction of the continent's linguistic and cultural locations represented the *sine qua non* of colonial subjugation, and more so in the mental colonizations of the people. Ironically, the idea of education leading to social well-being was turned over, and the new, formalized colonial schooling was to serve as a potent agent of extensive ontological inferioritizations and practical underdevelopment. Clearly, therefore, as Rodney in his magisterial work *How Europe underdeveloped Africa* (1982) so skillfully noted, the new unequal relationship created a situation where perhaps we should see the first problematizations of the ideas as well as the pragmatics of the relationship between education and development.

In my previous comments, I have quasi-equated social development with social well-being, which immediately gives a platform where we should relativize, without conditions, the definitional constructions as well as the possible operationalizations of education and development. If, for example, one agrees with my point on social well-being, then surely any social and politico-economic situation that assures the wellness of people (mainly in the way they perceive and analyze such well-being) should be regarded as development. Contrarily, any context that deprives the wellness of people should be presented as social malaise. From my readings and intentions here, people in pre-colonial Africa had certainly achieved a high level of social well-being that was situationally responsive to their needs, actualities and expectations using a combination of informal and quasi-formal learning systems that horizontally met the demands of the context. Here, again I am staying with the presumed relationship between education and development with both subsumed under the livelihood rubric of culture and its historical formations.

So what kind education led to this kind of social well-being, and what were its characteristics? To answer this central question of the story, I will again rely (as I have done few times before) on what I should tentatively call Rodney's (1982) contextual conditionalities where in order for any learning system to satisfy the implicated needs, it must meet, inter alia, the requirements of the social location of its formulators, implementers and modifiers. That is, who are the social actors and for whom are they designing this learning project? To be even more precise, pre-colonial African education was created by Africans, for African needs and for the future of Africans. Briefly, colonial education, regardless of its programmatic efficiency or organizational qualities, was the opposite of pre-colonial educational formations. It was foreign conceived, created for colonial needs that were destructive for Africans and was maintained to cement the epistemic-cultural colonizations of Africans. In interacting with wa Thiong'o's (1986) seminal work on decolonization, one should be able to clearly see how colonial education was designed to de-Africanize the African, surely a frightening life prospect no matter how you look at it. As we have seen in similar colonial experiences in the globe (e.g., the situation of Aboriginal peoples in Canada and Australia), the colonial attempts (with some success) to de-ontologize and de-epistemologize the natives is tantamount to the deliberate destruction of the concerned. Indeed, to appreciate my emphasis on culture here, one should realize how the process of de-ontologization actually involves the criminalization of speaking native languages, dressing with native attire and retaining native manners. As wa Thiong'o (1993) noted, African languages gave us a view of the world which was later distorted in school by a foreign language of domination, alienation and disenfranchisement.

Indeed, beyond the designers and implementers, one potent way of de-culturing education is to rescind, indeed, deride native languages as inferior and unfit as media of instruction. wa Thiong'o (1993) reports how speaking the mother tongue in colonial schools in Kenya was equated with being stupid. With such deliberate associative realities where intellectual failure is attached to one's cultural language, complemented by a myriad of other de-citizenizations (and all their concomitant subjectifications), the project of onto-epistemological de-Africanization was in full force, and certainly that did not bode well for African learning and social well-being. To see even more of the negative complexities of the situation, the type of de-Africanization empties *qofka wali jirkiisu joogo oo Afrikaanka ah* (the still physically present persona Africana) of what Charles Taylor (1994) terms as the essential self-esteem locations that could aid/affirm one's primordial agency to achieve social development. The problematic schemes Taylor is describing are dominant–subordinate issues that most of us should know. In submerging Africans in highly de-cultured systems of schooling, the processes of deconstructing learners and re-constructing them as colonial subjects follows the simple but inter-generationally impactful projects of misrecognition, imposition of false identities and the quasi-roboticization of new inter-subjective relations where what is admired, accepted and sought is the world of the colonial education and colonial prescriptions of development, frighteningly but in real time and space, complemented by the natives shunning anything that is native.

The even more problematic irony is that in these times of post-deconstruction border existentialities, the situation should be even more complicated. These internalizations of heavy doses of inferioritization are certainly more dangerous than the external imposed oppressions, for these represent some form of completing the circle of psychosomatic colonization where, as Albert Memmi (1991) so cogently discussed, once the colonized internalize their subordinate and deconstructed (indeed destroyed) ontologies, as normal, they come to a new existential location where they 'naturalize' their primordial and contemporaneously lowered being, thus eventually collaborating with the colonizer in their own oppression and marginalization. The self-denial here, as Fanon's classic *Black Skin, White Masks* (1967) so effectively described, is a learned behavior certainly achieved through colonial schooling. So de-cultured education clearly creates a de-cultured persona who instead of seeking schemes of social advancement actually de-advances himself or herself for they have been de-agentified via the negative onto-existential onslaught which renders them psychosocially alienated figures that precariously survive on a hitherto not fully comprehended borderland.

It is with these realities of psyche and self that Africans have moved into nominal post-colonialities that failed in one fundamental aspect of the liberation program: decoupling African education from pedagogically de-culturing colonial philosophies and ways of learning. This educational policy failure in 'post-colonial' Africa created a situation where the 'right' knowledge, the 'right' learning and the 'right' languages all emanate from European and American metropolises where even to validate the emergent epistemic clusters produced in Africa today by Africans could only acquire viable intellectual currency once they garner some external appreciation from extra-Africa locales. This was one situation that did not sit well with the man I dub the doyen of counter-colonial epistemologies, Chinua Achebe (2000, 2009), who expressed his disdain for this 'cocksureness' (his own word) where our intellectual production only makes sense if it first makes sense to Europeans or Americans. A fragment of this culture that amuses me is how Western reviewers of Achebe's work rate his literary weight with this snobbish false generosity: "the best writer in Africa", "the best work by an African". This should solicit the question (at least for me and others of related background), when does an author become a writer of global calibre, not even after his books are translated into 50 languages? To me, this is not too complicated to see. In a straight line analysis, it is a continuation of the colonial project where education (even with multiple certifications), achievement and epistemic sophistication are not associated with Africans because it contravenes the so-called European literary luminaries', philosophers' and thinkers' earlier exhortations (these include Hegel, Kant, Renan, Voltaire and Hobbes) who were somehow sure that Africans were not endowed in their intellectual and civilizational capacities (Abdi, 2008). So the tradition of epistemic colonization continues, and where things would have changed (at the public and educational policy levels), the now celebrated failure of African political leadership does not disappoint at all.

RE-CULTURING AFRICAN EDUCATION: SELECT CATEGORIES

For me, the need to re-culture African education is not an issue of contention; it is, ipso facto, essential and needed now more than ever. It is about infusing a lot of indigeneity into reconstructed knowledge systems, epistemologies and overall learning relationships. Looking at the continent's social development landscape, the current factors are not encouraging, and responding to such reality is important. That does not mean that I am fully buying into Western notions of development and the general indicators deduced from such contexts. What I am aware of is the factedness of the post-facto reality where Africa, as any other continent, is fully integrated into the global political, economic and educational systems. As such, Africa is not purely going back to the pre-colonial traditional systems of education, and has to retain something of current systems of formal learning for both its young and adult learners. As I have argued before, the post-facto event does not necessarily mean that the processes of epistemic colonization, which are a part of the overall event, cannot be neutralized. They can be, for Western education, especially in its technical notations, adopted in ways that do not rescind African life systems, basic educational philosophies and ways of learning and knowing. With the reliable assumption that shareable contemporary knowledge categories have been created by all humans from all corners of the world with Africans contributing as much of the original ideas as anybody else (Harding, 1998; Bernal, 1987), possibilities of selectively borrowing the 'good stuff' from any system of education is not only necessary but desirable.

With that other fact of knowledge histories in mind, therefore, some conditionalities will still be needed for the reconstruction of African education systems to represent and respond to the *adduunka Afrikaanka ah* (the African world) of perceiving, analyzing and establishing both epistemic and related contexts that indemnify the continent in the world's social development scales from which it should not, indeed, cannot currently delink. It is with this in mind that we should look at the possibilities of re-culturing the system by focusing on the select categories redeeming indigenous languages and re-aligning science and mathematics education. By focusing on these, we can also address two issues that are fundamental to African education: respect for oral languages and knowledges and the appreciation of community epistemologies.

As the case is with many colonized populations around the globe, some of the non-traditional requirements of Western education were the horizontal devaluing of the knowledges of oral cultures and the perforce elevating of text-borne ideas and epistemes, complemented by the introduction of non-communal learning platforms that are purely based on individualistic competition. Instead of the traditional African ways of prioritizing what is good for all, the needs as well as the rights of the person (as if the person is hermetically sealed from other needs and rights) are maintained through survival of the fittest learning. Individual advancement schemes when applied to the African context created a situation where those who have direct access to the means of production (to borrow a Marxian expression only for this purpose), which in most cases represented individualizing government managed public resources, as they have been so skillfully taught by their education, accorded all funds and other communally owned liquidities to themselves, their families and supporters.

The social development failure connections I am making here (again in the globally desired modernist notations and practices), may not be clear to all, but I submit they should be. Reading from Hamidou Kane's classic *An Ambiguous Adventure* (1963), and as we saw in the works of Achebe and wa Thiong'o, the greatest colonial damage to Africa is mental, and by extension, cultural, educational and enduringly psychological. With that comes the dislocation of values, relationships, social definitions and the primal meanings attached to success, failure and happiness. All of these are also directly linked to the cultural learning and all achievements thereof. In reconstructing African education with African cultural loci, therefore, we need to recast the space between the individual and community and realign the lost meanings of the body social, which will inculcate new modes of intergroup attention, concern and kindness. No, this is an oversimplification of complex things. It is actually the simplified attempt to re-equip fundamental ontologies and epistemologies torn asunder by the counter-African cultural and learning impositions that have done so much to de-Africanize *la persona Africana*, and that produced Africa's 'post-colonial' leadership decolonization shortcomings that directly affected more countries than we could count here. It is, indeed, this thick reality that many Africanist scholars seemingly missed the crucial need to critique the plethora of post-independence failures. Failures in policy, educational, cultural and attached development reconstructions that should have been systematically undertaken to reconstitute some viable historical conjecture and communal well-being via authentically decolonizing learning projects that contain in their kernel perceptions, values and livable undertakings that are onto-epistemologically and pedagogically African. As I said earlier, this new education should not aim for epistemic exclusions or any deliberate antithetical against anybody, but should just take what is good for Africa. As such, let me briefly focus on specific items that could be situationally realigned in the much needed cultural reconstructions of *pedagogia Africana*.

Language/Linguistic Re-Culturalizations

African nations are arguably some of the most multilingual societies in the world. Surely, this has prospects and problems that are attached to the history of colonialism, where in many instances national linguistic groups were broken up by the vulgaristic straight line drawing of the continent's boundaries by European powers. As important as this analysis is, I cannot accord too much space to it, so I will just speak about the importance of re-linguicizing that which has been de-linguicized in African education and development. As wa Thiong'o noted in his book *Re-membering Africa* (2009), one way to dismember people is to distill them of their languages. However, this does not necessarily mean that no one speaks the language, but that it is so devalued that it is, ipso facto, associated with being unlearned and mastering it does not advance your life chances. In many cases, it even limits the capacity to achieve in today's Africa where fluency in a European language is associated with knowledge, high social standing and professional success. From this viewpoint, we can historically and culturally analyze the benightedness that would befall upon peoples whose mother tongue, the carrier of one's cultural locations, is relegated to the scrap-heap of the concerned context in official circles of power and life management. Indeed, as Shizha (2012b, p. 148) notes, "any group of people's language is embedded in culture since culture expresses the way each group of people thinks and feels, and provides them with an identity".

What would be the condition, for example, of the French and the English if their languages were subjected to such fate by invading colonial entities? Surely, their memories of themselves will be constructed via negative reflections that debase their being so they de-constitute themselves from their culture, self-confidence and human agency. This is precisely what was (being) done to Africa, and without an urgent infusion of reconstructing the continent's linguistic realties and capacities, the promise of functional social development will not happen. As the brilliant analysis of Frantz Fanon (1967) can teach us, the world should belong to those in whose language it is expressed. My own example in this regard should serve me well; as a doctoral student many years ago in Montreal, Canada, I posed the question of my onto-social relationship with English, a language that I have mastered to an extent, and habitually try to manipulate its constructions, as I have attempted to do even in this chapter. In a direct format, I asked myself if, despite my relative mastery of English, this now globalized language belongs to me. Of course, I did not have a ready-made answer, and it took me a few moments to answer myself. My categorical conclusion, as I called it then, was *no*, I do not co-own English. I do not possess the necessary socio-historical and cultural attachments to it, and was therefore psycho-emotionally delinked from it. So what is my relationship with it? Basically it should serve me as literary mechanics with which I have familiarized myself, and due to immediate life exigencies, have decided to deploy for specific needs-triggered realities that were thrust upon me by the already established and savagely unequal global relationships where to make a living and communicate with the world (like I am doing now), I had to learn and excel in someone else's language. This is the center of the story of being educationally de-cultured, and it is so much worse for many others who even with some fluency in European languages, cannot live with some dignity in their daily lives.

With the previously-mentioned social and individual realities in mind, how should we then look into the possibilities of indigenizing the language of education in Africa? Generally, when one starts talking about the language or media of instruction debates in the continent, it is not difficult to find few voices that immediately use the multilinguality of many African countries as an impediment to using African languages in schooling and university settings. By and large, these arguments are not based on any reliable findings but are simply lacking the capacity to understand the thick relationship between indigenous languages, educational achievement, and by extension, social well-being. One example of not just general multilinguality but official multilinguality is the case of post-apartheid South Africa where despite the national/global power of English, some respect has been accorded, at least in official political corridors, to nine African languages, which along with Afrikaans, leaving South Africa with 11 official languages. With respect to expanding these languages, which are basically limited to some local primary school contexts and in mandated parliamentary interpretations, as important media of instruction even selectively, does not seem to be moving forward. Interestingly, the opposition to this is not limited to the powers that be which in economics, business and higher education would prefer everybody to be fluent in English, but as well, from many African parents who equate the mastery of this language with the assured employment success of their children (Evans & Cleghorn, 2012). That is understandable, but we need to see beyond the facade of the simplicity of people's Anglophone status and immediate job prospects. Indeed, the story is not so natural; it was created through domination, linguistic oppression and the outright devaluation of African education and its attached linguistic and epistemological realities.

Instead of relying on a historical alibi, one needs to realize even with those languages that are orally based in many parts of Africa, their epistemic equity with European languages cannot be minimized or pedagogically exiled from contemporary spaces of learning and social development. Surely, every language which is always a primary platform for the survival of concerned communities has sustained people over millennia to define their world, affirm their relationships and connections, responsibly (or with modernity, irresponsibly) use their resources, defend against both external and internal dangers and plan their futures with as much precision as those on the other side of the mountain, or for that matter, around the globe. Factually, the idea of complicating the role of local languages as effective media of instruction at all levels of education is unacceptable and more of concern to Africa than any other continent, particularly more in Sub-Saharan Africa than Arab North Africa, where Arabic is the main language of instruction in almost all aspects of schooling. It is not also a secret that on average, North Africa scores higher on the human development index (HDI) than those below the Sahara. The exception here is even more interesting. South Africans of European origin are doing better than Arab North Africans. Which should immediately beg the question, how is this attached to language and education? The important, timely answer to this concern, at least as far as I am concerned, is not at all difficult to find. The only people among the three groups who are not educated in their indigenous languages are Africans in South Africa, and of course, other Africans in other zones of the continent.

When one looks at social development in the global context today, Sub-Saharan Africa is depicted as the least developed zone; it is also where almost all education is conducted via foreign languages. So by accepting most of Sub-Saharan Africa as underdeveloped (not actually developing), one can also say that, more often than otherwise, all developed countries use their native languages as media of instruction, and so are most developing countries in Asia and Latin America. Perhaps the best examples among the latter are China, Korea, Brazil, Mexico and many others. Clearly, therefore, there is minimally a sizable conjectural evidence with respect to the relationship between indigenous languages and education and social development platforms. Certainly then, it is high time for African educational policymakers to re-think the language of education in the continent, and realize that the developmental move-forward cannot happen through linguistically de-cultured systems of education that marginalize the onto-epistemological realities of people that render their potentialities for well-being less viable.

Select Notations on Re-Culturing Science and Mathematics Education

With respect to culturing science and mathematics education, again, the issue is not to create some kind of science or mathematics that is purely African. In fact, in today's highly interconnected, networked world, there may not be such a thing as African science, Asian Science or European science for that matter. Whereas the global science domain is now dominated by the West, for example, the origins of science are historically and paradigmatically Eastern. Science is also socio-culturally constructed, and as Shizha (2012a) notes, less certain than otherwise believed, and can, be provisionally located against its contexts and users. So the claimed Western ownership of science stands on very shaky ground. In fact, most of the inventions we associate with advanced science today including advanced mathematics, astronomy, engineering and medicine have non-contemporary Western roots. This is one reason we should heed Sandra Harding's emphasis on the foundations of science as entirely multicultural (Harding, 1998, 2008). Clearly, therefore, it is necessary to fully comprehend the reality that Africans have brought as many bricks as anybody else to the edifice of science. As Van Sertima (1991) noted, for thousands of years, Africans were as advanced, if not more advanced, as anyone else in the practical applications of some scientific fields including astronomy and certain areas of engineering. Even more important is the fact that Africans were the first to introduce the use of iron without which most scientific applications would be obsolete. Needless to add that with the advent of colonialism, African science and science education which included projects in agriculture and related irrigation systems, medicine, veterinary medicine, meteorology and astronomy, which were mostly undertaken in quasi-informal learning contexts, were all derided as inferior to Western education, and along with elements of African development, excluded from the new imperialist dispensations of schooling.

With African pre-colonial science and scientific education historic-culturally emanating from African life and attached systems and humano-ecological connections, the rescinding of such learning programs represented another component of de-culturing African education, and by extension, indigenous possibilities of social well-being. As such and contrary to extensively biased arguments, the story is not and should not be about exporting Western science to the continent. More pragmatically, it is reconstructing hegemonically deconstructed local sciences and epistemologies of science that must now claim a viable, minimally equal place in current systems of learning. This scientific re-culturing will not be and cannot be an isolationist enterprise, but one that positively responds to the multicultural nature of all science, thus engendering a space of education where the best from Africa's science, including that which is practiced in the community's public spaces, should be intermeshed with what is practically useful for Africans from Western notions and practices of science. Here, the case is not at all as difficult as Western rationalists would want us to believe.

Needless to add that in our quest to reconstitute some useful scientific education for Africa's children, who as much as anybody else, acutely need such projects in the post-industrial and technologized societies claims, we are not necessarily looking for some kind of isolationism, non-practical African physics, biology or African electrical engineering. Simply, the general advocacy should be redesigning these subjects so that they contain certain foundational knowledge, concrete examples and epistemologies that can selectively Africanize the platform as well as the learning relationships of schooling. As I intend it here, therefore, my point on reculturing African science education is not a call to do away with Western systems of schooling but to acculturate or *selectively* post-modernize (i.e., a new version of anti-colonial post-modernization) the physical sciences and mathematics education, where these subjects are given a thick loci and foci that are minimally or partially African. It is with that happening that science education in Africa can assume an active decolonizing effect (Shizha, 2012a).

With respect to mathematics education, Bishop's points in his aptly titled article "Western Mathematics: The Secret Weapon of Cultural Imperialism" are still valid in that (if) to "decontextualize is in the heart of Western mathematics, and if your culture believes that everything belongs and exits in its relationship with everything else, then removing it from its context makes it literally meaningless" (Bishop, 1995, p. 74). Indeed, it does not only become meaningless, it also elevates the mathematicizable epistemological locations of those who come from such rationalist, decontextualizing and individualistically competitive communities in the West and willfully disadvantages the rest. As such, recontextualizing and resocializing mathematics and science education assists African learners to culturally relate to and appreciate the subjective connections they could establish with schooling so as to make it useful and recognizable in their daily lives. Certainly every group anywhere in the world including Africans have always counted and deciphered complex mathematical realities for the continuation of their immediate livelihood. The epistemological questions therefore are: how did this group vis-à-vis that group count? What counting methods did they develop and value in their specific situations and with respect to their emergent and expected needs?

In the African context, the methodologies of counting and cultural mathematical acquisition usually display a location of amicability and play where the whole exercise, although not entirely void of some competition, is collaboratively undertaken (Nabie, 2012). Clearly, therefore, in such contexts, mathematics becomes less of a project that advances its usually problematic loser syndrome, and represents something that is sought in ensemble, so it constructively creates a solution that meets the community's needs and expectations. Indeed, it is via the achievement of these combined epistemologies and methodologies of instruction that African science and mathematics education could be re-cultured and brought to the location of the African child, not as hegemonic archetypes of Western schooling, but as contextually inclusive possibilities of education that affirm their voice as well as those of their communities and families. Needless to add that when these subjects are conveyed via indigenous languages, the current instructional schemes of alienation will subside, thus assuring a world of learning where the day is not commanded by de-ontologized and de-epistemologized categories of knowledge, but by a concrete perception of historic-cultural and contemporary affirmations of self and society that will certainly aid the needed self-efficacy for conscious social development.

CONCLUSION

In this chapter, I have analytically and certainly critically engaged the colonial deformations and, by extension, de-culturings of African educational and social development contexts. In speaking about this, I have expressed the level of learning and general related problematics that this has caused in achieving viable advancement schemes that could have favored the lives of the African people. With the systematic de-culturing of African education and the rescinding of contextually important traditional platforms of education, the colonial was also determined to de-ontologize and de-epistemologize the overall existentialities of *dadka Afrikaanka ah*. With this in place, one would have expected 'post-colonial' African educational policymakers to re-establish systems of learning that are not counter-African culture, history and ways of knowing. Unfortunately that did not happen, and the continuities of colonial education, philosophies and structures mostly stayed intact, which should primarily explain the development difficulties the continent and its peoples face, especially in these times of globally interlinked post-facto realities where Africans cannot and should not withdraw from their connections with the rest of the world.

It is with these facts in mind that I have called for new and urgent ways of de-culturing African learning systems, including novel ways of re-introducing African languages as media of instruction and even aiming for possible ways of Africanizing science and mathematics education. These suggestions should not be as difficult as they might sound to some. Surely all languages have always served as media of education, and marginalized African languages continue to do so in the informal contexts of family, the playground and in communal public spaces. These languages also already possess the etymological constructions as well as the descriptive dexterity and analytical sophistication to respond to any epistemic contexts that could be embedded in contemporary learning relationships. The proof of this is abundantly located within and around pre-colonial traditional education systems where, as indicated earlier, almost all systems of complex learning in almost all subjects were created, operationalized and modified for community well-being and development. Therefore, the need as well as the viability to re-culture African education for inclusive African social well-being is as urgent as ever, and without some extensive reforms in this domain, Africans will continuously survive on the side of the global *precariate* in a world that belongs to those in whose language it is expressed.

REFERENCES

Abdi, A.A. (2006). Culture of education, social development and globalization: Historical and current analyses of Africa. In A. Abdi, K. Puplampu & G. Dei (Eds.), *African education and globalization: Critical perspectives* (pp. 13–30). Lanham, MD: Rowman & Littlefield.

Abdi, A.A. (2008). Europe and African thought systems and philosophies of education: 'Re-culturing' the trans-temporal discourses. *Cultural Studies*, 22(2), 309–327.

Achebe, C. (2000). *Home and exile.* New York: Oxford University Press.

Achebe, C. (2009). *The education of a British protected child.* Toronto: Doubleday.

Bernal, M. (1987). *Black Athena: The Afro-Asiatic roots of classical civilization: The fabrication of Ancient Greece 1785–1985.* New York: Scholarly Book Services.

Bishop, A. (1995). Western mathematics: The secret weapon of cultural imperialism. In B. Ashcroft et al. (Eds.), *The post-colonial studies reader* (pp. 71–76). London: Routledge.

Black, M. (2007). *No-nonsense guide to international development.* Toronto: Between the Lines.

Evans, R. & Cleghorn, A. (2012). *Complex classroom encounters: A South African perspective.* Rotterdam, Netherlands: Sense Publishers.

Fagerlind, I. & Saha, L. (1989). *Education and national development: A comparative perspective.* Toronto: Pergamon Press.

Fanon, F. (1967). *Black skin, white masks.* New York: Grove Press.

Harding, S. (1998). *Is science multicultural? Postcolonialisms, feminisms, epistemologies.* Bloomington, IN: Indian University Press.

Harding, S. (2008). *Sciences from below: Feminisms, postcolonialities and modernities.* Durham, NC: Duke University Press.

Kane, C.H. (1963). *Ambiguous adventure.* London: Heinemann.

Mandela, N. (1994). *Long walk to freedom: The autobiography of Nelson Mandela.* Toronto: Doubleday.

Memmi, A. (1991). *The colonizer and the colonized.* Boston: Beacon Press.

Nabie, M. (2012). Cultural games and mathematics education in Ghana: A theoretical analysis. In H. Wright & A. Abdi (Eds.), *The dialectics of African education and Western discourses: Counter-hegemonic perspectives* (pp. 163–179). New York: Peter Lang.

Nyerere, J. (1968). *Freedom and socialism: A selection from writing and speeches, 1965–67.* London: Oxford University Press.

Nyerere, J. (1974). *Man and development.* New York: Oxford University Press.

Rodney, W. (1982). *How Europe underdeveloped Africa.* Washington, DC: Howard University Press.

Shizha, E. (2012a). Are we there yet? Theorizing a decolonizing science education for development in Africa. In A. Abdi (Ed.), *Decolonizing philosophies of education* (pp. 163–175). Rotterdam, Netherlands: Sense Publishers.

Shizha, E. (2012b). Linguistic independence and African education and development. In H. Wright & A. Abdi (Eds.), *The dialectics of African education and Western discourses: Counter-hegemonic perspectives* (pp. 148–162). New York: Peter Lang.

Taylor, C. (1994). *Philosophical arguments.* Cambridge, MA: Harvard University Press.

Tutu, D. (1999). *No future without forgiveness.* Victoria: Image Publishers.

Van Sertima, I. (1991). *Blacks in science: Ancient and modern.* New Brunswick, NJ: Transaction Publishers.

wa Thiong'o, N. (1986). *Decolonising the mind: The politics of language in African literature*. London: James Curry.
wa Thiong'o, N. (1993). *Moving the centre: The struggle for cultural freedoms*. London: James Curry.
wa Thiong'o, N. (2009). *Re-membering Africa*. Nairobi: East Africa Educational Publishers.

5 Counter-Visioning Contemporary African Education

Indigenous Science as a Tool for African Development

Edward Shizha

INTRODUCTION

Knowledge and education that are socially and culturally constructed are significant to appropriate sustainable development. For centuries, indigenous African sciences have been neglected in education and development. The current neo-liberal globalization agendas promote Western epistemologies while marginalizing African indigenous knowledges (IK). This chapter interrogates the neglect of IK and sciences in African education and development programs in favor of elitist and positivist approaches and questions the failure of policymakers to utilize IK in promoting development. The chapter further argues, from a critical post-colonial perspective, for African development that emerges from implementing anti-colonial discourses and African IK. The conclusion made from the discussion is that education for social development in post-colonial Africa should be founded on the principle of heterogeneity of knowledges in creating a vision for socio-economic development through inclusive science.

CULTURE AND EDUCATION IN AFRICA

Culture is shared behavioral patterns of identity and how social values are transmitted among members of a community. The culture of any society has a historical basis and is passed on from one generation to another, and as the environment in which each generation finds itself changes, so does culture (Nicolaides, 2012). Broadly speaking, culture is both symbolic/material and non-material. There is a considerable relationship between cultural beliefs, values and knowledge and material culture that symbolizes social development. In Africa, cultures provide knowledge and systems of thought that guide and regulate social conduct and material production. These cultures are learned and transmitted through both formal and informal education.

Education is a socialization process for imparting knowledge and building individual personality. It is the process by which culture is learned. Often, education is supposed (although not always the case) to create shared meanings in a harmonious community and opportunities for thinking, planning and designing social programs. However, education takes place in contested cultural and socio-political contexts (Nieto, 1999). Culture and education are constantly changing resulting in people learning new ways of interacting with their social and natural environments. Thus, the content and context of education and development cannot be divorced from the people's culture and lived-experiences. The content of education, as determined by the most powerful people in society, is the main vehicle for transforming culture. In colonial Africa, power was used to impose Euro-centric education at the expense of indigenous African systems. That power was used to define knowledge, policies and programs for political and socio-economic development. While it is widely accepted and agreed that culture is dynamic, multifaceted, embedded in context and influenced by social, economic and political factors, how it can be used to colonize other cultures is of great concern to post-colonial and anti-colonial theorists.

Historically, in Africa, colonial education introduced inevitable risks to African cultural realities. The risks included the loss of individual and cultural identities and disrupted African legitimate socio-cultural order. Whereas traditionally indigenous education provided stability and socio-cultural progress, hegemonic European education disabled the 'cultural toolkit' (Bruner, 1990) for imparting wisdom to new generations. Culture as the toolkit for survival strengthened the capacities and capabilities to participate in community life. Unfortunately, the disruptive European education introduced individualistic and competitive attitudes that were alien to African collective societies.

Before colonization, traditional African cultural contexts were significantly favorable to the mental development and interpersonal relationships that involved symbolic exchanges between teachers (elders), parents and learners. Colonial education introduced an individualistic approach to learning that is not in sync with African communal realities. In current educational settings that adopted Western education, individuals are responsible for their success, and they work independently to determine their path to educational success. These 'universalistic' settings lack unique local realities and experiences that encourage collaboration and the reproduction of cultural particularisms and collectivisms.

CONCEPTUALIZING INDIGENOUS AFRICAN WORLDVIEWS AND SCIENCE

Knowledge does not exist in a vacuum, but depends on the socio-cultural environment in which it is created. All forms of knowledge (universalistic/global or particularistic/local), including science are socially and culturally created to benefit their creators. Indigenous science is grounded in indigenous cosmologies of place, cognition, affect and spirituality. In Africa, cultural knowledge determines social reality and the guiding principles of social action. It provides a worldview or cognitive lens for perceiving the world. Describing worldviews, Hart (2010, p. 2) states:

> Worldviews are cognitive, perceptual, and affective maps that people continuously use to make sense of the social landscape and to find their ways to whatever goals they seek. They are developed throughout a person's lifetime through socialization and social interaction. They are encompassing and pervasive in adherence and influence. Yet they are usually unconsciously and uncritically taken for granted as the way things are.

Worldviews are culturally determined frameworks for understanding lived experiences. In Africa, indigenous cultures provide insights and analytical tools/guidelines for creating socio-cultural experiences. An understanding of indigenous African ecological systems leads to an understanding of indigenous African sciences. Indigenous worldviews emerged as a result of the people's close relationship with their natural environment and their lived experiences. According to Asabere-Ameyaw, Dei and Raheem (2012, p. 5):

> Studies of African Indigenous knowledge systems attest to how the physical environment has been an important source of knowledge about herbal pharmacology and herbatology, indigenous farming technologies, traditional arts and crafts, including folkloric productions, knowledge of climatic changes and patterns, as well as local soil and vegetation classification systems.

From an indigenous African perspective, the natural environment is significant in understanding indigenous science/ecological knowledge. The physical environment is the source of scientific knowledge and it contributes to health promotion for both humans and animals. Currently, over "80% of the world's population depends on indigenous healthcare based on medicinal plants" (Eyong, 2007, p. 125). Indigenous people use at least 20,000 plant species for medicines and related purposes (Melchias, 2001, as cited in Eyong, 2007). Therefore, indigenous ecological systems support people's physical, spiritual, emotional and psychological well-being. For example in Cameroon, studies have confirmed that medicinal plants used in Central Africa are as efficient as the imported 'Western' prescription medicine and the U.S. National Cancer Institute reportedly signed a contract with the government following the discovery of a forest plant species with a potential anti-AIDS chemical (Nkuinkeu, 1999, as cited in Eyong, 2007). In Kenya, a study by Njoroge and Bussmann (2006) concluded that the Kikuyu use herbal remedies such as *Strychnos henningsii, Ajuga remota* and *Olea europaea* to cure malaria (as cited in Wane, 2010). In Tanzania in the Pangani District, traditional healers are reported to have treated opportunistic diseases of over 2,000 HIV/AIDS patients using medicinal plants. Some terminally ill patients have reportedly lived longer by five years (Scheinman, 2000, as cited in Gorjestani, 2000). These observations from rural indigenous communities confirm the medicinal value of indigenous African science.

New alternative worldviews that are now held by a majority of the African elite were introduced during colonization and led to contradictions and inconsistences in how African knowledge is perceived and conceptualized in the post-modern era. The education that was provided by colonial educators failed to create space for both linear-rational and non-linear metaphoric forms of knowledge production. The majority of Africans who have maintained their indigenous cultural views feel alienated from the new world order, which universalizes knowledge and science. For them, on one hand, dominant worldviews are not sufficient enough to provide solutions to their socio-economic needs. On the other hand, indigenous perspectives are also viewed as inadequate for the current development projects. Development work with indigenous peoples requires acting outside of the dominant worldviews while incorporating the views of the locals. Therefore, given the interdependence of knowledges, the ideal is to create 'interknowledges' for development.

INDIGENOUS AFRICAN ECOLOGICAL KNOWLEDGE

Definitions of indigenous ecological knowledges (IEK) rest on specific epistemological assumptions that they are about the relationship of living beings with one another and with their ecological environment. The knowledges are organized around a central principle of pragmatism and active practicalities over metaphysical or abstract explanations. They are place- and context-specific and situated in contexts of engagement. Place-based knowledge is scientific and essentially applicable and appropriate to the needs of users. Knowledge that is locally generated "encompasses an explicit understanding of relationships and processes, an embodied knowledge of community relationships and the ecology of place, an awareness of the layered nature of the interdependencies of life-sustaining processes" (Bowers, 2001, p. 152). Place is an important element in defining indigenous African science as it unites and solidifies the connections among ecosystems, cultures, learning and sustainable development.

IEKs include a system of classification, a set of empirical observations about the local environment, and a system of self-management that governs resource use (Maweu, 2011). Because of the broad and complex nature of IKs and their marginalization in contemporary societies, Islam (2012, p. 9) concludes that:

> In view of the marginalisation process, IK today means 'non-Western' or 'anti-Western' knowledge. IK includes the way people observe and measure what is around them, how they set about solving problems, and how they validate new information. Recently, the term indigenous

> knowledge has been used in different disciplines, such as sustainable development, environmental studies, agriculture, rural development, aqua-culture, animal husbandry, social sciences, health science, cultural studies, language and linguistics, and many other branches of social sciences.

IEK is holistic and an act of empowerment for indigenous people. It constitutes a whole range of possibilities for a community's adaptive strategy. The holistic relationship between indigenous people and their ecological system is explained by McKenzie and Morrissette (2003, p. 259) who state:

> All things exist according to the principle of survival; the act of survival pulses with the natural energy and cycles of the earth; this energy is part of some grand design; all things have a role to perform to ensure balance and harmony and the overall well-being of life; all things are an extension of the grand design, and, as such, contain the same essence as the source from which it flows (*Gitchi-Munitou*); and this essence is understood as "spirit," which links all things to each other and to Creation.

In practice, holistic relationships between people and nature are the core of human existence. This relational worldview (Graham, 2002, as cited in Hart 2010) explains the nature of relationships that are not conceived as vehicles for maximizing individual satisfaction but a common good. An individual does not exist outside his social and ecological environment. An understanding of the social and the ecological creates a symbiotic relationship between individuals, the family, the community and their ecological environment. Uncontrolled individualism promotes mistrust, disharmony and dysfunctional communities.

INDIGENOUS AFRICAN SCIENCES, GLOBALIZATION AND BIO-COLONIZATION

In his article "The Interface of Neo-liberal Globalization, Science Education and Indigenous African Knowledges in Africa", Shizha (2010, p. 27) asks the following important questions: "With the imposition of neo-liberal globalization and Eurocentric science education in Southern Africa, how do African people develop their African humanity and sensibilities? How can African students and people, in general, reclaim indigenous sciences to act upon their natural world?" Globalization has rekindled colonial memories that reify Eurocentric cultural values and predispositions that are presented as scientific or empirical (Shizha, 2011). A critical contributing factor that impacts the dynamics in the construction and legitimization of science knowledge is the influence of globalization and corporate power.

According to Nicolaides (2012, p. 121), "Globalisation implies a set of social processes that seem to alter the current social condition by seeking to weaken nationality so that one global post-modern 'nation' may emerge". When we consider the elusive and multifaceted effects of globalization and the complex nature of indigenous sciences, it is even harder to predict the impact of globalization on indigenous ecological issues. Nicolaides (2012) further contends that globalization is a set of integrative global processes working on different levels and in diverse dimensions for the purpose of convergence, greater development and less global conflict. However, there is adequate evidence that global conflict exists due to the global plunder and exploitation of resources by multinational corporations.

Indigenous ecologies are being monopolized and commodified for the global market by multinational corporations mainly from a few Euro-American nations (of course now joined by Chinese companies). Advocates of IK criticize Western development models for their concern with commodification and commercialization of knowledge for development without concern for sustainable use of resources. Resources are depleted to the extent of creating uncertainties in the future of indigenous ecological systems and biodiversity. Globalization of resources has the tendency to disrupt the socio-ecological relationship that is the key to the indigenous African existence. According to Ramakrishnan (2002, p. 235):

> Recently recognized human-induced ecological drift collectively termed '*global change*,' and the market driven '*globalization*' of economies have added another dimension to biodiversity management and its conservation. Both these phenomena affect socio-ecological systems in a variety of different ways depending upon the resources that are under the command of the societies in the '*developing*' and the '*developed world*'.

Through globalization, multinational corporations in the 'developed' world unfairly benefit from the expropriation and monopolistic control of genetic resources from indigenous African communities. Indigenous cultural sciences are being "positioned at the nucleus of globalization and within this ideology, multinational corporations are free to control events in a nation without any limitations" (Nicolaides, 2012, p. 122). The appropriated genetic resources are utilized in manufacturing bio-engineered products, which are then patented by the multinational corporation in question. This 'new' globalized relationship of exploitation has been described as bio-piracy and bio-colonization (Harry, 2001).

Bio-colonialism is in many respects more of the same—a continuation of the oppressive power relations that have historically informed the interactions of Western and indigenous cultures, and part of a continuum of contemporary practices that constitute forms of cultural imperialism (Whitt, 2009). Indigenous genetic materials have been patented and Westerners owning copyrights merely repackage the knowledge base from local

Africans. As noted in this chapter, a good example of bio-colonization is the repackaging of the San people's *hoodia* which is now being sold in pharmacies in Europe and North America.

The advent of the genomics revolution is fueling a new wave of scientific research in the form of bio-prospecting, and it is impacting the lives of indigenous peoples around the world. The commodification of knowledge and of genetic resources that bio-colonialism facilitates is sharply at odds with the web of prescriptions and proscriptions that guide the process of knowing within indigenous contexts (Whitt, 2009). There are concerns about global pilfering of indigenous plants through the so-called global diversity. The monopolization of intellectual property rights and the growth of biotechnology are causing conflict in indigenous communities. Western scientists, plant breeders and biotechnologists are at the forefront of multinationalizing and privatizing indigenous genetic material that they collect from indigenous communities. They are working with/for pharmaceutical biotechnological corporations that enforce patents that exclude the real owners (indigenous people and their communities) from being identified with the collected material and the processed product.

The expropriation of indigenous genetic material through biological invasion and the colonization of indigenous ecological systems are likely to result in biodiversity depletion (Ramakrishnan, 2002). For example, Whitt (2009) describes the concerns of the Guajajara in Brazil whose herbal/medical knowledge to treat glaucoma using *Pilocarpus jaborandi* has been jeopardized by bio-colonialism. *Pilocarpus* populations have been virtually depleted as Brazil has exported it for some $25 million annually, and corporations holding patents derived from it have earned far more than the Guajajara who have been subjected to debt peonage and slavery by the agents of the companies involved in the trade. Overconsumption through bio-prospecting by multinational corporations has the consequence of environmental degradation when viewed from the context of the great divide between the rich and poor nations. Therefore, indigenous resource management and control should be viewed with skepticism when it is introduced by the same organizations that are exploiting indigenous resources.

INDIGENOUS AFRICAN SCIENCE AND SUSTAINABLE DEVELOPMENT

There is crucial debate on whether global knowledge is more important than IK for a country's social development. Development is usually associated with changes in material culture, and the utilization of material culture to enhance people's livelihoods. Many indigenous people have intricate knowledge of their ecological environment and have developed technologies for sustainable management of their resources. Subsequently, indigenous communities have lived in harmony with their environment and have utilized resources without impairing nature's capacity to regenerate itself (Shizha, 2010). Their way of living is sustainable.

The advent of bio-colonialism and globalization, with their emphasis on neo-liberal knowledge, science and technology, has led to IK being either subsumed in the Western concept of "knowledge for sustainable development", or ignored altogether (Maweu, 2011). The concept 'sustainable development' became a common theme in development strategies since the Brundtland Commission of the mid-1980s. The Commission Report (World Commission on Environment and Development, 1987, p. 43) defined sustainable development as development that "meets the needs of the present without compromising the ability of further generations to meet their own needs". From an African indigenous perspective, the use of resources in a nature-friendly controlled way achieves sustainability.

Sustainable development should be considered in its wider framework for evaluating the development process and also for evolving suitable development for the future (Das Gupta, 2011). Sustainable use of biological resources means finding new drugs, crops and industrial products, while conserving the resources for future generations. This concern for sustainability is often viewed as less-profitable from the perspective of industrialized nations' neo-liberal market economy. The global market economy is exploitative, profit-making-oriented and not resource-sustainable. For example, Ramdas (2009) explains that the World Bank views climate change as an investment opportunity that will assist communities to use forests as a means of moving out of poverty and suggests that local ownership offers opportunities to capitalize on forest assets. This powerful convergence of global climate change policies and neo-liberal markets appears to be an overriding force in shaping the direction of development policies in 'developing' nations (Kapoor, 2010). Sustainable development, from indigenous perspectives, focuses on managing and controlling resources without creating imbalances in the ecosystem. Therefore, indigenous groups in Africa and other geographical regions should form political-ecological movements that challenge neo-liberal and capitalist paradigms that promote destructive and unsustainable development. They should resist exploitative and repressive capitalist relations of development. Although capitalism is gaining unabated momentum in Africa, indigenous people should learn from the Adivasi oppositional social movement in India which has resisted colonial and imperial projects that transgress their indigeneity (Kapoor, 2012).

Indigenous institutions, indigenous appropriate technology and low-cost approaches can increase the efficiency of development programs because IK is a locally owned and managed resource (Gorjestani, 2000). Gorjestani proposes that utilizing IK helps to increase the sustainability of development efforts because the IK integration process provides for mutual learning and adaptation, which in turn, contributes to the empowerment of local communities. Because efficiency, effectiveness and sustainability are key determinants of the quality of development work, harnessing IK has a clear development business perspective. The realization that IK has not become redundant in today's world is increasingly widespread. According to Kothari (2007), the Rio Declaration, the Convention on Biological Diversity, the World Summit on Sustainable Development, institutions such as the World Intellectual Property Organisation, the International Labour Organization, the Food and Agricultural Organization, the World Health Organization, UNESCO, UNEP, UNDP, the UN Commission on Human Rights and a number of other international organizations have similarly recognized and acknowledged the diversity, utility value and sustainability of IK.

IK is used in sectors like textiles, pharmaceuticals, household goods and so on. In health care, some systems of medicine are dependent on IK, or on combinations of IK and Western knowledge. Eyong (2007, p. 133) gives an illuminating example of how indigenous African resources promote the development of health in Africa and how this knowledge has been expropriated to Europe and North America:

> A multiple-use tree species *Prunus africana* has local as well as international economic and medicinal values. The bark is the major source of an extract used to treat benign prostatic hyperplasia. . . . This tree is found in Angola, Burundi, Cameroon, DR Congo, Equatorial Guinea, Rwanda, Sudan and Uganda. Its bark which contains *phytosterols* or *beta-sitosterol, pentacyclic triterpenoids* like *ursolic* and *oleaic* acids and *ferulic esters* of *docosanol* and *tetracosanol*, is exported to Europe for drug production.

This is evidence that African IKs are scientific and authentic. Another example of the value of indigenous sciences is the popularization of *hoodia* by Western pharmaceutical scientists (Shizha, 2011). The *hoodia gordonii* plant is a succulent that grows in Southern Africa. It contains cellulose, *croscarmellose* sodium, stearic acid, silicon dioxide, magnesium stearate and pharmaceutical glaze, and it is used as an appetite suppressant. *Hoodia* has found a large market in Europe and North America where it is used to control obesity. IK systems are no longer useful only to the local people in Africa, but they are also being exported to external markets.

According to Kothari (2007), numerous studies have demonstrated the contribution that IK makes to the modern pharmaceutical industry and modern health care with the World Health Organization estimating that 25% of modern medicines are made from plants/herbs first used traditionally. Unfortunately, those who have colonized indigenous sciences would want us to believe that indigenous remedies are unscientific. Far from it, indigenous sciences are as good as any other sciences. All sciences have their origins in the indigenous or traditional cultural practices of particular societies. Colonial misconceptions of indigenous African science, knowledge or development tended and still tend to disqualify what is outside the knowledge realms and realities of Western paradigms. From the perspective of these colonizing agents, Whitt (2009, pp. 1–2) aptly concludes that:

> The ideology that sustains biocolonialism is, in turn, rooted in the neo-positivist assumption of value neutrality and in a practice of value bifurcation which together enable it to deflect ethical and political critique. It both facilitates the marginalization of indigenous knowledge systems and provides thereby a legitimating rationale for biocolonialist practice.

The hypocrisy of neo-positivists has led to bio-colonization and the plundering of indigenous genetic resources in an attempt to establish the medicinal value of these genetic resources, an attempt to standardize scientific knowledge.

STANDARDIZED SCIENCE KNOWLEDGE VERSUS INCLUSIVE SCIENCE

Globalization and its acknowledgment of diversity, has meant that IEK is becoming increasingly prominent in many educational disciplines including in science education (Carter, 2008). If development theorists and practitioners strongly believe that IK is a critical factor for sustainable development, it is imperative that indigenous sciences make their way into the education curriculum. However, Western approaches to science have excluded IK and ways of learning that are traditionally practical and hands-on. IK learning requires attentiveness, presence of being and inter-related engagement that is not found in Western academic textbooks.

The Folly of Standardization of Science

The inclusion of IKs in development has been acknowledged as contributing to efficiency, effectiveness and sustainable development impact (Gorjestani, 2000). Indigenous science, like any other knowledge, needs to be constantly used, challenged and further adapted to changing local contexts. Schools are the institutions that can promote the importance of indigenous sciences. This means that in African education systems, policymakers, curriculum planners, educational administrators and teachers have to address complex challenges in terms of how 'official science' continuously disrupts the lived experiences and intercultural realities of students. School science has failed to address the social, cultural, political and socio-economic needs of local communities in Africa.

School science tends to be standardized. The curriculum and how it is taught is pre-programmed. Standardization is critical to Western science in that it is assumed that it ensures quality and the interoperability of scientific knowledge and research processes (Holmes, McDonald, Jones, Ozdemir & Graham, 2010). Standardization as promoted by positivist dominant theories and reductionist approaches creates absurdity in inter-cultural knowledges. Arguably, standardization ignores and distorts social life and social interactions that form the cornerstone of participation in classroom learning and community involvement. In the African contexts, knowledge standardization implies that schools and school knowledge exist "in a vacuum hermetically sealed off from the outside" (Brighouse & Woods, 1999, as cited in Shizha, 2011, p. 29). School science is characterized by scientism and excludes the presentation of other ways of knowing (Elliot, 2009). Conceptualizing science requires some degree of flexibility to be practical in different cultural sites. Therefore, students in African schools experience challenges in learning because of the dissonance between the school science and the cultural experiences they bring from their communities. In other words, for African students to succeed, they must renounce their culture and adopt Western approaches to science learning.

The manner in which standards are created, and by whom, impacts negatively those whose cultural science is regarded as illogical, irrational and unscientific. Historically, the academic environment in African schools has not enabled indigenous African students' academic success in any way other than from a Western perspective. Western approaches to learning have little relevance or applicability to students' lives, especially those who live in rural areas. This lack of relevance and failure to foster concept building from an indigenous perspective leads to feelings of isolation in an unwelcoming academic environment (Shizha, 2010). Science education in Africa requires transformation and not standardization. Standardized knowledge establishes a colonizing and hegemonic legitimacy of a particular scientific way of thinking. A new vision to restore African pride in their knowledge systems needs to be the core of curriculum designing across all subjects. The new science curriculum should provide a counter-vision to the dominant and hegemonic Western science that currently prevails in African schools.

Many of the current science education programs in Africa do not address the complexity of indigenous learners in the post-colonial environment and apply a 'one size fits all' instructional approach (Lee, 2001, as cited in Quigley, 2009) thus causing cultural and cognitive dissonance between 'formal science' and the experiences of students. Lahire (2008, p. 166) describes this dissonance as a boundary between "cultural legitimacy and cultural illegitimacy". The legitimacy/illegitimacy binary is a positivist's illusion that disregards the cultural and contextual diversities, complexities and interpretations of science in the post-modern era. What are required are teachers, academics, curriculum developers and policymakers who use multicultural and inclusive practices and methods of interpreting, mediating and implementing knowledge. Assertions of the transformative impact on public policy of post-modernity (or even modernity and globalism) can be greatly exaggerated due to lack of appreciation of the power and resilience of deep structural values (Houlihan, 2011) in African societies.

A science curriculum that depends on dominant perspectives leads to students' failure. Students' underachievement in schooling has been attributed to the standardization that creates 'cultural gaps' between the expectations of the official curriculum and those of the students. Furthermore, knowledge that is not endorsed by the elite is likely to be regarded as irrelevant and inappropriate and not seen as fit for sustainable development. Interestingly, Niemeijer and Muzzucato (2003), drawing on field evidence from Burkina Faso, argue that because much IK research has focused on taxonomies, rather than theories or processes, there has consequently developed a tendency to see IK as static. IK is flexible and open to changing circumstances. A science curriculum from a positivist paradigm is more alienating than invitational as it seeks primarily to promote standardized knowledge of the privileged elite that does not meet the needs of students in their personal and social contexts. A cultural mismatch between the values and philosophy of school science and the values and philosophy of indigenous communities, makes increasing the visibility of IK in science and technology a socio-cultural, political and educational necessity and requirement.

Inclusive Science Education for African Schools

One major criticism of standardized school science in Africa is that it is not culturally inclusive. The 'mainstream' science curriculum reflects unfamiliar knowledge, which is designed to produce scientists who are unlikely to give back to their communities. Western values are more exploitative, competitive, decontextualized, 'rational', materialistic and uncritically celebrate a view of humanity's progress as technological, economic and scientific development. Researchers on IK and school science in Canada found that, in Western science classrooms, Kickapoo indigenous students were unengaged and showed little evidence of learning; however, the very same students when faced with the very same lessons in a different context (i.e., in their own village) were active, engaged and showed evidence of learning by enthusiastically answering questions (Canadian Council on Learning, 2007). Shizha (2012) reports similar findings in Zimbabwe where students in primary school science classes are silenced by the learning environment, in which Western science is taught in a foreign language, but very active when they are using their indigenous language.

Western science can be very alienating to indigenous students "whose worldviews, identities and mother tongues create an even wider cultural gap between themselves and school science" (Aikenhead, 2001, p. 338). The Canadian Council on Learning (2007, pp. 3–4) reports conclusions on science education and indigenous students' forced choices between three problematic strategies for coping with science education:

1. Students can learn Western science by adopting a Western science world view and abandoning or allowing the marginalization of their indigenous values and ways of knowing.
2. Students can acquire enough surface knowledge of the material presented in science classes to achieve a passing grade without acquiring a meaningful understanding of the concepts—thus avoiding potential threats to their identity.
3. Students can avoid learning any science at all and accept the consequent failing grades and/or lack of participation in science education.

The three options are, however, not sufficient to assist indigenous students in making sense of school science. None of these strategies is likely to lead to exciting and engaging experiences with science education.

Indisputably, indigenous sciences are appropriate for education and the development of indigenous African communities. If rural communities, where most of the African population resides, are to develop, then traditional values and local knowledge and wisdom are crucial to sustainable development. According to Asabere-Ameyaw et al. (2012, p. 2):

> Among the ways to counter-vision contemporary African education, one can point to how we promote Indigenous science education to improve/enhance African science and technology development in general. There has been a longstanding push to re-examine local cultural resource knowings in order to appreciate and understand the nature, content and context of Indigenous knowledge science as a foundation to promote African science and technology studies in general.

However, we should not forget that knowledge changes with time and new knowledge can be integrated to current forms to establish inclusive knowledge/science for development. In this respect, indigenous African science and Western science should be integrated to design school science in Africa. Inclusive science is a body of knowledge that integrates the different or alternative worldviews in its content and ways of knowing, and disrupts scientism as a framework of knowledge production. In this sense, inclusive science is a tool for answering existential questions and making sense of the connections between people, their cultures, their ecology and their society at the same time making connections to Western ways of knowing.

Turnbull (1997) describes inclusive science and its integrated form as the 'third space'. In this third space, there is recognition that science depends on teachers' understanding of the interaction between Western and indigenous sciences and their ability to manage dispassionate and impartial classroom discourses. It is contended that science is "performance rather than representation" (Asabere-Ameyaw et al., 2012, p. 25). Subsequently, inclusive science enhances performance and is not a hostage to standardization, but open to innovation. Innovation arises when existing knowledge no longer sufficiently addresses current needs. Whereas standardization focuses on universalisms, innovative inclusive science is open to modification and transformation that may lead to the creation of new technologies that may contribute to human well-being through economic, health and social development.

CONCLUSION

Although there is an understandable dissonance between Western science and indigenous African ways of knowing, inclusive science opens up possibilities for sharing unbiased and balanced knowledge. According to Elliot (2009, p. 285), we need to dispel the myth of objectivity as well as the idea of scientism, "the belief that Western science gives the only real description and explanation of reality". Scientism excludes the ontological and epistemological understanding of the ecological world through other forms of knowledge, particularly indigenous African ways of knowing. Therefore, inclusive science is a new model that introduces new perspectives of human cognition and meaning-making from different worldviews and philosophies. It disrupts the effects of standardization that create discord between globally framed standards and the local implementation of those standards. A hybrid of Western and indigenous African perspectives will assist learners in being critical and analytical in their understanding and comprehension of science. It is important that when dealing with school knowledge the curriculum should include culturally relevant material across disciplines beyond the social studies and humanities. When IK is included across the curriculum, the notion that IK is relevant to a particular subject will be disavowed. It is important to keep in mind, however, the enormous diversity in African cultures across different countries. Curriculum materials developed in one country will not necessarily be transferable to another. Each nation will need to apply indigenous science that is relevant to its communities and its developmental needs. Any curriculum that includes African indigenous science content must be flexible enough to accommodate specific local knowledge.

Inclusive science, as a body of school knowledge, challenges the coloniality of 'science' and 'scientism' and the way dominant science has served to delegitimize certain indigenous cultural ways of knowing in social development. Locally constructed knowledge is the bedrock of sustainable development. Teachers and educators in general, should desist and resist the temptation to portray science from one dominant point of view. They should avoid an apparent depiction of learning and knowing about science that colonizes other ways of knowing. Usually, in African schools, there is an underlying sentiment and romanticism that there is one way to do science and students are not presented with any other method (Shizha, 2010). There should be a strong emphasis on creating multimodality and epistemological pluralism in social development and for a collaborative learning community because collaboration and working together as a community are a critical part of indigenous cultures and African development.

REFERENCES

Aikenhead, G.S. (2001). Integrating Western and Aboriginal sciences: Cross-cultural science teaching. *Research in Science Education*, 31, 337–355.

Asabere-Ameyaw, A., Dei, G.J.S. & Raheem, K. (2012). The question of indigenous science and science education: A look at the current literature. In A. Asabere-Ameyaw, G.J.S. Dei & K. Raheem (Eds.), *Contemporary issues in African sciences and science education* (pp. 1–28). Rotterdam: Sense Publication.

Bowers, C.A. (2001). *Educating for eco-justice and community.* Athens: The University of Georgia Press.

Bruner, J.S. (1990). Culture and human development: A new look. *Human Development*, 33, 344–355.

Canadian Council on Learning. (2007). *The cultural divide in science education for Aboriginal learners.* Ottawa: Government of Canada.

Carter, L. (2008). Recovering traditional ecological knowledge (TEK): Is it always what it seems? *TCI (Transnational Curriculum Inquiry), The Journal of International Association for the Advancement of Curriculum Studies*, 5(1), 16–25.

Das Gupta, A. (2011). Does indigenous knowledge have anything to deal with sustainable development? *Antrocom Online Journal of Anthropology,* 7(1), 57–64.

Elliot, F. (2009). Science, metaphoric meaning, and indigenous knowledge. Alberta Journal of Educational Research, 55(3), 284–297.

Eyong, C.T. (2007). Indigenous knowledge and sustainable development in Africa: Case study on Central Africa. In E.K. Boon & L. Hens (Eds.), *Indigenous knowledge systems and sustainable development: Relevance for Africa, tribes and tribals special*, 1, (pp. 121–139). Delhi: Kamla-Raj Enterprises.

Gorjestani, N. (2000). *Indigenous knowledge for development: Opportunities and challenges.* A presentation made at the UNCTAD Conference on Traditional Knowledge in Geneva, November 1.

Harry, D. (2001). *Biopiracy and globalization: Indigenous peoples face a new wave of colonialism.* Comments made for the International Forum on Globalization Teach-In held in New York City, February.

Hart, M.A. (2010). Indigenous worldviews, knowledge, and research: The development of an indigenous research paradigm. *Journal of Indigenous Voices in Social Work*, 1(1), 1–16.

Holmes, C., McDonald, F., Jones, M., Ozdemir, V. & Graham, J.E. (2010). Standardization and omics science: Technical and social dimensions are inseparable and demand symmetrical study. *OMICS: A Journal of Integrative Biology*, 14(3), 327–332.

Houlihan, B. (2011). Introduction. In B. Houlihan & M. Green (Eds.), *Routledge handbook of sports development* (pp. 1–4). New York: Routledge.

Islam, M.R. (2012). Indigenous or global knowledge for development: Experiences from two NGOS in Bangladesh. *International NGO Journal*, 7(1), 9–18.

Kapoor, D. (2010). Learning from Adivasi (original dweller) political-ecological expositions of development: Claims on forests, land and place in India. In D. Kapoor & E. Shizha (Eds.), *Indigenous knowledge and learning in Asia/Pacific and Africa: Perspectives on development, education and culture* (pp. 17–34). New York: Palgrave Macmillan.

Kapoor, D. (2012). Human rights as paradox and equivocation in contexts of Adivasi (original dweller) dispossession in India. *Journal of Asian and African Studies*, 47(4), 404–420.

Kothari, A. (2007). *Traditional knowledge and sustainable development*. International Institute of Sustainable Development. Retrieved October 12, 2012 from http://www.iisd.org/pdf /2007 /igsdtraditionalknowledge.pdf

Lahire, B. (2008). The individual and the mixing of genres: Cultural dissonance and self-distinction. *Poetics*, 36, 166–188.

Maweu, J.M. (2011). Indigenous ecological knowledge and modern Western ecological knowledge: Complementary, not contradictory. *Thought and Practice: A Journal of the Philosophical Association of Kenya (PAK) New Series*, 3(2), 35–47.

McKenzie, B. & Morrissette, V. (2003). Social work practice with Canadians of Aboriginal background: Guidelines for respectful social work. In A. Al-Krenawi & J.R. Graham (Eds.), *Multicultural social work in Canada: Working with diverse ethno-racial communities* (pp. 251–282). Don Mills, Ontario, Canada: Oxford University Press.

Nicolaides, A. (2012). Globalisation and Americanisation—The hijacking of indigenous African culture. *Global Advanced Research Journal of History, Political Science and International Relations*, 1(6), 118–131.

Niemeijer, D. & Muzzucato, V. (2003). Moving beyond indigenous soil taxonomies: Local theories of soil for sustainable development. *Geoderma*, 111, 403–424.

Nieto, S. (1999). *The light in their eyes: Creating multicultural learning communities*. New York: Teachers College Press.

Quigley, C. (2009). Globalization and science education: The implications for indigenous knowledge systems. *International Education Studies*, 2(1), 76–88.

Ramakrishnan, P.S. (2002). What is traditional ecological knowledge? In P.S. Ramakrishnan, R.K. Rai, R.P.S. Katwal & S. Mehndiratta (Eds.), *Traditional ecological knowledge for managing biosphere reserves in South and Central Asia* (pp. 17–48). New Delhi: Oxford and IBH Publishing.

Ramdas, S. (2009). Women, forest spaces and the law: Transgressing the boundaries. *Economic and Political Weekly*, 64(44), 65–73.

Shizha, E. (2010). The interface of neo-liberal globalization, science education and indigenous African knowledges in Africa. *Journal for Alternative Perspectives in the Social Sciences (JAPSS)*, 2(3), 27–58.

Shizha, E. (2011). Neo-liberal globalization, science education and indigenous African knowledges. In D. Kapoor (Ed.), *Critical perspectives on neo-liberal globalization, development and education in Africa and Asia* (pp. 15–31). Rotterdam: Sense Publishers.

Shizha, E. (2012). Linguistic independence and African education and development. In H.K. Wright & A.A. Abdi (Eds.), *The dialectics of African education and Western discourses: Counter-hegemonic perspectives* (pp. 148–162). New York: Peter Lang Publishers.

Turnbull, D. (1997). Reframing science and other local knowledge traditions. *Futures*, 29(6), 551–562.

Wane, N.N. (2010). Traditional healing practices: Conversions with herbalists in Kenya. In D. Kapoor & E. Shizha (Eds.), *Indigenous knowledge and learning in Asia/Pacific and Africa: Perspectives on development, education and culture* (pp. 229–243). New York: Palgrave Macmillan.

Whitt, L. (2009). *Science, colonialism, and indigenous peoples: The cultural politics of law and knowledge*. Cambridge: Cambridge University Press.

World Commission on Environment and Development. (1987). Our common future. Oxford: Oxford University Press.

6 Reclaiming the Education for All Agenda in Africa

Prospects for Inclusive Policy Spaces

Musembi Nungu

INTRODUCTION

African states are still far from realizing the Education for All (EFA) goals set at the Dakar Forum in 2000 especially with regard to educational equity, quality, universal access and inclusion. What we have, instead, are dropping participation rates, increased functional illiteracy and a near chaotic educational policy landscape all over the continent. The project's failure implicates the inability by African governments to assume full control over the continent's educational and overall development agenda. Such impotence on the part of African governments has spawned the now pervasive shifting of democratic legitimacy away from responding to the demands and needs of local citizenry towards the demands of dominant international institutions. This chapter critically examines the EFA program in Africa, as both a discursive and political project. It also highlights the limitations of externally driven policy agendas, and eventually, suggests possibilities for locally driven and inclusive policy spaces that are guided by an Afrocentric discourse or philosophy of education.

EDUCATION FOR ALL: HISTORY AND DISCOURSE

The education for all idea was born at the World Conference on Education for All in Jomtien (Thailand) in March 1990. The participants, drawn from 155 governments, 20 intergovernmental bodies and 150 non-governmental organizations (NGOs), deliberated a broad array of educational issues leading to what was termed a "world wide consensus on an expanded vision of basic education and a renewed commitment to ensure that the basic learning needs of all children, youth and adults are met effectively in all countries" (UNESCO, 1990, preface). Yet, 10 years later, in 2000, the world community congregated again in Dakar, Senegal, to assess the progress made since Jomtien.

The Dakar conference noted that there was little progress towards achievement of EFA and that, in fact, more than 100 million youth were out of school, more than 800 million adults were illiterate and gender discrimination was still rampant in schools (UNESCO, 2000). At the Dakar conference six broad goals, later referred to as the Education for All goals, were set namely:

1) Expanding and improving comprehensive early childhood care and education, especially for the most vulnerable and disadvantaged children,
2) Ensuring that by 2015 all children, particularly girls, children in difficult circumstances, and those belonging to ethnic minorities, have access to and complete free and compulsory primary education of good quality,
3) Ensuring that the learning needs of all young people and adults are met through equitable access to appropriate learning and life skills programmes,
4) Achieving a 50 per cent improvement in levels of adult literacy by 2015, especially for women, and equitable access to basic and continuing education for all adults,
5) Eliminating gender disparities in primary and secondary education by 2005, and achieving gender equality in education by 2015, with a focus on ensuring girls' full and equal access to and achievement in basic education of good quality, and
6) Improving every aspect of the quality of education, and ensuring their excellence so that recognized and measurable learning outcomes are achieved by all, especially in literacy, numeracy and essential life skills. (UNESCO, 2000, p. 8)

The fact that one of the two key EFA conferences was held in Africa should be of particular symbolic significance to the continent—at least to the extent that Africa's voice and concerns would shape the policy dialogues around EFA. More importantly, one would hope that Africa would have a front-seat opportunity to contribute to global policy suggestions towards an EFA agenda specific to the educational needs of the continent. After all, the EFA agenda was to be delivered on a platform of participation, partnership and policy ownership (Samoff, 1999). The question that remains unanswered is whether, and to what extent, the three elements, participation, partnership and ownership, still guide the EFA quest in Africa.

A brief examination of some of the terms used extensively in the EFA discourse is in order here. A quick scan of the EFA goals shows an emphasis on two key elements, namely, inclusiveness and equity. Phrases such as, 'equitable access', 'gender equality' and 'eliminating disparities' highlight equity whereas 'ethnic minorities' and 'most vulnerable and disadvantaged' allude to inclusiveness. Such allusions to equity and inclusiveness, thus, frame EFA as a rights-based discourse (Nguyen, 2010). The EFA process is often linked to the expansion and sustainability of universal rights, democratic processes and political systems. Indeed, EFA policies, particularly with regard to universal primary education (UPE), have been tied, discursively and in practice, to creating an environment in which political democracy can flourish (Kendall, 2007). However, the success stories of EFA and UPE are varied across countries and continents.

Where education-for-all has been reduced to schooling-for-all, success has been measured by the number of school-age students enrolled in school as a proportion of the total number of children of that age, or even as the number of students who complete primary school (King, 2011). If we reflect and focus on these indicators alone, many developing countries would declare, and they have declared, success in their progress towards reaching the EFA goals. Indeed, even in low-income countries, according to King (2011), the net enrollment rate at the primary level has increased from an average of less than 60% in 1990 to over 80% by 2008, and the completion rate has gone up from 44% in 1990 to 63% by 2008. Over the past 20 years, these are what governments have been measuring as the outcomes of EFA and commitment to UPE.

Linked closely to the idea of inclusiveness is the development of partnership. Partnership arrangements open the way to sharing information and better coordination of educational programs. Both the Jomtien and Dakar conferences, as well as the subsequent regional forums, emphasized the need for partnerships at the local, national, regional and international levels, noting that such partnerships could help "harmonize activities, utilize resources more effectively, and mobilize additional financial and human resources where necessary" (UNESCO, 1990, p. 25). In the Dakar Forum for Action document (UNESCO, 2000), for example, the word partnership(s) is used 54 times. The assumption, therefore, is that the various stakeholders in the EFA process would be enjoined as partners acting in concert and collaboratively towards the realization of education for all.

Another popular term in the EFA discourse is policy ownership. Ownership is a willing assumption of responsibility for an agreed program of policies (Boughton & Mourmouras, 2002). From the late 1990s, the donor community started emphasizing local ownership of development initiatives and policy processes. This shift was prompted by the World Bank's Comprehensive Development Framework (CDF), which called for recipient countries to both own and direct their development agenda, with the Bank and other partners playing a supporting role (World Bank, 2002, 2004). However, whereas the CDF was a shift from the strict oversight of the Structural Adjustment Program era, it only amounted to a transformation of conditionality (Pender, 2001) as aid would only be given to countries with a 'good policy environment'. The definition and determination of the good policy environment, however, would be solely at the discretion of the Bank and the donor community. Such a scenario, doubtlessly, puts to question the quality and extent of ownership envisioned in the CDF as aid would still be conditional (Collier, 1999). Such conditionality, couched as partnership, is problematic and, as Dean (1999) posits, it is an abuse of the technologies of partnership to entrench the hegemonic grip of the North over the South.

Ultimately, although we are appreciative of the relevance of inclusiveness, partnership and ownership in the EFA quest in Africa, we must treat with caution such apparently value-neutral policy articulations that give the impression that policy processes are linear and unencumbered (McGee, 2004). Indeed, policy processes are messy and laden with vested interests, a power game wherein "truth is constructed through the selection, construction and representation of policy text that aims to shape a desirable image of the reality and the conditions in which it operates" (Barton 2004, p. 69). An important concern for us here, therefore, is to interrogate the relations of power between the different policy players in the EFA discourse especially within the framework of the idea of partnership. In particular, we examine: (1) how different stakeholders, especially African governments and civil society are positioned vis-à-vis the donor governments and multilateral organizations; (2) the nature and extent of their participation in the EFA policy conversations; and (3) their understanding and interpretation of the EFA discourses—is EFA, in their understanding, a genuine effort to provide education to Africans for the stated purposes of poverty eradication and economic advancement (UNESCO, 2000) or do they see it in the same way that Nguyen (2010) views it, as a hegemonic project of neo-capitalism?

In the following sections, we will examine two measures that in our thinking may bring African people closer to owning the EFA process. First, we examine the issue of participation in policy conversations, especially at the grassroots level. To this end, we look at coalition building spearheaded by civil society organizations such as the African Network Coalition on Education for All (ANCEFA) as a viable vehicle for grassroots voices to find their way to such policy conversations. Second, we will highlight the need to revisit the idea of an Afrocentric education, which we consider to be the foregrounding of African traditional ways of knowing and being as the drivers of policy and practice in education.

PARTICIPATION THROUGH COALITION BUILDING: THE CASE OF ANCEFA

From our earlier discussion, we discern three key strands that bestride the EFA discourse, namely, participation, partnership and ownership. These strands are neither discrete nor exclusive of each other but are processes that frame the prospect for an inclusive policy terrain in the quest for the realization of the promise of EFA in Africa. There has been a lot of talk, and even practical attempts, to make the management of education in Africa a participatory project especially with regard to the involvement of non-government participants ranging from non-governmental organizations, community based organizations and community members. A key project in this regard has been decentralization of education management in numerous African countries (Bray & Mukundan, 2003; Lugaz, Grauwe & Baldé, 2010). However, the decentralization project has had little impact in terms of participation in policymaking as the said participation, particularly by grassroots stakeholders, has been largely limited to financing the shortfall arising from government cutbacks (Kane & Mbwavi, 2007). That said, however, there has been a growing movement towards more meaningful participation at the policy level by grassroots stakeholders in the EFA effort. This movement has been especially spearheaded by the African Network Coalition on Education for All (ANCEFA).

Right from its beginnings in Abuja, Nigeria, in 2000, ANCEFA was born on a platform of inclusive participation. In fact, the formation of ANCEFA, immediately after the World Education Forum in Dakar in Senegal in the year 2000, was a response to the exclusion of African civil society in the early EFA discussions and policy processes. At the conference, the highly fragmented African civil society organizations quickly realized that their fragmentation highly constrained their meaningful participation in the deliberations at the Forum. From the Dakar experience, African civil society organizations quickly realized that they could not just sit back and wait for invitation into the EFA discursive spaces but that they had to stake their claim. The immediate response to this realization was to embark on coalition building as a strategy for making their voices heard at the policy table. Once the civil society organizations are in a coalition, ANCEFA helps to build their capacities in communication, research, policy formulation influencing, documentation and advocacy in education to ensure that governments are kept on their toes to meet the promises they make to the public, and also to see that governments maintain reasonable budgets for education (ANCEFA, 2002; Strutt & Kepe, 2010).

The coalition approach favored by the ANCEFA frames an acute awareness of the skewed power relations among the EFA stakeholders in favor of governments and donor organizations (Kane & Mbwavi, 2007; Mercer, 2003). Within such a set up, individual civil society organizations have little chance of making any impression on the policy landscape. Such power imbalance, moreover, led to a repeat, in the post Dakar Forum era, of the mistakes that constrained the implementation of the Jomtien resolutions, notably lack of inclusive participation, thus unilateral decision making by the donor community. Whereas the Dakar Forum emphasized partnership in policy processes and countries were encouraged to enjoin civil society organizations in the drafting of EFA national action plans, such mechanisms were largely ineffective as the donor community "shifted their agendas from the inclusive Dakar Framework to a more selected group of targets based on new action plans and coordinating mechanisms" (Kane & Mbwavi, 2007, p. 17). Thus, coalition building is intended as a countervailing measure to such unilateral decision making by the donor community as it is intended to ensure a critical mass of civil societies acting together to keep the EFA agenda a priority policy issue for African governments as well as the donor community. To this end, currently, ANCEFA brings together 35 education coalitions spread in countries all over Africa. A basic requirement for each coalition is the presence of an inclusive structure that accommodates the media, teachers' unions, academia, human rights activists and researchers.

ANCEFA coalition members have, on the one hand, responded to the EFA discourses by opposing certain aspects that they deem inappropriate for the African context. A notable example, in this regard, is the coalition's opposition to aspects of the Fast Track Initiative (FTI). The FTI, which started in 2002, is a partnership effort bringing together donor and developing country partners to focus on the Millennium Development Goal (MDG) of providing universal primary education by the year 2015 (FTI, 2004). ANCEFA and other African civil society organizations have opposed some of the aspects of the initiative owing to the following three reasons. First, the initiative underscores the donor community's proclivity to unilateral decision making, which, in this case, amounted to reneging on the Dakar agreement by unilaterally initiating new priorities (Kane & Mbwavi, 2007). A key point of contention is the initiative's conditionality of limiting expenditure on teachers, a fact that ANCEFA coalition members see as shifting the focus from quality education to economy-oriented imperatives. In Kenya, for instance, education civil society organizations under the umbrella of the Elimu Yetu Coalition (EYC) have opposed the move towards enrollment expansion at the expense of quality (EYC, 2010, p. 14), arguing that what indeed needs fast tracking is the "deployment of additional teachers and expansion of existing facilities".

Second, the FTI is a narrow program addressing only two MDG goals, thus shifting focus from the broad framework of the EFA to the narrow focus of the MDGs framework (ANCEFA, 2004, 2007). ANCEFA expressed their frustration by this shift in focus in a letter to (then) President Bush of the United States The letter, dated June 6, 2003, stated in part, "African civil society perceives that the international community, led by the USA, has backed out of its international commitment at Dakar and has pulled the rug from under our feet" (ANCEFA, 2003). While recognizing the potential of the FTI particularly with regard to the quick disbursement of funds (EYC, 2010), ANCEFA was emphatic that "pressure from in-country donors to reduce the focus of education plans to just primary or formal schooling must be resisted as there is a clear inter-dependency in the EFA goals" (ANCEFA, 2007, p. 2). To ANCEFA, moreover, the narrow view of EFA enshrined in the FTI is problematic as it excludes the educational aspirations of large sections of the African population whose interests lie outside of primary school education. Finally, ANCEFA's opposition to the FTI was because of the initiative's highly problematic mechanism for identifying potential beneficiaries. Although the FTI process was criticized for locking out countries that were most needy and off-track (Kitamura, 2007; Rose, 2005), the bigger problem was that the benchmark for qualifying for FTI funds, that is, credible and participatory country plans, was highly questionable and unreliable. Whereas donors believed that qualifying countries had instituted participatory policy processes, ANCEFA had reason to question the credibility of such country plans as "we know from civil societies on the ground that the plans have been cobbled together in the backroom somewhere" (ANCEFA, 2002, p. 4).

On the other hand, ANCEFA coalition members have embraced aspects of the EFA discursive frameworks such as partnership and inclusion in various ways to further the quest for EFA in Africa. The ANCEFA secretariat has, for example, prioritized capacity building to help coalition members to better understand and engage the policy process. ANCEFA also encourages coalition members to actively participate in policy discussions and forums all the way from the grassroots to the national level. In Ghana, the Ghanaian National Education Campaign Coalition (GNECC) has made important contributions to EFA policy in Ghana as a member of two important committees namely, the Education Sector Technical Advisory Committee and the National Thematic Group Committee (Kane & Mbwavi, 2007). The two are powerful committees that advise government on education sector reforms particularly with regard to the education strategic plan.

In Kenya and Zambia, too, ANCEFA coalition members have participated in key EFA policy initiatives. In Kenya, the Elimu Yetu Coalition is a member of the Education Development Consultative Group (EDCG) comprising government, civil society and private sector stakeholders. The group has been instrumental in formulating education policy within the framework of the Kenya Education Sector Support Program (Elimu Yetu Coalition, 2010). A notable victory by the coalition was its successful campaign for constitutional amendments guaranteeing free primary school education in Kenya. Starting in 2003, EYC led a campaign called 'Basic Needs as Basic Rights' whose aim was to mobilize popular and legislative support for education as a fundamental human right. The campaign culminated in the guarantee to free and compulsory basic education for every child in the new constitution promulgated in 2010 (National Council for Law, 2010). The coalition has also participated actively in various EFA initiatives including Ministry of Education free primary education and EFA taskforces (Mwendwa, Munene & Kibui, 2008).

In Zambia, members of the Zambia National Education Coalition (ZANEC) have embarked on campaigns to entrench an expansive approach to EFA within policy and practice spaces. In this regard, some of the ZANEC members such as The Anti-Voter Apathy Project (AVAP) have undertaken to educate Zambians, particularly those in rural areas, about their rights as voters (AVAP, 2009). Besides educating citizens on their constitutional rights, the organization also involves the citizens in monitoring elections to ensure transparency in the electoral process. Such watchdogging is important as it enjoins the citizens in the governance project as well as ensuring that the government remains accountable to the people (Crawford, 2003).

Ultimately, although the ANCEFA is a viable platform for African civil society and other community groups to coalesce and have a strong policy voice in the EFA project, the coalition must remain wary of various forces that may blunt its effectiveness. First is the issue of funding. Dependency on external funding, particularly from the same developed countries whose domination of the EFA agenda ANCEFA aims to challenge, is problematic. A quick review of the 'partners' section in the ANCEFA secretariat and the coalition members' websites shows that most of the so-called partners are foreign organizations and governments. Other problems include inadequate human resources as well as inordinate influence by external organizations such as the Global Campaign for Education (GCE) on some of the member coalitions (Strutt & Kepe, 2010).

SHIFTING THE EPISTEMIC GAZE: RE-ENGAGING AN AFROCENTRIC EDUCATION

An EFA effort that mirrors the aspirations of the African people must necessarily begin at the epistemic level and in the overarching philosophy and ideological constructs that undergird educational policy and practice. This calls for re-examination of the philosophy of education that informs the educational objectives, structures and processes on the African continent.

The packaging of certain discursive aspects of EFA as universal truths could be seen as part of the project of the coloniality of knowledge and being that African scholars (e.g., Achille Mbembe, 2000, 2002; Claude Ake, 1996; Ngugi wa Thiong'o, 1986, 2009, among others) have discussed extensively. The coloniality of knowledge and being (Mignolo, 2000) entails the use of subtle forms of domination such as language to exclude certain groups from participating as equal partners in the naming of their social, economic and political realities and imaginations. In the context of education, such exclusions lead, inevitably, to policies and practices completely delinked from the existential realities of the very people education aims to serve. Unfortunately, what we have are policymakers who believe these policies which are literally manufactured outside of Africa, because they privilege and sustain them. The idea of Africanizing education and utilizing indigenous discourses in Africa is, therefore, closely tied to the continent's colonial history and the quest for total emancipation.

Even though the concept of Africanization has been assigned various meanings (Shizha, 2005), it basically speaks to a shift in values, such as the privileging of an interpretive lens that restores dignity to African ways of being and thinking. The colonial project, including the attendant missionary and settler involvement, entailed a deliberate scorched earth approach aimed at complete domination of African people. Franz Fanon, in *Black Skin White Masks* (1967), describes how colonialism succeeded in Africa largely because of the subconscious acceptance by the Africans that 'white[ness]' was superior to 'black[ness]'. The privileging of whiteness through the education system had the desired result of delinking and alienating the educated African from their African roots. The 'civilizing mission' of Western education thus created educated elite who loathed their Africanness (Obbo, 2006). This practice is still alive and strong today. Enough said. There is an abundance of very rich and engaging literature—including novels, poetry, scholarly papers and books—on the whys, hows, and so-whats of the colonial project (see, for example, Abdi, 2007, 2008; p'Bitek, 1972; Rodney, 1982; wa Thiong'o, 1986, 2009). Our concern in this section is to examine how we can re-energize a movement towards an Afrocentric education within the framework of the EFA agenda. The task, we must quickly add, is not a simple one as the colonial project of demonizing and rendering primitive and backward everything African is still deeply entrenched in the education systems of post-colonial Africa.

A first step towards a genuine attempt to reclaim ownership of the EFA project in Africa is to revisit the meaning of the 'all' in education for all. Right from its inception, EFA assumed formal schooling as the default vehicle for acquiring education. Along the way, the meaning of EFA was whittled down to include only formal primary school education. The privileging of formal schooling, for instance, is a furtherance of the colonial project of divorcing education from the indigenous everyday realities of the people and perpetuation of the myth that Africans did not have systems of education prior to the advent of Western schooling. Emerging from this scenario is what Zulu (2006, p. 41) calls "a web of slack reforms that fail to educate the overwhelming majority in Africa".

An Afrocentric education would, in this regard, bring to the fore the 'all' in education, thus the central role of the community in traditional African ways of being and knowing. Within such a system, education is not a product packaged elsewhere and delivered to an audience but an interactive and spontaneous process that involves everyone in the community (Mbiti, 1990). Such a process does not necessarily preclude the necessity for formal structures that ensure efficient administration of education. What we are suggesting, ultimately, is an expansive approach to education that entails the broader objective of linking education to the everyday experiences of the people, whether within formal school settings or outside of such settings. Such a system would entail investing heavily in mass education especially through adult education programs.

Recentering the African sense of identity, history and culture (Dei, 1994) should inform the approach to EFA that we are suggesting here. According to Dei (1994, p. 5), the import of the project of Afrocentricity is to rescue and dignify the subjectivity of Africans:

> It is about Africans taking up their right to the experiences of the continent, the enjoyment of their culture, the celebration of their historicities, and the continued survival and togetherness of African peoples, irrespective of where they have decided to reside.

Such a celebration of Africanness entails education that recognizes and seeks to uphold the cultural specificity (Krätli, 2001) of educational practices and experiences, particularly at community level. In the context of the EFA agenda in Africa, the interruptive marginalization of local values, especially the cultural and relational aspects of African traditional community life, by the imposition of external values is of great concern. For example, the use of hegemonic foreign languages (e.g., English, French, Portuguese, Spanish and Italian) for instruction is counterproductive to the broad goals of EFA as it delinks parents who do not speak those languages from participating in the education of their children. Furthermore, the elevation of the said foreign languages to the status of official languages, therefore the benchmark for literacy, locks out the 'illiterate' from participating in policy conversations and processes that are conducted in those languages. There is need, thus, for changes to foreground cultural and relational dimensions in policymaking and practice.

African governments have made attempts to Africanize school curricular particularly through language policy as well as inclusion of African and local specific content in subjects such as history, geography, literature and religion. The language question in particular has drawn a lot of attention particularly because of the politics of sub-national groups that constitute the different African countries. The debate over 'national' and 'official' languages is still alive in many African countries. South Africa, for example, has a multilingualism policy. Within this policy, nine local languages are recognized as official languages and the use of mother tongues is encouraged in the lower levels of primary school education. However, there is still a steep disconnect between intent and performance as most of government business is still transacted in English (Beukes, 2009). In Tanzania, the use of Kiswahili for all official and social communication was heavily promoted by president Nyerere, not only to unite the people, but also as a tool for reenergizing pride in African ways of knowing and recreating an egalitarian society (Nyerere, 1968). However, with Tanzania embracing capitalism in the post-Nyerere era, the country has moved more towards the universal adoption of English as the language of instruction (Swilla, 2009).

The staying power of foreign languages, especially English, even as African countries implement policies that aim to privilege local languages, is largely a function of the neo-liberal market forces. Thus, the language policies aimed at foregrounding African languages on a platform of Africanization of education have to confront the equally urgent demand for credentials that are competitive in the global market. Ngugi wa Thiong'o (1986) took the bold step to stop writing in English and instead write in his mother tongue, Kikuyu, in line with his thesis on decolonizing the mind. Such a commitment, at an ideological level, is laudable and worthy as it privileges the use of local languages while at the same time preserving valuable folklore. At the policy and practice levels, however, such a project is problematic especially given the highly sensitive tribal and clan politics that dot the African political landscape. Ultimately, in the so-called interests of national cohesion, as well as the exigencies of the market, English still reigns as the premier language of instruction and official communication. Notably, wa Thiong'o may have ultimately succumbed to the market forces and re-embraced English as his latest publications *Re-membering Africa* (2009) and *Globalectics* (2012) demonstrate.

We are not suggesting that the language question is unimportant, or that we should quickly acquiesce to the dictatorship of the global markets in our endeavor to craft language policies that privilege African languages in schools and other educational spaces on the continent. There is need for African governments to invest in promoting African languages to a level where they can be used on national and global platforms. Alexander (2007) suggests that, in fact, multilingualism in Africa should, and can be, a tool for social empowerment and democratic participation rather than a linguistic handicap. An Afrocentric EFA effort would, indeed, offer a credible rationale and platform for multilingual policies that would open up "accessibility, equality and political participation for Africans in their own societies" (Brand, 2011, p. 173). However, beyond the language question, there is need for a broad view approach to the whole issue of an Afrocentric education effort. A more urgent focus should be on the curriculum content. The school was a highly successful and strategic site for the 'civilizing' and colonizing mission of the European missionaries and colonial governments. African art, music, dance, history, geography, science and religion were banished in the curriculum and replaced with those of the occupying forces (Ofori-Atta, 2006). Civilization and modernization were thus, and continue to be, defined from a Western worldview. We suggest that an Afrocentric discourse on education should entail a deliberate attempt to reclaim the school as a site for an expansive education that privileges an African definition of life, civilization and modernization.

CONCLUSION

In sum, the quest for EFA in Africa cannot rest on a platform of unquestioning acquiescence, on the part of African governments and local stakeholders, to externally imposed global agendas that give little regard to contextual imperatives and the immediate needs of the African people. African civil society organizations through coalitions such as ANCEFA have responded to these global discourses in ways that seek to disrupt the entrenchment of hegemonic control by the donor community over the African policy spaces.

Such coalitions offer a powerful model and opportunity for grassroots policy stakeholders, especially to participate in the quest for education for all. African scholars (e.g., Abdi, 2008; Dei, 1994; p'Bitek, 1972; Mbembe, 2000; wa Thiong'o, 1986) have strongly argued for African education systems that heavily draw on African philosophical and ontological traditions. Ultimately, the realization of the promise of EFA in Africa hinges on genuine commitment by all stakeholders to the ideals of participation, partnership and local ownership. Such ideals must necessarily draw on and privilege local indigenous languages, histories and worldviews.

REFERENCES

Abdi, A.A. (2007). Global multiculturalism: Africa and the recasting of the philosophical and epistemological plateaus. *Diaspora, Indigenous and Minority Education*, 1(4), 251–264.

Abdi, A.A. (2008). Europe and African thought systems and philosophies of education: 'Re-culturing' the trans-temporal discourses. *Cultural Studies*, 22(2), 309–327.

Ake, C. (1996). *Democracy and development in Africa*. Washington, DC: Brookings Institution.

Alexander, N. (2007). Language diversity in Africa in a global perspective. In N. Alexander & B. Busch (Eds.), *Literacy and linguistic diversity in a global perspective: An intercultural exchange with African countries* (pp. 13–23). Strasbourg: Council of Europe Publishing.

ANCEFA. (2002). *ANCEFA statement to the high level group meeting in Abuja*. Retrieved November 19, 2002 from http://www.ANCEFA.org/francais/download_files /ANCEFA

ANCEFA. (2003). *Letter to George Bush*. Retrieved September 24, 2004 from http://www.ANCEFA.org/en/docs/bush.html

ANCEFA. (2004). *The challenge of achieving EFA goals in Africa*. ANCEFA position paper for GCE World Assembly, Johannesburg, South Africa, December 1–4. Retrieved May 26, 2011 from http://www.commonwealtheducationfund.org/downloads/country%20information/ANCEFA%20POSITION%20PAPER%20FOR%20GCE%20WORLD%20A

ANCEFA. (2007). *Writing the wrongs*. Paper presented at the High Level Workshop on adult literacy, Abuja, Nigeria, February 16. Retrieved September 15, 2012 from www.ANCEFA.org/francais /downloadfiles/abujacallforaction.doc

AVAP. (2009). *Strategic Plan 2009–2012*. Retrieved December 12, 2012 from http://www.antivoterapathyproject.org/images/downloads/Avap%20Strategic%20Plan%202009%20-%202012.pdf

Barton, L. (2004). The politics of special education: A necessary or irrelevant approach? In L. Ware (Ed.), *Ideology and the politics of (in) exclusion* (pp. 63–75). New York: Peter Lang.

Beukes, A. (2009). Language policy incongruity and African languages in post apartheid South Africa. *Language Matters: Studies in the Languages of Africa*, 40(1), 35–55.

Boughton, J.M. & Mourmouras, A. (2002). *Is policy ownership an operational concept?* (EPub). Washington, DC: International Monetary Fund.

Brand, G. (2011). African philosophy and the politics of language in Africa. *Language Matters: Studies in the Languages of Africa*, 42(2), 173–189.

Bray, M. & Mukundan, M. (2003). *Management and governance for EFA: Is decentralisation really the answer?* Comparative Education Research Centre, Faculty of Education, University of Hong Kong.

Collier, P. (1999). Learning from failure: The international financial institutions as agencies of restraint in Africa. In A. Schedler, L. Diamond & M. Plattner (Eds.), *The self-restraining state: Power and accountability in new democracies* (pp. 313–332). Boulder, CO: Lynne Rienner.

Crawford, G. (2003). Partnership or power? Deconstructing the 'partnership for governance reform' in Indonesia. *Third World Quarterly*, 24(1), 139–159.

Dean, M. (1999). *Governmentality: Power and rule in modern society.* London: Sage.

Dei, G.J.S. (1994). Afrocentricity: A cornerstone of pedagogy. *Anthropology and Education Quarterly*, 25, 1–13.

Elimu Yetu Coalition (EYC). (2010). *Education financing and aid effectiveness.* Nairobi: A Policy Brief on Assessment of the Role and Place of Official Development Assistance in Kenya.

Fanon, F. (1967). *Black skin, white masks.* New York: Grove Press.

Fast Track Initiative (FTI). (2004). *Education for all—Fast track initiative: Framework.* Retrieved May 24, 2007 from http://www.educationfasttrack.org /media/library/EFAFTI Framework2004-English.pdf

Kane, L. & Mbwavi, E. (2007). *African civil society involvement in policy dialogue and EFA processes: A study conducted for the Collective Consultation of NGOs in Education.* Abuja: ANCEFA report funded by UNESCO.

Kendall, N. (2007). Education for all meets political democratization: Free primary education and the neoliberalization of the Malawian school and state. *Comparative Education Review*, 51(3), 281–305.

King, E. (2011). *Jomtien, 20 years later: Global education for all partners must renew commitment to learning.* Washington, DC: Education for Global Development.

Kitamura, Y. (2007). The political dimensions of international cooperation in education: Mechanisms of global governance to promote education for all. *International Perspectives on Education and Society*, 8, 31–72.

Krätli, S. (2001). *Education provision to nomadic pastoralists.* Brighton, UK: Institute of Development Studies.

Lugaz, C., Grauwe, A. & Baldé, D. (2010). *Schooling and decentralization: Patterns and policy implications in Francophone West Africa.* Paris: UNESCO, International Institute for Educational Planning.

Mbembe, A. (2000). *On the postcolony.* Berkeley: University of California Press.

Mbembe, A. (2002). African modes of self-writing. *Public Culture*, 14(1), 239–273.

Mbiti, J.S. (1990). *African religions and philosophy* (2nd ed.). Oxford, UK: Heinemann.

McGee, R. (2004). Unpacking policy: Actors, knowledge and spaces. In K. Brock, R. McGee & J. Gaventa (Eds.), *Unpacking policy: Knowledge, actors, and spaces in poverty reduction in Uganda and Nigeria* (pp. 1–26). Kampala: Fountain Publishers.

Mercer, C. (2003). Performing partnership: Civil society and the illusions of good governance in Tanzania. *Political Geography*, 22(7), 741–763.

Mignolo, W. (2000). *Local histories/global designs: Coloniality, subaltern knowledges, and border thinking.* Princeton, NJ: Princeton University Press.

Mwendwa, J., Munene, J. & Kibui, A. (2008). *Commonwealth Education Fund—Kenya: End of Project Evaluation Report.* Retrieved May 13, 2010 from http://www.commonwealth educationfund.org/downloads/EPEs/CEF%20Kenya%20End%20of%20Project%20Evaluation%20Report.pdf

National Council for Law. (2010). *The Constitution of Kenya, 2010.* Retrieved June 1, 2011 from http://www.kenyalaw.org/klr/fileadmin/pdfdownloads/Constitution_of_Kenya__2010.pdf

Nguyen, T.X.T. (2010). Deconstructing education for all: Discourse, power and the politics of inclusion. *International Journal of Inclusive Education*, 14(4), 341–355.

Nyerere, J.K. (1968). *Education for self-reliance.* Dar-es-Salaam: Oxford University Press.

Obbo, C. (2006). But we know it all! African perspectives on anthropological knowledge. In M. Ntarangwi, D. Mills & M. Mustafa (Eds.), *African anthologies: History, critique and practice* (pp. 154–158). New York: Zed Books.

Ofori-Atta, K. (2006). The British and curriculum development in West Africa: A historical discourse. *International Review of Education*, 52(5), 409–423.

p'Bitek, O. (1972). *Song of Lawino and song of Ocol.* Nairobi: East African Publishing House.

Pender, J. (2001). From 'structural adjustment' to 'comprehensive development framework': Conditionality transformed? *Third World Quarterly*, 22(3), 397–411.

Rodney, W. (1982). *How Europe underdeveloped Africa.* Washington, DC: Harvard University Press.

Rose, P. (2005). Is there a 'fast-track' to achieving education for all? *International Journal of Educational Development*, 25(4), 381–394.

Samoff, J. (1999). Education sector analysis in Africa: Limited national control and even less national ownership. *International Journal of Educational Development*, 19(4–5), 249–272.

Shizha, E. (2005). Reclaiming our memories: The education dilemma in postcolonial African School Curricula. In A.A. Abdi & A. Cleghorn (Eds.), *Issues in African education: Sociological perspectives* (pp. 65–84). New York: Palgrave Macmillan.

Strutt, C. & Kepe, T. (2010). Implementing education for all—Whose agenda, whose change? The case study of the Ghana national education campaign coalition. *International Journal of Educational Development*, 30(4), 369–376.

Swilla, I.N. (2009). Languages of instruction in Tanzania: Contradictions between ideology, policy and implementation. *African Study Monographs*, 30(1), 1–14.

UNESCO. (1990). *World declaration on education for all and framework for action to meet basic learning needs.* New York: UNESCO.

UNESCO. (2000). *The Dakar framework for action.* Paris: UNESCO.

wa Thiong'o, N. (1986). *Decolonising the mind: The politics of language in African literature.* Nairobi: Heinemann.

wa Thiong'o, N. (2009). *Re-membering Africa.* Nairobi: East African Publishers.

wa Thiong'o, N. (2012). *Globalectics: Theory and the politics of knowing.* New York: Columbia University Press.

World Bank. (2002). *World Bank announces first group of countries for 'Education for All' fast track.* Press release dated on June 12, 2002, News Release No. 2002/345/S.

World Bank. (2004). *Education for all-fast track initiative newsletter.* Retrieved from June 12, 2012 from www.worldbank.org/education/efafti

Zulu, I.M. (2006). Critical indigenous African education and knowledge. *The Journal of Pan African Studies*, 1(3), 32–49.

7 Education Inequality and Economic Development in Eastern and Southern Africa

Oliver Masakure

INTRODUCTION

Economic development in Sub-Saharan Africa has trailed most other world regions over the past four decades and education inequality explains part of the story. Econometric evidence from developed and developing countries suggests that education is associated with an increase in long-run economic growth (Hanushek & Woessman, 2009). At the individual level, education directly increases workers' productivity and thus increases their incomes. However, educating children in an uncertain economy where everybody's livelihood is being threatened is a great challenge. There are also many second-round non-monetary benefits from education at the individual and country level, such as improved health, reduced fertility rates, education of children and building of institutions and a sense of nationhood. Education is equally important for promoting tolerance, peace and fighting discrimination of all kinds, political stability and thus lower crime (UNESCO, 2011). These analyses all underscore the value of improving a country's human capital and provide the motivation for developing countries to invest in the skills of their populations.

Policymakers in developing countries generally recognize the value of education for social and national development, and have with the aid of donors, increased investments in education, but progress across African countries has been varied. In 2008, the World Bank published a report, "Accelerating Catch Up: Tertiary Education for Growth in Africa", advocating rapid increases in the quantity and quality of tertiary education in Africa to accelerate economic and income growth and poverty reduction in an increasingly knowledge based global economy (World Bank, 2008). Another publication that focused on the development and provision of education was the 2010 Education for All Global Education Monitoring report that was on "Reaching the Marginalized" in which emphasis was placed at ensuring that children across the world have the right to education (UNESCO, 2010). Of course, the report was preceded by the World Conference on Education for All in Jomtien (Thailand) in March 1990, which set the notion of education as a fundamental human right and urged countries to intensify efforts to address the basic learning needs of all (Inter-Agency Commission, 1990), and Dakar Framework for Action for Education for All in 2000, which reaffirmed goals to support educational equity, quality, universal access and inclusion (UNESCO, 2000).

Whereas many Sub-Saharan African countries have been impressive in reducing hunger, poverty, child and maternal mortality (UNESCO, 2010) and registered large gains in primary and secondary school enrollment, other countries continue to lag behind (UNESCO, 2010). Whereas educational inequalities are marked within countries, the Africa Education Barometer (Brookings Center for Universal Education, 2012) shows that these are more salient in Botswana, Lesotho, South Africa, Uganda, Malawi and Zimbabwe. The roots of these inequalities lie in deeply entrenched disparities in socio-economic circumstances, gender, ethnic and rural and urban differences (Brookings Center for Universal Education, 2012), and are accentuated by political indifference (UNESCO, 2011). For example, in 2008, there were nearly 69 million children who were out of school worldwide (UNESCO, 2010) and about 17 million of Africa's 128 million school-aged children are not in school. In terms of specific countries in Eastern and Southern Africa, the data from the Children Out-of-School Report (UNESCO Institute for Statistics, 2005) suggests that about 39.8% of school-aged children in Kenya were out of school, 33.5% in Zambia, 40.3% in Mozambique, 45% in Tanzania and up to 57% in Eritrea. In Somalia, 90% of the children were out of school, the highest national rate in the world. In Central and West Africa, up to 65% of school-aged children are not in school in Burkina Faso and Democratic Republic of Congo (UNESCO Institute for Statistics, 2005). The quality of student learning is very mixed at best and extremely poor in much of Sub-Saharan Africa. It is estimated that 37 million children in Africa are not mastering basic literacy and numeracy skills upon completion of primary education (Brookings Center for Universal Education, 2012).

Even if these standard education indicators are indicative of varied levels of progress across Sub-Saharan African, they do not reflect the absolute and relative distribution of human capital which is important for economic growth (Thomas, Wang & Fan, 2001). Persistent and widening inequalities in education are both unjust and unfair (Pritchett, 2004; UNESC0, 2010) and we should care as much about education attainment as about its distribution. Indeed most people would detest the idea that children's educational achievements should be dictated by the wealth of their parents, their gender, their race or their ethnicity (see Roemer, 1998).

This chapter considers the extent to which inequality in education impacts growth in Eastern and Southern Africa. It is organized as follows: section 2 provides a brief overview of studies on the relationship between economic development and inequality (wealth and education). Section 3 describes the research methodology, followed by empirical results in section 4 and conclusions in section 5.

LITERATURE REVIEW

There is large theoretical and empirical literature that documents the relationship between wealth inequality and economic growth, and a subset that links education inequality to economic growth. This review section thus does not aim to be exhaustive and will admittedly not do justice to this expansive literature, but is meant to summarize the main findings from this literature. The main finding is that inequality reduces growth because it undermines the creation of human capital for the next generation.

Some earlier theoretical and empirical studies suggest that wealth inequality (Galor & Moav, 2004) and inequality in education (Barro & Lee, 2010) should stimulate capital accumulation and thus are good for economic growth. However, recent studies starting in the 1990s based on better data and econometric methods have challenged the view that inequality is growth enhancing. Based on cross country regressions of gross domestic product (GDP) growth on income inequality, they find a consistently negative correlation between the average growth rate and wealth inequality (Alesina & Rodrik, 1994; Alesina & Perotti, 1996; Persson & Tabellini, 1994; Aghion, Caroli & Garcia-Penalosa, 1999; Benabou, 1996) and average growth rate and inequality in education (Klasen, 2002; Klasen & Lamanna, 2009) in addition to other inequality measures. In addition, some studies find that in the last 30 years, the growth–inequality relationship has been ambiguous partly because of other forces that have shaped global economic patterns: trade liberalization, technical change and the emergence of new organizational forms (Bruno, Ravallion & Squire, 1996; Goudie & Ladd, 1999; Rehme, 2007).

The literature suggests a number of channels through which inequality reduces growth. We consider four channels. Firstly, inequalities in education reduce the average amount of human capital in a society and this attenuates economic growth. Policies and processes that perpetuate education inequality artificially restrict the pool of talent from which to draw for education and skilled workers, and because this excludes highly talented individuals (see Dollar & Gatti, 1999), it reduces the average ability of the workforce (Esteve-Volart, 2004). Inequality in education could also reduce the investment rate and thus indirectly affect growth because countries with lower human capital levels have lower returns on investment (Klasen, 2002). The resultant differential abilities act to limit innovation, investment and economic and social development (Watkins, 2012).

A second argument concerns the externality of education. The idea is that promoting education (especially female) reduces fertility levels, child mortality rates, dependency rates and promotes the education of the next generation. Other studies suggest that a lower fertility rate will increase the relative income for the poor, which in turn increases economic growth, thereby reducing income inequality (de la Croix & Doepke, 2003). These arguments complement the life expectancy model of de la Croix and

Licandro (1999). In this model investment in human capital is intergenerational: it depends on parental human capital, the number of children born by their parents and the individual's life expectancy, which then depends on the environment where individuals grow up. For example intergenerational models assume that a reduction in family size increases private savings and enables households to invest more in their children, raising the workforce's productive capacity which boosts growth (Galor & Weil, 1996; de la Croix & Doepke, 2003; Galor, 2005). In addition, reduced fertility rates allow women greater labor force and boosts growth indirectly through the impact of demographic factors on investment (Klasen, 2002; Knowles, Lorgelly & Owen, 2002; Klasen & Lamanna, 2009; Bloom, Canning, Fink & Finlay, 2009). Declining fertility rates imply decreasing youth dependency rates and thus a relative increase in the share of the working age population, which in turn increases output per capita and therewith per capita income (Bloom, Canning & Sevilla, 2003; Bloom, Canning, Fink & Finlay, 2010). New growth theories suggest that an effective and equitable education system will have a positive effect on long-run productivity and growth through increasing the efficiency of innovation technologies and investments (both are highly skill intensive) and by reducing the cost of skilled labor which in turn increases profits that accrue to successful innovators. A higher stock of human capital increases countries' ability to both innovate and also to imitate advanced technologies (Benhabib & Spiegel, 1994).

The third argument relates to international competitiveness of countries and the functioning of capital markets. Empirical studies show that emerging economies especially South Asian countries that have reduced gender inequalities in education have attained global competitiveness through female-intensive export oriented manufacturing industries (see Klasen, 2002), indicating that reducing barriers to female education and employment aids the global competitiveness of developing nations. In terms of capital market imperfections, Aghion et al. (1999) argue that wealth inequality reduces investment opportunities, worsens borrowers' incentives and generates macroeconomic volatility. The model by Aghion et al. (1999) shows that in the presence of imperfect capital markets, greater inequality reduces aggregate incentives to accumulate wealth and that redistribution through education and other instruments such as taxes will create opportunities for investment and economic growth.

The fourth channel suggests that inequality reduces economic growth because of the political economy effects and negative incentives of redistribution (Alesina & Rodrik, 1994; Persson & Tabellini, 1994). Persson and Tabellini's (1994) political economy model suggests that as income inequality rises, more voters will prefer higher taxes and more social spending, which discourages investments, and thus lowers growth. Some studies show that inequality (through unequal access to investment opportunities) directly increases macroeconomic volatility (Aghion et al., 1999) and some argue that inequality affects macroeconomic stability through social-political instability (Alesina & Perotti, 1996). Both channels weaken the capacity of the government to respond to external shocks, hence lowering economic growth. As well, when inequalities are large, the poor may engage in disruptive activities that are usually at the cost of the rich, leading to reduced efficiency, less investment and weak growth (Benabou, 1996; Alesina & Perotti, 1996; Alesina & Rodrik, 1994).

As a collective, there is a large amount of empirical evidence that gaps in wealth and education detract from economic growth. According to Shaffer (1994), both the persistence of poverty in many parts of the world after decades of so-called 'development' and the sea changes occurring more generally today in political, social and cultural life have once again made education an issue of critical importance. However, studies on gaps on wealth, education and human resource development do not focus their empirical analysis on specific countries. The availability of new data on educational achievement and economic performance that now stretches to 2010 allows one to update the findings of the impact of educational inequality on economic growth. In particular, no study has focused on Eastern and Southern Africa which has been identified by the African Education Barometer as worryingly lagging behind other regions of Sub-Saharan Africa in terms of educational inequalities. There is also evidence of persistent wealth inequality and growing marginalization within countries and South Africa is a good example. The end of Apartheid in 1994 brought about tremendous change in social and political life, but unemployment has remained high and economic growth has been low (Rodrik, 2008). Keswell (2010), who estimated returns to education in South Africa, found that although the opportunity gap between 'whites' and 'blacks' has narrowed, a new form of racial inequality has emerged. This is not operating directly through income, but indirectly through inequality in the rewards for effort and where one receives his or her education. Keswell (2010) warns that if not addressed, this new incentive structure may reverse the gains made in the equalization of schooling attainment.

DATA AND METHODS

To assess the impact of education inequality on growth in 12 countries in Eastern and Southern Africa, we combine data from World Bank's Education Statistics, World Development Indicators (WDI) and Barro and Lee's (2012) data on education. The countries are Botswana, Kenya, Lesotho, Mozambique, Mauritius, Malawi, Namibia, Swaziland, Tanzania, Uganda, South Africa and Zambia. Zimbabwe is excluded due to problems with availability of data. The panel data covers the period 1990 to 2010 and the data were measured in 5-year intervals—1990, 1995, 2000, 2005 and 2010. The dependent variable is the natural log of GDP per capita measured in purchasing power parities (PPP) and in constant dollars (year

2000=100). This variable comes from the World Bank's World Development Indicators. We use constant-price measures of GDP to filter out the increase in GDP per capita that is due to price inflation without relating to any increase in consumption basket. The use of the natural logarithm of GDP per capita is standard in most macro-econometric works because the logarithmic form reduces absolute increases in the levels of GDP per capita and therefore captures proportional rather than absolute differences in the distribution of GDP per capita levels.

The key identifying variable is education Gini index. Education Gini index, which was first used by Thomas et al. (2001), enables the measurement of relative inequality of education distribution and thus seems to be an appropriate measure of inequality. Education Gini index, which is similar to other Gini coefficients used to measure income distribution, wealth, land, etc., ranges from 0 (perfect equality) to 1 (perfect inequality). Education Gini coefficients can be calculated using enrollment, financing or attainment data (Thomas et al., 2001). The data on education Gini index is taken from the World Bank's EdStats database (Porta, Arcia, Macdonald, Radyakin & Lokshin, 2011). The Gini coefficients are for the years 1990, 1995, 2000, 2005 and 2010. Where there were missing values for the desired year, the Gini coefficient from either one year earlier or one year later is used as a proxy for the Gini coefficient in the year under examination. If one assumes serial correlation for these data, this proxy value should be a reliable estimate of the true value for the desired year. However, the World Bank's Education Statistics lack data on some countries such as South Africa and Botswana. For these countries, the education Gini index is calculated from Barro and Lee's (2012) Barro-Lee Educational Attainment Dataset. This data set extends the 2000 Barro-Lee data set to 2010. The online version is at www.barrolee.com. We include a number of regressors that are known to affect economic growth in the literature, including fertility rate, urbanization rate, foreign direct investment (FDI) and military expenditure both measured as a proportion of GDP.

One complication with the education Gini index and economic growth relationship is that they could be jointly determined and mutually reinforcing so that it is difficult to find a causal relationship between the two (Thomas et al., 2001). It may also be that educational inequality indirectly affects economic growth through its effects on fertility rates and urban population. Thus, the most appropriate strategy is to capture both the direct and indirect effects of educational inequality on economic growth. One common econometric strategy under such circumstances would be to estimate a simultaneous equation. The alternative used here is to estimate the system equation-by-equation. Granted this approach is not efficient (in the way that a system estimator like a 3-stage least squares-3SLS estimator would be) but the results will be consistent, and will have the advantage over a system estimation in that if one equation is misspecified, it will not spill over and contaminate the estimation results for the other equation.

For the cross-sectional (OLS) analysis, we estimate equation-by-equation models rather than simultaneous equations using equations 1–4 specified next.

(1) $GDP = \alpha + \beta_1 Edu + \beta_2 Fert + \beta_3 Urban + \beta_4 FDI + \beta_5 Military + \varepsilon$

(2) $Fert = \alpha + \beta_6 Edu + \beta_7 Urban + \beta_8 FDI + \beta_9 Military + \varepsilon$

(3) $Urban = \alpha + \beta_{10} Edu + \beta_{11} Fert + \beta_{12} FDI + \beta_{13} Military + \varepsilon$

(4) $GDP = \alpha + \beta_{14} Edu + \beta_{15} Military + \varepsilon$

(5) $GDP = \alpha + \beta_{16} Edu + \beta_{17} Fert + \beta_{18} Urban + \beta_{19} FDI + \beta_{20} Military + \varepsilon$

Equation (1) measures the direct effect of inequalities in education as it controls for fertility rates, urbanization, military spending and FDI. Inequalities in education, however, influence fertility rates and urbanization. Thus, it is important to consider the indirect effect of inequalities on economic development through these factors (equations 2–3). The total effect of educational inequality on economic development is calculated through path analysis by summing the direct effect (equation 1) and indirect effects (equations 2–3) of education inequalities on growth. This is the approach used in Klasen (2002). Equation (4) is the 'reduced form' regression. This regression excludes fertility rates, urbanization and investment variables. In Klasen (2002) and Klasen and Lamanna (2009) the expectation is that the coefficient on education inequality in this regression captures the total effect of education bias on economic development. This estimate should be comparable to the sum of the direct and indirect effects calculated using path analysis.

In order to account for unmeasured country-specific factors, we use panel data with equation (5). A fixed effects (FE) estimator is used to eliminate unobserved country-specific variables that are constant over time and that have an impact on growth. One might, for example, think of the country's degree of national feeling that might be correlated with economic development as well as with a country's education inequality. The fixed effects estimator also captures norms and attitudes that do not necessarily change much over time but impact growth, for example, attitudes towards gender roles.

The summary statistics for the sample data are presented in Table 7.1. The data reveals that economic development is low; inequalities in education are high, averaging 0.39; whereas fertility rates average five children, but both indicators show little variation across countries. Urban population averages 32% across countries, but foreign direct investment is relatively low, whereas military spending as a proportion of the gross domestic product is 2%, with a maximum of 8%.

Table 7.1 Summary Statistics of Sample Data

	*Mean**	*St Dev*	*Min*	*Max*
LogGDP-PPP	7.808	1.141	5.981	9.990
logGDP-PPP$_{1990}$	7.682	3.068	5.981	8.984
Education Gini	39	7.640	31	64
Fertility	4.483	1.512	1	7
Urban population (%)	32.583	13.962	12	62
FDI (% GDP)	3.516	5.110	-2	34
Military spending (% GPD)	1.983	1.408	0	8
Max N	63			

*Unweighted averages

RESULTS

Table 7.2 details the results. All the direct and reduced form regressions pass the omitted variable test. The substantive results confirm many of the empirical findings from the growth literature. The coefficient of the education Gini index is negative and statistically significant, consistent with extant studies on education inequality and economic growth (Thomas et al., 2001; Klasen, 2002; Klasen & Lamann, 2009). We also note that although the sum of the direct and indirect effect (regressions 1 to 4) is dissimilar to the direct estimate from the reduced form (regression 4), the full model (regression 1) is very close to the fixed effects model (regression 5). As expected, fertility rate dampens economic growth. Consistent with extant studies, high urbanization boosts economic development. Bloom et al. (2009) show that urbanization is highly correlated with level of income; urban areas offer economies of scale and richer market structures, and there is strong evidence that workers in urban areas are individually more productive, and earn more, than rural workers. The downside of rapid urbanization is crowding, environmental degradation and other impediments to productivity. However, overall, Bloom et al. (2009) show that the level of urbanization does not reduce the rate of economic growth.

Columns 2 to 3 estimate the indirect effect of education inequality on growth through the effects they have on fertility and urbanization. The fertility regression shows that higher education inequality encourages higher fertility rates, a finding that is consistent with extant studies on growth. High urbanization reduces fertility rates. Military spending and foreign direct investment have no significant effect on economic growth. This is not surprising because the level of FDI in Eastern and Southern Africa since the 1990s has declined. In column 3, education inequality has no significant effect on urbanization, although fertility rates reduce urbanization.

Table 7.2 The Effect of Education Inequality on Economic Development—OLS and Fixed Effects (FE)

	OLS (1)	OLS (2)	OLS (3)	OLS (4)	FE (5)
	LogGDP	Fertility	Urban	logGDP	logGDP
logGDP_PPP$_{1990}$	0.0420	0.0606	0.253	0.0164	—
	(1.29)	(1.15)	(0.57)	(0.44)	
Education Gini	-0.0191*	0.0477***	-0.0272	-0.0768***	-0.0198*
	(-1.90)	(3.91)	(-0.23)	(-5.78)	(-1.83)
Fertility Rates	-0.421***	—	-6.365***	—	-0.419***
	(-6.35)		(-6.52)		(-5.91)
% Urban Population	0.0304***	-0.0644***	—	—	0.0311***
	(4.72)	(-8.42)			(4.51)
FDI (% GDP)	0.000724	-0.000126	-0.00737	—	0.00128
	(0.05)	(-0.01)	(-0.02)		(0.09)
Military (% GDP)	0.0454	0.0356	-0.106	0.00837	0.0521
	(0.70)	(0.29)	(-0.13)	(0.07)	(0.95)
Constant	9.295***	4.560***	61.96***	10.81***	9.343***
	(15.94)	(6.16)	(11.90)	(15.38)	(15.63)
R^2	0.8160	0.5561	0.4771	0.2449	
Overall					0.804
Between					0.941
Within					0.803
Ramsey Reset Test for omitted variables	F(3, 50) = 1.22p p = 0.3114	F(3, 54) = 1.00p p = 0.3994	F(3, 54) = 2.44p p = 0.073	F(3, 55 = 1.15p p = 0.335	
N	60	63	63	62	60

t-statistics in parentheses
* $p < 0.05$, ** $p < 0.01$, *** $p < 0.001$

Column 4 shows the reduced form regression which omits fertility rates, urbanization and FDI and provides a direct estimate of the effect of education inequality on economic growth. Column 5 displays the results from the fixed effects regression. The coefficient on education inequality has a negative and significant effect on economic growth, but the magnitude of the estimate is not dissimilar to the OLS estimate in column 1. Fertility rates also decrease economic growth whereas rapid urbanization is associated with growth as indicated earlier. Overall, the estimations show that educational inequality and high fertility rates continue to be detrimental to growth. If policies aimed at educational expansion are intended to level income inequality, policymakers and development organizations must realize that these effects are interdependent and may differ based on the specific economic policies adopted in any given country.

CONCLUSIONS

Education shapes the welfare of economies. There are many comprehensive studies investigating the relationship between economic development, education inequality and income distribution, but none that focus on Eastern and Southern Africa. This chapter used school attainment and economic development data for 12 Eastern and Southern African countries covering the period 1990 to 2010 to estimate the relationship between education Gini and economic growth. Controlling for a number of covariates, the results show that a higher education Gini is both directly and indirectly detrimental to economic growth, all things equal. This is consistent with extant studies which find that inequality negatively impacts economic development. As with land or other assets, equality in education is one of the preconditions for economic growth; it improves individual productivity, builds assets and improves social welfare.

Like any study, the study has some shortcomings. First, because the study covers a relatively short period 1990 to 2010, it is not clear to what extent the results can be generalized to other parts of Sub-Saharan Africa and over a longer period of time. Second, due to data constraints, the data lack information on the quality of education, which in addition to inequality, matters for development. As well, the regressions did not adjust for employment of the educated people; higher unemployment, underemployment or engagement in rent-seeking activities among the educated mean that development impact of education will not be maximized (Rogers, 2008). In spite of these caveats, the results have policy and research implications.

There is increasing evidence that in spite of the twin forces of globalization and technical innovation that have narrowed inequality globally, there is increasing income and education inequalities within developing countries and Eastern and Southern Africa in particular (see Keswell, 2010, for South Africa). Whereas economic theory suggests that some measure of inequality creates incentives for hard work, risk taking and rewards to entrepreneurs who drive economic progress, higher inequality can lead to inefficient allocation of resources and to less equality of opportunity particularly for the poor and the marginalized groups. Profound inequalities are not conducive for growth. The time period (from 1990 to 2010) considered in this chapter and the results give credence to these growth concerns.

Indeed, whereas income and wealth inequality is a growing concern and a macroeconomic risk (see Rajan, 2010), this chapter merely focused on equality of educational opportunity and the effects on growth. Attewell (2010) documents a paradox that comes with expansion of education at a global level. Whereas education expansion provides an important route out of poverty for individuals from disadvantages groups, it also at the same time may act to maintain or intensify existing social inequalities. Education has become a competitive tool among individuals and classes and inevitably creates winners and losers (Attewell, 2010; Keswell, 2010). There are particular disadvantages for the already marginalized as well as those who fail to reach higher levels of education when their age mates (or their nations) are becoming more credentialed. At the same time, government budgets are under even greater pressure and funding education is especially vulnerable. This poses a significant threat to developing countries in general and Sub-Saharan Africa in particular. As Keswell (2010) argues in the case of South Africa, it is important that countries protect the education gains already made and create incentives for sustainable growth. The critical challenge is on how to promote distributive public policies (such as taxation and regulation) and use the needed revenue to invest in quality social services and equitable education, good health and infrastructure. Evidence elsewhere across the world shows that successful societies, that is, the ones that protect their citizens, ensure that their lives are not merely determined by the circumstances of their birth but by public and economic policies targeted at educational expansion to reduce the education and learning gaps.

Some of the policies that governments and the international community need to alter to protect spending in education may include the development of more inclusive approaches that address the root causes of marginalization in education (for example, access, affordability, bringing schools to marginalized communities) and protect vulnerable populations (see UNESCO, 2011; Berejena-Mhongera & van Fleet, 2012). Another dimension involves improving the learning environment through equitable distribution of skilled teachers, provision of additional bonus for teachers who accept positions to teach in rural schools, targeting financial and learning support to disadvantaged schools and groups. Some entail promoting policies that alleviate rural poverty such as improving infrastructure, health and sanitation conditions and modernizing the agricultural sector. In addition, although urbanization is good for Africa's industrialization and growth, a synergy between rural and urban development needs to be maintained if the quality of education in rural areas is to be improved.

RECOMMENDATIONS

The underlying story is that education inequality is detrimental to growth in Eastern and Southern Africa but there are no easy answers to solving the educational crisis. Each country faces its own distinctive kinds of challenges and how to go about it, but there is one core issue that stands out: political leadership. For Africa to achieve transformative progress, policy solutions must come from African sources. Far too often, for political expediency, politicians view education as a second- or third-order priority. This perspective is misplaced. Education is critical to more inclusive and dynamic growth and innovation in addition to fostering human development and social justice. Although market reforms (labor, education, financial, etc.) and active labor market policies can increase economic and social development and thus reduce inequality, the greatest impacts are likely to come from policies and public actions designed to enhance quality education, skills training and good jobs. Political leaders need to take responsibility for driving the institutional reforms that are needed and commit to them over many years. Although universal education (improved teacher training and support, increasing attention to early childhood development, addressing inequalities in educational systems that are marginalizing the poor and girls) must remain a priority, post-secondary education must be given importance and skills be made to match the demands of the market, otherwise unemployment will continue to be a problem. In addition spending on social services is important to mitigating social inequalities in education. Yet all too often governments pay insufficient attention to the pressing need for more equitable spending between rural and urban areas.

Educational reforms must be made despite the difficulties of doing so given the limitations both of current economic and political conditions in many parts of Africa. Reform efforts must at least in part be based upon broader partnerships and more participatory development processes. Policy making and governance, including the setting of school goals and targets, the planning of school policies and programs and the managing of school budgets and personnel, and the instructional process, including determining the content of education, should aim at equalizing educational opportunities.

Indeed the opportunity for effective political leadership has never been so urgent. African governments face tough reform challenges (including educational reform) and they will continue to do so, but this should stop being used as an excuse for delayed action. Africa is progressively shaking off its image of a 'doomed continent' and significant educational, economic and social developments across the continent are showing that Africa offers great opportunities for educational advancement and equity. Even the once skeptics are seeing the region as 'emerging Africa' because of the positive changes that have taken place and continue to take place across the continent. African political leaders must realize that without sustained measures aimed at tackling inequalities that hold back progress in education and skills development, the positive gains made thus far may be reversed. Growth and stability has lifted millions of Africans out of poverty over the last 10 years (except in a few countries like Sudan, Somalia and Zimbabwe). Africa can bridge the resource gap with strong political leadership, leveraging the strong economic growth and by adopting innovative political and economic policies. Through growing unity, the voice of Africa could be heard. African leaders should advance a continental vision for integration and accountability that includes enhancing access to education, trade and transportation and promoting stronger collaboration among Africa's Regional Economic Communities. Now is the time to build recipient ownership and indigenization of development finance, strengthening existing country resources and capacities and transforming and promoting Africanized development in a way that contributes to the end of aid dependency for Africa.

REFERENCES

Aghion, P., Caroli, E. & Garcia-Penalosa, G. (1999). Inequality and economic growth: The perspective of the new growth theories. *Journal of Economic Literature*, 37(40), 1615–1660.

Alesina, A. & Perotti, R. (1996). Income distribution, political instability and investment. *European Economic Review*, 40, 1203–1228.

Alesina, A. & Rodrik, D. (1994). Distributive politics and economic growth. *Quarterly Journal of Economics*, 108, 465–490.

Attewell, P. (2010). Education and inequality in a global context. In P. Attewell & K.S. Newman (Eds.), *Growing gaps: Educational inequality around the world* (pp. 3–32). Oxford: Oxford University Press.

Barro, R.J. & Lee, J. (2010). *A new data set of educational attainment in the world, 1950–2010*. NBER Working Paper No. 15902.

Barro R. and J.W. Lee. 2012. A New Data Set of Educational Attainment in the World, 1950- 2010 Retrieved August 5, 2012 from http://www.barrolee.com/data/full1.htm.

Benabou, R. (1996). *Inequality and growth*. Cambridge, MA: Bureau of Economic Research.

Benhabib, J. & Spiegel, M. (1994). The role of human capital in economic development: Evidence from aggregate cross country data. *Journal of Monetary Economics*, 34, 143–173.

Berejena-Mhongera, P. & van Fleet, J.W. (2012). *Patchwork model won't work: A call for a holistic education approach for orphans and vulnerable children in Zimbabwe*. Retrieved September 10, 2012 from http://www.brookings.edu/blogs/up-front/posts/2012/07/12-zimbabwe-education-van-fleet/

Bloom, D., Canning, D., Fink, G. & Finlay, J. (2009). Fertility, female labor force participation, and the demographic dividend. *Journal of Economic Growth*, 14, 79–101.

Bloom, D., Canning, D., Fink, G. & Finlay, J. (2010). *Fertility, the demographic dividend and economic growth*. Presented at the Fourth Annual Research Conference on Population, Reproductive Health, and Economic Development, Cape Town, January.

Bloom, D.E., Canning, D. & Sevilla, J. (2003). *The demographic dividend: A new perspective on the economic consequences of population change*. Santa Monica: Population Matters Monograph MR-1274, RAND.

Brookings Center for Universal Education. (2012). *Africa education barometer*. Retrieved May 9, 2012 from http://www.brookings.edu/research/interactives/africa-learning-barometer/

Bruno, M., Ravallion, M. & Squire, L. (1996). *Equity and growth in developing countries: Old and new perspective on the policy issues*. Policy Research Working Paper, No. 1563. Washington, DC: The World Bank.

de La Croix, D. & Doepke, M. (2003). Inequality and growth: Why differential fertility matters. *The American Economic Review*, 93, 1091–1113.

de La Croix, D. & Licandro, O. (1999). Life expectancy and endogenous growth. *Economics Letters*, 65, 255–263.

Dollar, D. & Gatti, R. (1999). *Gender inequality, income and growth: Are good times good for women*. Washington, DC: The World Bank.

Esteve-Volart, B. (2004). *Gender discrimination and growth: Theory and evidence from India*. SPICERD Discussion Papers DEDPS42, London School of Economics.

Galor, O. (2005). The demographic transition and the emergence of sustained economic growth. *Journal of the European Economic Association*, 3(2–3), 494–504.

Galor, O. & Moav, O. (2004). From physical to human capital accumulation: Inequality and the process of development. *Review of Economic Studies*, 60, 35–52.

Galor, O. & Weil, D.N. (1996). The gender gap, fertility and growth. *American Economic Review*, 86, 374–387.

Goudie, A. & Ladd, P. (1999). Economic growth and poverty and inequality. *Journal of International Development*, 11, 177–195.

Hanushek, E. & Woessmann, L. (2009). *Schooling, cognitive skills, and the Latin American growth puzzle*. NBER Working Paper No. 15066.

Inter-Agency Commission. (1990). *Meeting basic learning needs: A vision for the 1990s*. World Conference on Education for All, Jomtien, Thailand, March 5–9.

Keswell, M. (2010). Education and racial inequality in post-apartheid South Africa. In P. Attewell & K.S. Newman (Eds.), *Growing gaps: Educational inequality around the world* (pp. 83–104). Oxford: Oxford University Press.

Klasen, S. (2002). Low schooling for girls, slower growth for all? Cross-country evidence on the effects of gender inequality in education on economic development. *The World Bank Economic Review*, 16(3), 345–373.

Klasen, S. & Lamanna, F. (2009). The impact of gender inequality in education and employment in economic growth: New evidence for a panel of countries. *Feminist Economics*, 15(3), 91–132.

Knowles, S., Lorgelly, P.L. & Owen, P.D. (2002). Are educational gender gaps a brake on economic development? Some cross-country empirical evidence. *Oxford Economic Papers*, 54, 118–149.

Porta, E., Arcia, G., Macdonald., Radyakin, S., & Lokshin, M. (2011). Assessing Sector Performance and Inequality in Education: Streamlined Analysis with ADePT Software. © World Bank. Washington DC.

Persson, T. & Tabellini, G. (1994). Is inequality harmful for growth? *The American Economic Review*, 84, 600–621.

Pritchett, L. (2004). *Towards a new consensus for addressing the global challenge of the lack of education*. Washington, DC: Working Paper 43, Center for Global Development.

Rajan, R. (2010). *Fault lines: How hidden fractures still threaten the world economy*. Princeton, NJ: Princeton University Press.

Rehme, G. (2007). Education, economic growth, and measured income inequality. *Economica*, 74, 493–514.

Rodrik, D. (2008). Understanding South Africa's economic puzzles. *Economics of Transition*, 16(4), 769–797.

Roemer, J. (1998). *Equality of opportunity*. Cambridge, MA: Harvard University Press.

Rogers, M. (2008). Directly unproductive schooling: how country characteristics affect the impact of schooling on growth. *European Economic Review*, 52(2), 356–385.

Shaffer, S. (1994). *Participation for educational change: A synthesis of experience*. Paris: UNESCO: International Institute for Educational Planning.

Thomas, V., Wang, Y. & Fan, X. (2001). *Measuring education inequality: Gini coefficient of education*. Policy Research Working Paper, No. 2525. Washington, DC: The World Bank.

UNESCO. (2000). *The Dakar framework for action*. Paris: UNESCO.

UNESCO. (2010). *EFA global monitoring report 2010. Reaching the marginalized*. Paris: United Nations Educational, Scientific and Cultural Organization (UNESCO).

UNESCO. (2011). *Education for all global monitoring report 2011. The hidden crisis: armed conflict and education*. Paris, United Nations Educational, Scientific and Cultural Organization (UNESCO).

UNESCO Institute for Statistics. (2005). *Children out of school. Measuring exclusion from primary education*. Montreal: UNESCO Institute for Statistics.
Watkins, K. (2012). *The power of circumstance: A new approach to measuring education inequality*. Retrieved September 12, 2012 from http://www.brookings.edu/research /papers/2012/01/measuring-educational-inequality-watkins
World Bank. (2008). *Accelerating catch up: Tertiary education for growth in Africa*. Washington, DC: World Bank Publications.

8 Learning by Doing

Julius Nyerere's Education Policy for Self-Reliance in Tanzania

Grace John Rwiza

INTRODUCTION

This chapter focuses on the influence of the 'learning by doing' principle, a philosophy that was articulated in Tanzania's education and training policies and practices. Learning by doing was the main thrust of the philosophy of *Education for Self-Reliance*, which is a brain-child of Julius Nyerere (1922–1999), the first president of Tanzania. The Education and Training Policy (ETP) initiative was formulated and approved by the government in 1995 to govern all education systems and practices in the country, pre–primary, primary, secondary and higher education. Other areas which are guided by the policy include adult and non-formal education, the inspectorate, technical education, vocational education and training and curriculum development and assessment. There are other sector specific policies that reinforce ETP which include the Technical Education and Training Policy of 1996, Higher Education Policy of 1999 and Science and Technology Policy of 1996. Specifically, these policies aim at improving the quality of education and training, expanding the provision of education and training and promoting of science and technology (United Republic of Tanzania [URT], 1999). The overarching objective of the education policy and system is to develop competencies among learners. It is believed that with appropriate skills, learners can enhance both their personal lives and that of their communities at large. This chapter, first, discusses the principle of learning by doing in light of available scholarly literature. Second, the chapter analyzes philosophical foundations of Education for Self-Reliance (ESR) policy and the principle of learning by doing and their influence on teaching and learning. Third, in light of ESR and the learning by doing principle, some suggestions are offered for improving teaching and learning practices in schools and training institutions.

CONCEPT OF LEARNING BY DOING

Learning by doing is basically an experiential form of learning through reflecting on the acquisition of new behaviors by performing a definite task.

This type of pedagogy focuses on the learning process for each individual and on meaning-making through direct experience. Learning by doing is normally contrasted with rote learning, repetition and memorization of information. The involvement of learners in their own learning fosters better understanding of new knowledge and longer retention of information than does rote learning. Psychologists and progressive educators correlate understanding and retention of knowledge with the act of using many senses in the process of learning. Confucius, the ancient Chinese philosopher (see Ishumi, 1978, p. 53), supported learning by doing, stating that, "Tell me and I will forget, show me and I may remember, involve me and I will understand".

Psychological studies have also confirmed that 'doing' is an important factor in learning. Scholars such as Dewey (1916) in *An Introduction to the Philosophy of Education*, and Freire (1972) in *The Pedagogy of the Oppressed* emphasize 'doing' in the learning process. Plato argues that one needs to practice in order to be a good doer, whereas Dewey presupposes that education should engage with enlarged experience and that students must freely interact with their environment to construct knowledge. Nyerere's (1968) *Education for Self-Reliance* also emphasizes the principle and practice of learning by doing. African philosophy, where work is seen as part and parcel of human life, supports Nyerere's ideas on education. Nyerere believed that appropriate knowledge, skills and attitude could be developed through education. The core elements of Nyerere's ESR philosophy and the principle of learning by doing were deeply rooted and had origins in what education should do for societies. When Tanzania gained independence in 1961, the country had three interdependent enemies, namely, disease, ignorance and poverty. The battle against the three enemies of development, in Nyerere's thinking, could be won by using ESR as an effective learning weapon. For this reason, ESR confirms the argument put forward by some critical theorists, including Anderson (1990), that meanings are the products of social and material forces.

PHILOSOPHICAL FOUNDATIONS OF ESR

In 1961, Tanzania (then known as Tanganyika) gained its independence, and Julius Nyerere became the country's first president. Colonial Tanzania was characterized by racism, and only a few individuals controlled the means of production. Elements of racism were also present in the education system, whereas the content of the curriculum was not relevant for the Tanzanian society. Nyerere (1968, p. 269) argues that:

> The education provided was not designated to prepare young people for the service of their own country; instead, it was motivated by a desire to inculcate the values of the colonial society. . . . [It] induced attitudes

> of human inequality and in practice under-pinned the domination of the weak by the strong, mainly in the economic field.

Nyerere's observation was supported by Nasongo and Musungu (2009) who note that the colonial education system tended to promote the values of the elite class and alienated most learners from the realities of their indigenous society and discouraged students from working hard. Similarly, Nyerere declared that "one of the effects of colonial re-socialisation was the disregard for manual work" (Ishumi, 1978, p. 37).

In 1967, Tanzania promulgated the Arusha Declaration which defined the vision of the country. The declaration articulated socialism and self-reliance as the official ideology of the country upon which all development policies had to be anchored. Nyerere's vision under the Arusha Declaration was to build a people-centered society where humanity could reach its full potential instead of merely creating wealth. He believed that in order to attain socialism and self-reliance, education could be used as a tool for the transmission of the new values, transformation of society and liberalization of the country and its people from dependency to self-reliance. Therefore, in March 1967, the policy of ESR was launched to guide Tanzania's education system at all levels. The policy identified the needs of the country which could be attained by using education as a tool for development and social transformation. As a philosophy, ESR not only established the core features of Tanzania's education system, but also reflected on the three key features of rational and consistent thought. In their analysis of ESR policy Ishumi and Malyamkono (1995, p. 51) conclude:

> [ESR] was speculative in the sense of being a wide-ranging survey, and synthesis, of the goals and purposes any education system serves in society; goals which in a normal, politically uninterrupted situation converge on the one value of upholding and maintaining the norms of society for the survival and posterity of society itself and its upcoming generations.

Another Tanzanian scholar, Kassam (1983), noted that Nyerere's philosophy of ESR had two main components namely, 'adult education and lifelong learning' as well as 'education for liberation'. In addition, Kassam realized that the aim of ESR was to counteract the legacy of colonial assumptions and domination of the formal education system, which was oriented to suit colonial demands and interests as well as inculcating colonial values and norms.

Commenting on ESR, Nasongo and Musungu (2009) identify two parts of the policy, the 'self' and 'reliance'. To them, 'self' refers to being human, and 'reliance' to the state of being dependent. In this case, 'self-reliance' denotes a situation where a person relies upon him/herself for his or her being. They assert that from philosophical and psychological points of view, the 'self' refers to the specific entity to be liberated from mental or physical constraints. Using the lens of ethical liberation, Njoroge as cited in

Nasongo and Musungu (2009) asserts that ESR has to do with the ethical worthiness of the value committed to the process of liberation. Thus, Nyerere's ESR was a form of education that could make people more independent and liberated both mentally and ethically. Based on the prevailing context, this was considered the appropriate form of education in Tanzania.

The main thrust of ESR was to merge theory and practice and eventually to enhance competencies among learners. This implies involvement of all the developmental domains in the process of learning, the cognitive, affective and psychomotor. Nyerere (1968, p. 282) refers to this kind of education in one of his seminal works this way:

> The object of teaching must be the provision of knowledge, skills and attitudes which will serve the student when she or he lives and works in a developing and changing socialist state; it must not be aimed at university entrance.

Nyerere believed that education has an important role to play in building a socialist state. Therefore, he identified the basic areas which education had to focus on in the process of putting ESR and learning by doing principle into practice. However, Nyerere failed to define the preconditions for effective implementation of ESR in order to realize its envisaged goals and objectives.

AREAS THAT NEED(ED) ATTENTION

ESR by its nature was meant to answer the question of what is to be done and to prescribe measures for correcting previous learning and development mistakes. Unlike colonial education, ESR aimed at fostering social goals with commitment to the whole community, assisting pupils to learn the values relevant to our future and to provide education that went beyond training for the labor market and the skills for earning salaries. In Nyerere's (1968) views, the ultimate goal was human well-being. In order to bring about change, three major aspects of the education system required attention: the entry age for primary schools, the content of the curriculum and the organization of the schools.

For Nyerere, the emphasis now was on learning by doing (practical learning). Along with integrating education into local life, education was to teach people basic skills such as functional literacy (reading and writing skills) and numeracy. The aim of education was also to instill a sense of curiosity into learners' mindsets. In order for primary school graduates to be useful to themselves and society, it was suggested that the primary school entry age be increased. It was expected that such an increase would make children older and, ideally, more mature by the time they graduated. Also, the increase of the school entry age was intended to enable pupils to learn more quickly while at school. The major thrust of the decision was completion of primary education at a tender age sufficient enough to make the recipient engage in self-reliance activities. This idea was based on the fact that only about 13% of primary school graduates were continuing to secondary education. This measure was meant to ensure that primary schooling would be complete in itself as a way of preparing school leavers for the lives they would lead (Nyerere, 1968).

Similarly, meaningful changes were made regarding the content of the curriculum. These involved a review of the school curricula and teaching and learning packages including the syllabi and textbooks. On the organization of schools, Nyerere (1968, p. 283) explained his expectations especially on secondary and higher education saying:

> They must contribute to their own upkeep; they must be economic communities as well as social and educational communities. Each school should have, as an integral part of it, a farm or workshop which provides the food eaten by the community, and makes some contribution to the total national income.

However, all was not well following the promulgation of the ESR policy. During the implementation stage, the policy was misinterpreted and the learning by doing principle was misunderstood. For example, ESR was misconstrued as the implementation of agricultural projects at almost every school. Productive work is one orientation, and the merging of theory and practice is another orientation of implementing ESR. The two are mutually reinforcing and in practice complement each other instead of one replacing the other. The process should have involved the identification of the skills to be enhanced and which theories and practices were to be merged to ensure effective learning. However, as Ishumi and Malyamkono (1995) reported, in most places the policy was narrowly-defined as agricultural projects; pupils were preoccupied with the tilling of land of which the realization of the intended dialectical link of theory and practice remained unattained.

Generally, the intention was to ensure that practice would be included in the process of learning. Practically, the merging of theory and practice was expected to occur in all subjects including mathematics, physics and geography. But ESR was misread as 'income-generating activities'. Scholars including Mhina and Abdi (2009) argue that not many people understood Nyerere's ideas clearly enough to ensure their effective implementation. The problems associated with failures of the implementation of ESR included inadequate manpower and material resource, and the dominant top-down approach that originated from Western models of education. Despite the misconceptions and misinterpretation, however, ESR and the learning by doing principle had a remarkable influence on education policies and practices in Tanzania.

INFLUENCE OF ESR AND LEARNING BY DOING ON THE ETP (CURRENTLY UNDER REVIEW)

Access and Equity

The Tanzania Development Vision 2025 and the National Strategy for Growth and Reduction of Poverty (NSGRP) both recognize the role of education for social and economic development. Also, Tanzania has ratified and is committed to international conventions on the development of education including the 1990 Jomtien Education for All Accord and the 2000 UN Millennium Development Goals. Consistent with objectives of Vision 2025 and international conventions, and based on the ideology and philosophy of education for social transformation and liberation, the government has guaranteed access to pre-primary, primary and adult literacy classes to all citizens as a basic right (URT, 1995). Primary education is universal and compulsory for all children aged 7–13 years (URT, 2011a).

In order to put this commitment into practice, in 2001, the government designed the Primary Education Development Program (PEDP) with specific strategic objectives, including expansion in enrollment, quality improvement, capacity building and institutional arrangement. To ensure enrollment expansion, school fees and all mandatory contributions were abolished in 2002 raising the enrollment of Grade 1 to 1.6 million from 851,743 in 2000. This was a big achievement. However, the main challenge to primary schooling was the quality of education provided. Indicators of inefficiency were observed in repetition rates, dropouts and failure rates at tests for basic literacy skills. In 2012, there were 218,120 repeaters whereas the 2011 data also indicate that 22% of primary school pupils were older than the minimum starting age when they began school. This may partly be associated with dropouts. Other challenges include the shortage of 33,636 primary school teachers in 2011, shortages of teaching and learning materials and the declining pass rate (URT, 2009, 2011a).

PEDP also targets the out-of-school youths and adult learners. According to URT (2011a), there are about 76,867 out-of-school youth in the Complementary Basic Education in Tanzania (COBET) centers. COBET is for children aged 11–18 years who either never enrolled in schools or enrolled and later dropped out. In such a situation PEDP provides a second chance for schooling for those who have never attended school. For both cohorts 11–13 and 14–18 they normally do standard four or Primary School Leaving Examination respectively before they are mainstreamed to formal education. There are 907,771 adult learners in adult and non-formal education. The programs in the adult centers include basic literacy, income generating activities and vocational and life skills (URT, 2012). These programs are based on learners' needs and are practically oriented. The challenge is to retain COBET learners until they are mainstreamed in the formal system and to satisfy a wide range of adult learners' needs.

Equally important, adult education, especially functional literacy, is given due weight. The Local Government Authorities (LGAs) are directed to have budget allocations in order to implement adult education activities (URT, 2006). However, the challenge is on the availability of resources and priorities. This problem has led to weak implementation of the programs in some areas (URT, 2009). Effective implementation of adult education programs has been observed where different stakeholders participate and provide support. However, with meager resources, maintaining a sustainable program has been difficult. As a result, the implementation of adult programs has been disappointing.

Tanzania is currently implementing the Secondary Education Development Program II (SEDP; 2010–2014) in order to expand enrollment and improve the quality of education. The enrollment has increased tremendously at the Ordinary level from a 30.5 Gross Enrollment Ratio (GER) in 2007 to 50.2 in 2011 and at the Advanced level, from 3.7 in 2007 to 5.0 in 2011 (URT, 2011a). Despite the efforts to expand secondary education, few students gain access to higher education. Available statistical data show that in 2010 a total of 416,977 (53%) of the primary school students qualified to join the ordinary level of secondary education, but only 50.4% passed the Certificate of Secondary Education Examination (CSEE) in 2010 and thus qualified for admission to Advanced Secondary School level (URT, 2011a). However, in today's globalized world, a well-educated public is necessary for any country's social and economic development. Primary education alone is no longer sufficient enough to enable people to contribute significantly to the development of their countries.

In Tanzania, opportunities for higher education have been expanded to respond to an unprecedented increase at lower levels of the educational ladder, specifically primary and secondary enrollment following the implementation of the PEDP and SEDP respectively. For example, under the first phase of SEDP which was implemented in the 2004–2009 period, the enrollment rose from 432,599 (2004) to 1,466,402 (2009). The Gross Enrollment Ratio (GER) rose from 11.7% in 2005 to 31.3% in 2009, whereas the Net Enrollment Ratio (NER) increased from 10.1% in 2005 to 27.8% in 2009. Moreover, the transition rate increased from 36.1% in 2005 to 51.6% in 2009 (URT, 2010, 2011a). Basically, all these successes have exerted pressure on the capacity of higher education institutions to absorb the ever-increasing demand. However, although in 2004/05 Tanzania had 24 universities and university colleges with a total student population of 37,667, which rose to 95,525 in what became 31 universities and university colleges in 2008/09, the ratio is still relatively low when compared with the country's total population of 44.8 million in 2010. Also, compared to other countries in Sub-Saharan Africa, Tanzania still has a relatively low ratio of the population that access higher education (URT, 2010, 2011a; World Bank, 2011).

Official Entry Age in Primary Schools

One of the current challenges involves the official entry age in primary education. After independence, Nyerere (1968) proposed to increase the entry age so that students would be old enough and sufficiently mature to engage in self-reliance and productive work after graduating from primary school. Although the official primary school entry age is 7 years, younger children also attend primary school. For example, 15% of the students in 2011 were under age (URT, 2011a) because some parents, especially in urban areas, enrolled their children in pre–primary schools even though these children were younger than the recommended age of 5–6 years. Many parents prefer their children to complete their education in fewer years than expected. However, in some rural areas where the population is scattered, and where there are no boarding schools (especially in pastoralist areas), overage students are a feature of the student population. The whole issue of access is associated with the geography-based rural–urban dichotomy, the parents' preferences and the availability of services.

Nyerere (1968) also wanted to make primary education complete in itself rather than just serving as a means to higher education. Although the curriculum has been reviewed to make it competence-based, 12- or 13-year-old primary school graduates still have difficulty in starting a meaningful career. The issue of prolonging the length of basic education to 9 or 10 years in Tanzania is a hot debate in the public domain. There is no consensus over the time frame for the primary school cycle. Moreover, in light of the preceding account, Tanzania is in line with the 2007 Kigali call for action that deliberated on UNESCO's advice to advocate and assist countries in formulating legal, policy and curriculum frameworks for expansion of basic education to 9–10 years. The logic behind this declaration was based on the importance of free and compulsory basic education of at least 9 years. By having competence-based curriculum in place coupled with free and compulsory basic education and with increase of basic education duration, it was anticipated to achieve quality education for all and productive primary school graduates. However, in the current context of the market economy, higher education is perceived to be necessary for the challenges of globalization (Tendon, 2005).

Objectives and Content of the Curriculum

In relation to access and equity, another area that Nyerere focused on was the objectives and content of the curriculum that would reflect the society's needs. Responding to that, for example, the URT (1995, p. 51) clearly states that "the formal school curriculum will focus on the teaching of languages, science and technology, humanities and life skills". This focus has influenced the nature and type of subjects taught in schools. For example, Kiswahili, English and other foreign languages are promoted whereas

Kiswahili and English are compulsory subjects. Samoff (1990, p. 253) states that the "curriculum materials gained distinctively Tanzanian flavour and schooling used local language forms". In the ETP, the emphasis is placed on Kiswahili language (the country's *lingua franca*), which is compatible with the Tanzanian curriculum. The medium of instruction in most public primary schools is Kiswahili. English is taught and studied as a distinctive subject, and as a foreign language. In most private primary schools, the medium of instruction is English, and Kiswahili is studied as a stand-alone subject from Grade 1.

The best way for pupils to handle the transition from their mother tongue to Kiswahili (the national language) and English and for educators to build concepts of curriculum content has been a subject of debate within the community of educators-cum-teachers and parents in Tanzania. Advocates of local languages refer to countries like Uganda, India and some parts in South Africa, which use clustered local languages in lower level classes in order to facilitate concepts-building and understanding. Also India has been cited to have about 420 tribes and yet uses clustered local languages. Currently, Tanzanians are debating which language, in the current context, is most relevant for use as the medium of instruction in primary schools. No conclusion has been reached yet by the concerned government authorities.

In order to ensure that learners are the main actors in the teaching and learning processes, the primary education curriculum was reviewed in 1995 to make it learner-centered. With this approach to teaching and learning, the teachers assume the role of facilitators rather than instructors who should know it all. To ensure effective classroom interaction, all 175,449 primary school teachers had to be retrained. However, currently, no coordinated, systematic and sustainable national in-service program is in place for all teachers. The existing programs depend on support from the central government, LGAs or other partners. The lack of a national capacity-building program and strategy limits the ability of teachers to support the learning and teaching process. However, the Ministry of Education is still working on the findings and recommendations of the study it commissioned in 2009/10 regarding issues pertaining to the Education Sector Capacity (URT, 2009, 2011b).

The Ministry realizes that the methods of teaching contribute to the development of appropriate attitudes among learners. The emphasis is on cooperation and the belief that education for liberation is education for cooperation among citizens. Through cooperation one can liberate oneself and this perspective has influenced the methods of teaching in Tanzania. Group work and other projects are recommended, particularly in the primary education curriculum (Nyerere, 1978; Samoff, 1990; URT, 2005). Life skills are also important for every human being's survival. As stated in the ETP (1995, p. 54), "The curriculum at all levels of education and training shall emphasize and promote the merger of theory and practice and the general application of knowledge". This requirement has been put in practice. For example, 'vocational skills' is one of the subjects in the primary education curriculum. The 11 fields in this subject are basketry, theater art, music, cookery, photography, small business, laundry, needle work, shoe and bicycle repair, agriculture, livestock keeping and fishing and pictorial art, print marking and modeling decoration. The teaching of these activities is intended to nurture the students' talents at the lower levels of schooling. The teachers have to choose four trades that are relevant to the local environment and needs. The teaching also allows invitation of experts from surrounding communities to address the students. However, the program has been facing a number of challenges that includes inadequate capacity-building in relation to the teaching of vocational skills, irrelevant teaching and learning materials, and inadequate and irregular disbursements of funds. For example in the fiscal year 2008/09, each school received an average of 6,000 Tanzania shillings per pupil (equivalent to US$4) instead of the targeted 10,000 (URT, 2009, 2011b). These challenges have led to loss of interest among teachers in theoretical teaching, thus, making the application of practical teaching difficult. Moreover, no matching stream of vocational skills is available at the secondary level.

Post-Primary Technical Centres (PPTCs) and Multi-Purpose Folk Development Colleges (FDCs) were introduced as part of the post-primary training programme (URT, 1995). In addition, there are Vocational Training Centres (VTCs) that offer programs with relevant knowledge and practical skills for some trades. Vocational training is available in agriculture and food processing, automotive, clothing and textiles, construction, electricity, mining, hospitality and tourism. Currently, Tanzania has 672 institutions (FDCs and VETs) with a total enrollment of 102,217, including 50,190 female learners (URT, 2011a). Tanzania also has 358 PPTCs nationally. Most students who join PPTCs and FDCs are those unable to get into ordinary secondary schools, whereas VETs accommodate secondary education graduates. Basically, classes in this area include practical activities. There are quality assurance and control mechanisms in place (URT, 2011a). The challenge has been the LGAs' management of the PPTCs. The LGAs oversee all social services including education, but their budgets are not large enough to satisfy all the demands in their areas of jurisdiction. Thus, the status of these centers differs greatly across councils (URT, 2009).

Like vocational skills, practical skills are strongly emphasized in science subjects. To ensure that practical skills are taught in schools, the government has supported schools by providing specific teaching and learning materials. For example, science subjects' kits have been distributed to all primary schools. However, in some schools, the kits have remained unused for years, and some teachers are not competent in using those kits. Measures are in place to develop a science practical guide to support teachers who have no sound science background. These measures are necessary because at the primary school level, there is no subject specialization. At the secondary level, practical science guides have been developed to ensure the teaching of skills in schools. However, qualified teachers, appropriate infrastructure and enough qualitative teaching/learning materials are not always available. For example, the Ministry of Education and Vocational Training (MoEVT) data indicate an acute shortage of teachers in science subjects (URT, 2011a). This also limits the teaching and learning processes in schools. All these measures indicate intentions of putting ESR learning by doing in practice despite shortcomings in the implementation process.

Assessment

The assessment of curriculum implementation at the primary level is based mainly on the students' cognitive achievements as measured by examination (pen-and-paper tests) results for selection and placement. For example, the primary education cycle ends with a final examination which assesses learning achievement that is used to select students for secondary education. However, Ishumi (1978, p. 64) argues, "Evaluation should go beyond the cognitive by measuring behavioural and technical competencies as well as attitude change and performance inside and outside the classroom". Similarly, Nyerere (1968, p. 281) pointed out that evaluation should include "character, the assessment of a student's ability to reason and willingness to serve his society". Unlike in primary schools, in secondary and teacher education, continuous assessment has been formalized (URT, 1995). The students' final grade comprises marks achieved on the final examination and selected marks from classroom assignments. One of the achievements of continuous assessment is the Block Teaching Practice (BTP) component, which is mandatory for all student teachers before they qualify for their teaching certificates/diplomas. Normally, eight weeks are allocated for BTP every year for university undergraduate pre- and in-service students who are preparing to become teachers in secondary schools or junior colleges. However, attitude assessment is still a challenge to both teachers and education managers. The way curriculum is implemented and performance is assessed impacts the organization of schools.

Organization of Schools

Nyerere had a vision of schools becoming self-reliant communities with close relationships with their villages. School communities were expected to be involved in farming or other income-generating activities. According to URT (1995), work was made an integral part of curricular to provide meaningful learning experiences by merging learning and experience. With Tanzanian schools expected to have 'education for self-reliance projects', most of these projects consisted of farms and gardens, especially in rural schools, and poultry, animal husbandry and shops and tea rooms in urban areas. In practice, not all schools have 'self-reliance projects'. The schools that have these projects usually have effective leadership. Good examples are primary and secondary schools that are producing their own food (meals or light meals like porridge). This practice is occurring in schools that are implementing food-for-education-program although they are not in a project catchment area supported by development partners. Nyerere's (1968) vision was that if there was a school farm, the pupils working on it would learn the techniques and tasks of farming and that the welfare of the pupils would depend on its output.

The challenge was whether the motive for projects included learning or if it was simply to earn income. Another challenge was related to policy implementation. Not all schools have such projects. The question is how many supervisors have plans to follow-up and support schools to ensure the realization of this objective? Also, to what extent are those supervisors supported to visit schools in their working areas? These unanswered concerns and questions have implications on budget and commitment aspects. Experience has shown that in some cases, projects fail because of lack of transparency among the school-community members. Moreover, income-generating projects are not practical in universities because their charters and philosophies are based on different goals (Ishumi & Malyamkono, 1995). Also, because of neo-liberal policies, services normally provided by the public service have now been contracted to the private sector leaving higher education institutions to focus on their core functions of teaching, research, consultancy and public service (URT, 2010).

The previous discussion demonstrates that, at the policy level, ESR and learning by doing are being incorporated into Tanzania's education system. However, as Pal (2010) argues, most policies have shortcomings in design and implementation. Although, implementation makes a distinct contribution to the success or failure of a policy, an inappropriate policy, no matter how well implemented, cannot alleviate the problem for which it was designed. Learning by doing is closely linked to quality education, which gives learners competencies and skills. Also, the question of quality needs to be extended to issues of internal efficiency such as minimizing drop-out rates and repeating rates. Similarly, any education initiative that does not pay attention to teachers, the key players in the education system, is unlikely to achieve its intended objectives.

Although efforts have been made to train teachers to respond to PEDP and SEDP requirements, goals and objectives, trends in teacher training have not matched the enrollment expansion in primary and secondary schools. This problem has significantly undermined the delivery of primary and secondary education in both qualitative and quantitative terms. For example, at the primary education level, the national average teacher pupil ratio is 1:46 instead of 1:40. Nevertheless, there are variations across regions where the highest ratio is 1:70 (URT, 2012). It seems plausible to point to the fact that Tanzania's population increase has been exerting enormous pressure on the education sector. The Tanzania Education System Analysis Report of 2010 indicates that in the year 2010, 44.4% of Tanzanians were youth under 15 years, which exceeds the average of 43.1% of the Sub-Saharan African (Swarts & Wachira, 2010). Moreover,

> The primary school aged population (aged seven to 13 years) for mainland Tanzania is projected to reach 10.2 million by 2020. Given that 8.44 million children were enrolled in all primary schools in 2009, this implies that the place offered by the primary education system will have to expand by 21 percent by 2020. (URT, 2010, p. 59)

In this situation, unless there are deliberate efforts to respond quickly to the demographic dynamics and deal with the phenomena of overcrowding in classrooms, as well as shortages of teachers, teaching and learning materials, inadequate infrastructure and personnel for management and supervision, and above all, commitment, these challenges are inescapable and will consequently, undermine the achievement of the intended objectives. Based on the influence of ESR philosophy and the principle of learning by doing enshrined in ETP, Technical Education and Training Policy (1996), Higher Education Policy (1999) and Science and Technology Policy (1996), I devote the last section to recommendations for the purpose of revitalizing education philosophy and practice in Tanzania.

RECOMMENDATIONS

The MoEVT, which is mandated with educational policy development in Tanzania, must ensure effective implementation focusing on the quantity and quality of teachers because they are the key actors in the facilitation of the learning process. In the same innovative spirit, a nation-wide sustainable capacity-building program needs to be established. Additionally, the teaching and learning environment should support the learning process by having appropriate and adequate teaching and learning resources, including support staff, infrastructure, adequate furniture and supervisory mechanisms. The current context shows that neo-liberal ideological agendas and policies have influenced social and learning relations compared to the 1967 period. Therefore, guidelines for learning by doing should be reviewed, strictly adhered to, monitored, evaluated and feedback mechanisms set in place. With the current context, curricula at all levels should incorporate elements of entrepreneurship whereas assessment processes must include cognitive, affective and psycho-motor domains. To ensure effective policy execution and accountability at institutional levels, arrangements must be made to establish an organ which would be responsible for the harmonization of policies as well as coordination and enforcement of accountability. Equally important, the government should allocate sufficient budget for undertaking key educational activities in order to achieve educational objectives from schools across the nation.

CONCLUSION

In conclusion, learning by doing is important in ensuring effective and meaningful learning because this form of learning enhances students' ability to acquire knowledge and relevant competencies that are retained for a long time. It also enables them to cope with the challenges of their daily lives. However, although some achievements have been made in implementing the principle of learning by doing through the philosophy of ESR, the expectation of merging theory and practice is yet to be fully attained due to some limiting factors. The system still does not enable all students to value and engage in productive work. To some extent, there is still a belief that education is identical with Western formal schooling. The manner of examining students must be re-examined with a view to aligning it with the spirit of ESR and learning by doing strategy. Thus, serious and comprehensive reforms in the education system are required in order to put into practice the basic premises of ESR policy and the basic tenets of the strategy of learning in line with Nyerere's educational philosophy.

REFERENCES

Anderson, G. (1990). Toward a critical constructivist approach to school administration: Invisibility, legitimation, and the study of non-events. *Educational Administration Quarterly*, 26(1), 125–156.
Dewey, J. (1916). *Education and democracy*. New York: The Free Press.
Freire, P. (1972). *Pedagogy of the oppressed*. London: Continuum.
Ishumi, A. (1978). *Education and development*. Dar es Salaam: Eastern Africa Publications.
Ishumi, A. & Malyamkono, T.L. (1995). Education for self-reliance. In C. Legum & G. Mmari (Eds.), *MWALIMU: The influence of Nyerere* (pp. 46–60). London: James Currey.
Kassam, Y. (1983). *Nyerere's philosophy and educational experiment in Tanzania*. Dar-es-Salaam: University of Dar-es-Salaam.
Mhina, C. & Abdi, A. (2009). Mwalimu's mission: Julius Nyerere as (adult) educator and philosopher of community development. In A.A. Abdi & D. Kapoor (Eds.), *Global perspective on adult education* (pp. pp. 53–69). New York: Palgrave Macmillan.
Nasongo, J.W. & Musungu, L.L. (2009). The Nyerere's theory of education to contemporary education in Kenya. *Education Research and Reviews*, 4(4), 111–116.
Nyerere, J. (1968). Education for self-reliance. In J. Nyerere (Ed.), *Freedom and socialism: A selection from speeches and writings* (pp. 267–290). London: Oxford University Press.
Nyerere, J. (1978). Development is for man, and of man: The declaration of Dar-es-Salaam. In B. Hall & R. Kidd (Eds.), *Adult learning: A design for action* (pp. 27–36). Oxford: Pergamon Press.
Pal, L.A. (2010). *Beyond policy analysis: Public issues management in turbulent times* (4th ed.). Toronto: Nelson Education Limited.
Samoff, J. (1990). Modernising a socialist vision: education in Tanzania. In M. Carnoy & J. Samoff (Eds.), *Education and social transition in the Third World* (pp. 209–273). Princeton, NJ: Princeton University Press.

Swarts, P. & Wachira, E.W. (2010). *Tanzania: ICT in education situational analysis*. Global e-Schools and Community Initiatives. Retrieved August 3, 2013 from http://www.gesci.org/assets/files/Knowledge%20Centre/Situational%20Analysis_Tanzania.pdf

Tendon, S. (2005). *Globalisation: Impact on education*. Retrieved September 14, 2012 from http://www.satishtandon.com/globaledu.html

UNESCO. (2007). *An expanded vision of basic education for Africa*. Seminar presentation on basic education held September 25–28, Kigali.

United Republic of Tanzania [URT]. (1995). *Education and training policy*. Dar-es-Salaam: Adult Education Press.

URT. (1999). *Tanzania development vision (2025)*. Dar-es-Salaam: Planning Commission.

URT. (2001). *Primary education development plan*. Dar-es-Salaam: Ministry of Education.

URT. (2005). *Kiswahili primary education syllabus*. Dar-es-Salaam: TIE.

URT. (2006). *Education circular letter number 2 of 2006 on budgeting for adult education programs*. Dar-es-Salaam: Government of Tanzania.

URT. (2009). *Education sector performance report and development program 2008/2009 report*. Dar-es-Salaam: Government of Tanzania.

URT. (2010). *Higher education development programme 2010–2015*. Dar-es-Salaam: Government of Tanzania.

URT. (2011a). *Basic education statistics in Tanzania*. Dar-es-Salaam: Adult Education Press.

URT. (2011b). *Tanzania education sector analysis beyond primary education: The quest for balanced and efficient policy choices for human development and economic growth regional bureau for education in Africa*. Dar-es-Salaam: Adult Education Press.

URT. (2012). *Basic education statistics in Tanzania*. Dar-es-Salaam: Adult Education Press.

World Bank. (2011). *World development indicators*. Retrieved November 14, 2011 from http://www.google.ca/publicdata

9 A Diploma for a Debt

Students' Perception of Their Student Loan Program in Burkina Faso

Touorouzou Herve Some

INTRODUCTION

This chapter is based on a study that was conducted to elicit the meanings that students at the University of Ouagadougou in Burkina Faso make about the student loan in the framework of cost sharing, through ethnographic interviews (Taylor & Bogdan, 1984). Cost sharing is conceptualized by Johnstone (2001, 2003) as the shift of higher education costs burden from an exclusive reliance on government or taxpayers to some reliance upon parents and/or students in the form of tuition to cover part of the costs of instruction. It is also a user charge to cover the cost of governmentally or institutionally provided room and boarding. It is best implemented when associated with a student loan.

PARTICIPATION AND ACCESS

Higher education in Burkina Faso remains the preserve of a privileged few in spite of a robust enrollment rate. In April 1974, the Centre d' Enseignement Supérieur de Ouagadougou was upgraded to the status of a university with a total of 350 students. In the 1998–1999 academic year, the gross enrollment figure in the public universities was 9,339 students distributed on three sites as follows: University of Ouagadougou, 8,241 students; University Polytechnique de Bobo- Dioulasso, 418 students; and L'Ecole Normale Supérieure de Koudougou (ENSK) had 680 trainee teachers. This is barely 1% of the age group in the general population.

Women constitute 52% of the Burkinabe population. But female students have always made up less than one-third of the overall student population. In 1993–1994, there were 2,131 female students out of a student population of 8,125 whereas in 1994–1995, there were 2,089 female students (22% of the student population) compared to 7,363 male students (78% of the student body). Female students are especially concentrated in some fields. For example, they are 96% in secretariat, 40.5% in English, 39% in sociology, 35% in French and 27% in Law and Political science. Current statistics reveal that only 25% of the student population is female students. The economic crisis in the country has led to a restructuring of the budget allocated to higher education, resulting in cost-cutting measures such as the reduction of the amount and the number of beneficiaries of scholarships and the implementation of a student loan. Already in 1993–1994 there had been 4,884 students who received scholarships (55% of the 8,815 enrolled students). The number of those receiving government scholarships has been shrinking and continues to recede.

ISSUES PERTAINING TO STUDENT LOANS IN AFRICA AND THE DEVELOPING WORLD

Student loans are perceived as the fulcrum of cost sharing. They ensure access and participation as the poorest students can contract loans to defray the costs of their studies. According to Woodhall (2004, p. 39):

> Loans give potential students from poor families, who would otherwise be denied access to higher education on grounds of poverty, the chance to invest in their own future, by providing them with financial aid when it is needed and allowing them to repay it when they can afford to do so.

However, student loans all over the world have a grim story to tell. Albrecht and Ziderman (1991) documented at least 50 loan programs that have crashed. This has brought Johnstone (2004) to put it graphically that the world is littered with the bones of student loan programs. The most known examples of failures in Africa are the examples of Ghana (Takyiwaa, Gariba & Budu, 2007), Kenya (Otieno, 2004) and Nigeria (Okuwa, 2004). But there are "several newer and lesser known programs such as those in Tanzania and Burkina-Faso also looking like failures, at least on the criteria of cost recovery" (Johnstone, 2004, p. 24). In Sub-Saharan Africa, loan programs suffer from excessive subsidization further compounded by insignificant cost recovery to the extent that they incur a heavy cost for collection and maintenance. This has been observed by Johnstone (2004, p. 25) who reports:

> Student loan programs . . . are frequently doomed to fiscal failure by a built-in taxpayer subsidy that would fail to generate a sufficient cost recovery (measured by the present discounted value of the reasonably anticipated stream of future repayments) regardless of the successful execution (e.g., as signaled by low defaults) of the loan plan.

Johnstone diagnosed an insignificant present value of the future payments made worse by especially inflation-prone economies. One would argue that, perhaps, the problem does not rest on subsidization per se. The South African government forgives up to 40% of its loan to excellent students who pass all their courses. This is a clear political choice. What is troubling is the unplanned over-subsidization in many loan plans; the faulty recovery of the loans in Sub-Saharan Africa because of unemployment or brain drain; and perhaps the non-realization by the students that the loan that they willingly contracted was a loan, and perforce and legally, must be paid back. In this sense, the government is also part of the problem. African governments have often been remiss in the loan collection, probably to mollify feisty students. There are also cases where governments have lost entire records of borrowers such as in Kenya (Otieno, 2004).

The ordinary difficulties attached to student loan collection seem to be magnified in the case of Sub-Saharan Africa. It is difficult to trace borrowers. The amounts to recover are generally small, making the administration and servicing costly as said earlier. As Johnstone (2004, p. 27) argues:

> The very little culture of credit, uneven postal and telephone services, generally inefficient governmental bureaucracies, and unevenly enforced official machinery for keeping track of people (such as a taxpayer or pension contribution numbers required of all employees)—it is little wonder that regular repayments are the exception and that borrowers are frequently lost altogether to the systems.

In spite of this less than satisfactory recovery situation, Woodhall (2004, p. 54) believes that student loans can work in Africa, only under the following conditions:

1. Objectives must be clear (is the main emphasis equity or cost recovery?);
2. Subsidies for student support must be well targeted and efficiently administered to ensure effective use of public funds and achieve equity;
3. Explicit subsidies (e.g., grants) are more effective than 'hidden' subsidies (e.g., interest subsidies);
4. To ensure access for the disadvantaged students loans should be combined with means-tested (needs-based) grants or scholarships, rather than be the sole form of student support (e.g., the combined loan-bursary provided under NSFAS in South Africa).

Woodhall recognizes that "[m]any countries have had . . . problems because their loan schemes have not been delinked from government current expenditures, budgeted annually as part of education allocation" (2004, p. 99). She acknowledges the difficulties assailing loan programs.

STUDENT FINANCIAL AID SYSTEM IN BURKINA FASO

Burkina Faso is a resource-poor, landlocked country located in the heart of West Africa. Before the introduction of the structural adjustment programs (SAPs) in 1991, all students passing the high school examination, the 'baccalauréat' before age 23, were entitled to a state grant of 412,500F (US$795). The new students received $50,000F ($100), 'le trousseau', to allow them to get settled. The students' health care and food were/are 80% subsidized by the state.

The year 1991–1992 was a watershed in students' lives in Burkina Faso as they experienced drastic conditions with the introduction of merit-based financial aid. Those students with an average grade below 11 on a 0–20 point scale were only entitled to half of the regular grant. The grant itself was reduced severely. Freshmen had to start with 25,000F (about US$50 per month) with a $10 increase when the student passes the grade. Beside the 'Prêt FONER', the government has come up with L'Aide that denied the many students *la bourse*, or the scholarship. During the first and second years, these non-scholarship holders apply for l'Aide. L'Aide amounting to 130,000 cfa francs (about US$250) is meant for beginning students annually and is only renewable twice during their studies.

Fonds National Pour L'education ET La Recherche (National Fund for Education and Research [FONER])

In 1994, the Fonds National pour L'Éducation et la Recherche (FONER) was set up under the instigation of the World Bank (WB) with the aim to support students in their studies and research activities, continuing faculty training and to provide for equipment to the public high schools. The student financial assistance managed by the FONER includes two components: L'Aide allocated to new students freshly enrolled in a public university in Burkina Faso and the Prêt FONER that gives loans to students in their third year of study in a public university.

In order to benefit from the loan or the Prêt FONER, the third-year students need to be citizens of Burkina Faso who has filed a complete application for the loan. They must sign a form stating that they agree to voluntarily give up part of their salary or income to repay the loan; they must not hold a grant nor get l' Aide, nor hold a permanent job nor be enrolled in the one-year national service. The Prêt FONER is renewable. The student is not entitled to the Prêt FONER in one of these situations; if the student repeats more than once in a cycle; repeats for the second time in the same year/class; obtains a grade of less than 9 on a 0–20 point scale; is involved in undocumented or unauthorized dropping out; is expelled from the university; does not show up one month after the list of the beneficiaries is posted on the bill board; enrolls in a private university; or enrolls in the national service. All sums paid out to the student will be reimbursed if the student gets a job or is enrolled in a training institution following a test organized by the civil service that recruits civil servants; or files forged documentation; or aids or abets violence, or show downright insubordination; or if perceived to have received the Prêt FONER and l' Aide concurrently.

Students who are already in a second or third cycle of a public university in Burkina Faso are the ones eligible for the Prêt FONER. The family income of the student must not exceed 5,000,000/year, or ($9,615). The amount of the loan awarded for FONER is 165,000F (about US$320) with an interest rate of 3% against 5–6% inflation. Since 1994, more than 36,639 loans have been paid out to the students to the tune of 5,850,795,000F (Bama, May 16, 2005). As of April 30, 2003 out of the 9,917 beneficiaries of the FONER, the loan and l'Aide, 7,189 loanees are still to repay the loan. Thus, the bad debts amount to 818,270,000F plus 24,548,100F of interest rate. Only six million coming essentially from the private sector and the informal sector has been recovered.

The loan carries a one-year grace period. The maximum duration of repayment is six years with the amount theoretically directly withheld on the salary at pay point. The amount of the student loan has frequently been the subject of student protests because it is considered inadequate. The FONER officials are aware of the legal and organizational obstacles that limit the efficiency of the loan scheme. These obstacles include the ambiguity of the legal personality of the FONER; the invalidity of the form signed by students to the effect that they will repay the loan in its current wording; the absence of guarantors; lack of motivation and training among FONER personnel; lack of recovery procedures; and unskilled use of the computer system.

METHODOLOGY

For data collection, I used semi-structured interviews to collect data from 40 participants (20 university students, 10 high school students, 5 parents and 5 authorities) in the education ministry, from the student loan office and from the university. The interviews were conducted face-to-face on a one-on-one basis. In addition to the interviews I held 18 focus group discussions. Because I was looking for a wide range of representations, I drew participants from a diverse socio-economic background that included gender. The 18 focus groups reflected the characteristics of students sampled in the individual interviews that lasted for one hour, and the focus group discussions lasted from one and a half hours to two hours.

THE PRÊT FONER: FAULT LINES AND DEBT AVERSION

Woodhall (2004, p. 41), talking from the vantage point of her wide international experience with student loans, proffered that:

> Loans give potential students from poor families, who would otherwise be denied access to higher education on grounds of poverty, the chance to invest in their future by providing them with financial aid when they can afford to do so. The rationale can be summed up in the slogan of the first student loan program in Latin America: ICETEX in Colombia: We lend to the student and the professional pays us back"

In the absence of scholarships, the FONER allows students to enroll at the university and take care of themselves more or less effectively. It has become the main source of income of the Burkinabé student. Zgr, a medical student, confesses that the Prêt FONER is 'The Manna from God'. In effect, Francisco, the vice-director of the FONER institution, stresses the importance of the Prêt FONER for studies by stating that:

> It's thanks to this loan program that some can make the two ends meet. As the population is poor in its majority, when some students reach the university, the parents say that they have got a source of income and the student is left to fend for himself.

Students agree that the Prêt FONER is useful in the absence of any other viable alternative. Without the FONER, many students would not be able to pursue their studies in Ouagadougou. Yet, they stress the smallness of the loan amount. Both l' Aide and the loan have remained static in spite of the tuition increase. Students think that they should also double at least to keep pace with the inflation that has flared up in the country.

The effect of the inadequacy of the student loans has been reported in other Sub-Saharan African universities. For example, they have caused income generating activities at the University of Nairobi often on the margins of the permissible. The Higher Education Loan Board set up in 1995 agrees that loans are far below the students' basic needs. The same scenario seems to be replicated at the University of Ouagadougou. Students bitterly complain about the inadequacy of the funds served by le Prêt FONER. If adequate, the loan could offset the adverse effects of cost sharing. It may be noteworthy to point out that the loan fuels ambiguous feelings. At its inception in 1994, it was frowned upon by students because it is not in their culture to take loans to pay for higher education studies. From nearly a free higher education coupled with generous pocket money to a stage where students had to borrow for the same studies, we had come a long way. A study conducted by Korbeogo (1999) found that only 22.2% of the students positively appreciate the FONER against 48.6% who had negative attitudes towards it.

As the years went by without the government clamping down on the first borrowers' unwillingness to repay—at least those who had completed their studies and who could avail themselves of an income—students became not bothered by a system that had no 'teeth'. The government could keep calling it a loan or whatever it pleased but in actuality the students get away with it. Johnstone (2003) perceived what he calls a paralyzing factor in the success of student loans in developing countries, especially in Sub-Saharan countries where higher education institutions are awash with the bones of dead student loans. Sometimes, government collusion in the failure to recoup the loans is often established beyond doubt. Authorities have not always prepared enough grounds for the loans to be repaid, and students have not necessarily perceived the loan for what it is. The negligence extends to sloppy record keeping and downright fishy disappearance of files as was the case with the Kenyan student loan in its former version (Oketch, 2003).

Eleven years after the Prêt FONER was set up, students are still asking questions about its objectives. The Department of Education (DE) sees the student loan as designed to replace the scholarships that have become rare. Students admit to ignoring the very motives of the loan and its mode of operation, pointing to the lack of preparation of the candidates to the loan (Johnstone, 2004). For example, an official in the DE argued:

> I think that the Prêt FONER is full of ambiguities. We don't really know the objectives of the FONER. Students engage themselves in it because they need money. We don't know anything about its functioning. I think they have to carry out improvements to the FONER.

The loan scheme is the object of other incriminations. The scheduling of the payout often baffles logic. The money does not usually come at sensitive moments when students are in dire financial needs. DE thinks that:

> The FONER was supposed to assist students in their studies. But we notice that the last scheduling was done after the final exam. The minimum for this service is to know our realities on campus.

Students do not quite know when the next installment is going to be paid. They take a poor view of portions being paid out at the end of the semester when all the course work is over and when there is practically no academic rationale. One student ironically put it that "the FONER loan comes in July when the student has already died", it has come in vain. Some students suspect the director of FONER to be fiddling with their money by being slow at withdrawing from the bank in order to maximize the interest that goes to line his pockets. It is also their view that the organizational skills of the FONER are so poor and that the FONER staff does not have a sense of organization. Students find it difficult to trace their names on the payout rolls and this does not allow for a smooth disbursement of funds. On a more substantive note, the criteria for eligibility to the loan are not clear and sometimes found not valid. As the World Bank (1994, p. 45) advised in *The Lessons of Experience*, cost sharing will only be equitable if there is a student loan program in order "to make funds available to all students who need to borrow for their education". Students are abrasive about the age and grade criteria. They wonder what age has got to do with a loan whose objective is to assist students in their studies. The following points were raised by students during a focus group discussion.

> X3: Also, the rate of coverage of the Prêt FONER is very low because when you look at the criteria of eligibility, somewhere, I think that it's unfair because they talk about age.

> X2: They say that the Prêt FONER is to help students to succeed in their studies. In reality, the amount is so small that it can't take care of anything. And still, many students are left out and they dare introduce conditions of age, grade average and all that.

Age should not be a factor in determining the eligibility for the loan. Bourdieu and Passeron (1970) have shown that students bring to school different cultural capitals. The cultural capital of the middle-class family children is regarded as the 'legitimate' one. This explains the inequitable distribution of educational outcomes. It is infrequent to graduate from high school at age 20 because of the high level of attrition. If Prêt FONER is a loan, it should be given to all students regardless of age. Therefore, meritocracy, which the administrators purport to apply, is a phony criterion. Students understand the nefarious effects of class on school performance and show their empirical grasp of reproduction theory. Francisco acknowledges these complaints in part when he observed that the Prêt FONER experiences problems that hinge around limited resources. Because of this, it was forced to assist a limited number of beneficiaries and to pay out a flat rate to all applicants. The FONER managers are well aware that no two students have the same needs. One official noted that in some loan systems:

> They look at your application and the loan is given according to your needs. That's not the case here. It's a system where a lump sum is imposed. It can be perhaps too much for some but too small for others.

This raises the question of the necessity to devise a means testing mechanism especially in an agricultural economy where income goes undeclared most of the time. Also, Francisco points out that the interest rate of 3% does a disservice to the loan as it does not compensate for the inflation that is around 5–6% in the West African Economic and Monetary Union (WAEMU) zone. Interestingly enough, students take a dim view of the principle of the interest rate altogether. They lament the fact that, not only has the government implemented a loan where there used to be a scholarship, but in the bargain, students are obligated to pay an interest rate as if the government were a commercial bank. According to (Korbeogo, 1999, p. 53):

> FONER is a means of dissuasion, of division of the student body in its political activism, and 22.6 percent want it to be cancelled. For the

latter, the FONER is just a speculating financial institution aiming at putting the students who have a bleak future into debt.

Korbeogo quotes an excerpt from *L' Etudiant burkinabé* that reads:

> The FONER is a juicy enterprise on the back of students and has no regard for the future conditions of the latter. It seems that in business there is no room for feelings: thus, by giving the loan to 1,000 students, the government will reap at the end of four years a net profit of 38,642,000 francs (*L' Etudiant burkinabé* as cited in Korbeogo, 1999, p. 53).

The fact that the student loan is construed as a lucrative business speaks volumes for the students' inability to conceive borrowing for their education. This seems to be the inevitable consequence of a culture of the university as something that should be free as it was during French colonial rule. All of a sudden the university is flooded by young people aspiring and reasonably believing that they deserve higher education after graduating from high school. There is a sense that these youths reproach the government for not meeting its responsibility to educate its children. This could explain the self-righteousness perceptions in the students' attitudes. The government and the students are reasoning at cross-purposes. Whereas the former is interested in the financial health of the university, the latter see higher education as a student's social and humanitarian right and a means for social mobility. Students in developing countries represent the elite and are expected to increase their personal earnings as they graduate (World Bank, 1994). But most students and their parents, like Assy, a sociology student and mother of two students, thinks that the country has not reached the stage where children can take loans for their studies. She commented, "For the loans you must be sure to get a job after the studies". Parents fear that they might be the ones who may end up being forced to pay for their sons' or daughters' loans if their children are not employed or are not gainfully employed.

THE PRÊT FONER AS A REAL LOAN: THE STUDENTS' SUDDEN DEBT AVERSION

Students did not seem to take the Prêt FONER as a serious loan that they were obliged to repay until very recently. One of the students, Assy, claims that:

> If the loan scheme has only recovered a handful of millions after a decade into its existence, this is proof that it is a 'deal' between government and students; in this case, it is no different from hidden small scholarships arranged to avoid student upheavals.

However, students realize to their amazement now that the Minister of Higher Education has addressed the question before the National Assembly. His intervention has been followed by a beginning of recovery of the loan and the students have suddenly realized that «it is a real loan». A focus group discussion held with second-year students in Law is instructive in this regard. The students revealed the following:

> X5: According to me, the loan, I don't think it's a deal between students and government. Because from the moment when we know that our country is highly indebted, this is the reality, if at one point in time, we are asked to take loans instead of giving us scholarships, maybe they can ask us to repay.
>
> X4: For me, not long ago, if you asked all the students, they would tell you that the loan is a deal between government and students, that we would never repay this loan. Even when we came, we wanted to register, our senior brothers told us that it is a way of talking; we do not repay the loan in reality. But recently we realized that all those who took the loan, once you are declared at the National Security office, they send you a notice to propose a repayment plan. All the students on campus are aware of this. So nobody doubts it now, it's a loan like any other and what's more, it's a loan with a 3% interest rate. So nobody doubts it today. If you take the loan, tomorrow if you start working and you are declared at the National Social Security, you pay.

It is interesting to point out how X4 situates his story in time. He uses the past to set off the time when there was no obligation to repay the loan without any consequence whatsoever. So it was a de facto arrangement. But times have changed. In his last two sentences he shows the discontinuity of a practice that was prevalent by the repetition of time markers such as 'now' and 'today' in contiguous sentences. The present thus becomes a milestone in the history of the student loan. X4 opens up his argument on the collective mode, 'all the students', 'they', the 'students', 'we' and 'our senior brothers' signaling the imagined symbolic kinship among students. However, at the end, there is a sharp contrast as he shifts the focus from the collective to the individual: 'You' in 'once you are declared', 'you' in 'you are told', 'you' in 'if you benefit'. In no uncertain terms, students have been brought to their senses. The responsibility to pay back is an individual onus. The loan is to be repaid, with a 3% interest rate.

Clearly, students have been brought to their senses by the clarification of the Minister of Higher Education. In a focus group, SS invited his peers to join him in outrage as he compared the student loan to the debt owed by developing countries.

> SS: The Prêt FONER today is for the Burkinabè students what the foreign debt consented by the international institutions is to the developing countries because you take without thinking about what will happen in the future with the interest rates.

In any case, today, the Prêt FONER causes a debt aversion as the government is poised to collect the bad debts. It follows that students show a distinct debt aversion unsuspected so far. SS went on to say:

> Look at this! A student taking a loan! He has not even started working and here he is with already a loan on his back. That's dangerous!

To show that the threats of the Prêt FONER are no figment of his imagination, SS ran a simulation of a medical student who borrows, at least, for seven years of study. The total debt is appalling to him.

> Imagine a student who is in medicine. He has 7 years and he is going to borrow 165,000F that must be repaid. How many millions is he finally going to pay?

The government is bent on taking steps, legal and administrative, in order to save the FONER. It is increasingly probable that the management of the FONER will be totally entrusted to the Ministry of Finance and Budget. That is why the loan, surprisingly, proves so frightening. Those students who are yet to be unruffled by the loan are only doing so out of ignorance. Ghilchrist, one of the students, thinks that they are living in a fool's paradise. Because the Minister of Higher Education has been called before the National Assembly to account for the Prêt FONER, students seem to have understood that from now on, it would be difficult to get away with the government's money because, according to NA:

> Even if you pass away, in your grave you are bound to repay because before the paperwork for the FONER, you must produce the certificate, you must produce the ID of one of your guardians to show that just in case . . . he is the one who is going to be caught.

The Director of Studies and Planning, Debie, confirms that the FONER is far from an arrangement. It is a false impression that people gather simply because the government is still searching for the best formula for recovering the money. The government is trying to figure out how to recover the loan at the level of the Ministry of Civil Service and thinks that it is very easy with the personal identification numbers. The only problem is that there is no legal provision to recover at pay point. Debie argues :

> There are no legal provisions to recover the funds. If one day a student decides, hey, I don't pay, do we arrest him or what do we do to

> him? There should be a legal arrangement that allows for example the FONER to get in touch with the Ministry of Finance that will agree to deduct from the salaries of debtors at pay point.

The inclusion in her argument of such terms as 'legal provisions' and 'a legal arrangement' expressing the much-wanted instrument that can greatly shield the loan scheme from bad debtors who could exploit the loopholes of a loosely conceived student loan points to the legal disempowerment of the recovery system.

In actual fact, the MPs from the ruling party requested the Minister of Higher Education to answer oral questions before the National Assembly about three issues: (1) the financial evaluation of the Fund; (2) the number of students and structures that benefitted from the Prêt FONER; and (3) his commitment to recover the loans by inviting institutions such as the Ministry of Finance, the National Council of Employers (CNPB), the major companies, the banks, and financial institutions to help track the defaulters. One big problem of the Prêt FONER that complicates recovery is the lack of legal provision likely to constrain students to pay as said earlier. The consent form they sign has, in fact, no legal value. Unless the National Assembly votes a law in this direction, no recovery can be conducted in this way. Students are certainly cognizant of this legal stricture and are exploiting the loopholes to the maximum.

From the previous discussion, it follows that most of the student loans in Africa have not been set up based on a mapping of the social, legal and technical parameters. They seem to have been reactive responses to quench the fire of student rebellion. They may be good at bringing temporary quiescence on campus, but show themselves to be poor instruments that fail to enhance cost sharing. In effect, Woodhall's (2004) admonitions towards making loan programs workable do not seem to have been heeded. In her attempt to improve student loan schemes in Africa, Woodhall (2004) strongly recommended that the objectives of such loans must be clear. For instance the following questions have to be addressed: what is the government looking for in the case of the Prêt FONER? Is it equity or cost recovery? It is, arguably, the case that neither equity nor cost recovery measures are met. Furthermore, the public money is not effectively used because the subsidies for the student support are not well-targeted and efficiently administered (Woodhall, 2004). Woodhall also recommended that loans be combined with means-tested grants or scholarships. Unfortunately, the disappearance of grants lends credence to the idea that the loan tends to be the only support program. If the support programs are not forthcoming, the odds are that student loans will be rejected.

Meanwhile, in the long run, social development in Burkina Faso and the whole of Africa for that matter (most African countries having to come to terms with a best formula about funding their higher education) is severely at stake. It has now become an accepted fact that the calendar of the new academic year remains in the laps of the gods. On 'normal' school years, classes started in October and ended in July. Now, it is a hit-or-miss affair. Several cohorts have missed starting courses in time, thus, creating dangerous bottlenecks of angry youths waiting to scramble for a much-vaunted higher education share, which taxes the fragile facilities of universities to breaking point. Members of faculty are already contending with 1,000 to 2,000 students in their courses (no pun intended). I, myself, had a batch of more than 1,700 students as a part-time instructor in the Faculty of Law and Political Science at the University of Ouagadougou from 1998 to 2002. For lack of seats, we had to hold classes in a big hall on the premises of the Salon International de l' Artisanat de Ouagadougou (SIAO), the International Artcraft Showcase of Ouagadougou. Needless to say that it is difficult for best practices to take place in such a context. If some students can still assimilate the content of the lessons in such unusual circumstances, it is also true that many generations are thus sacrificed. What kind of education and for what kind of development can we expect with such sub-standard conditions when it is unanimously acknowledged that higher education is the sine qua non of development? The World Bank that was quite skeptical about higher education as the engine of social engineering has made amends since the year 2002, at least when it embraced the concept of higher education as the stepping-stone to the knowledge and information economy.

CONCLUSION

The obstacles to student loans are mostly political, cultural and technical. For example, students find it difficult to move from a situation where higher education was free, a situation where they were even given grants, to one where they have to take loans for their university studies. For francophone students taking their cue from the "metropole", France, where a free higher education system is in place without a student loan program, this is hard to conceive. Also, loans, an important part of any cost-sharing scheme, are heavily subsidized with no means testing. Student loans fail to be collected in Sub-Saharan Africa because of high unemployment rates and student activism. The technical issues related to taxation are a sobering reminder that the implementation of student loans in Burkina Faso, and in Sub-Saharan Africa as a whole, is a complex endeavor evidenced by the unusually large amount of failed loan programs throughout the developing world.

REFERENCES

Altbrecht, D. & Ziderman, A. (1991). *Deferred cost recovery for higher education: Student loan programs in developing countries*. Washington, DC: The World Bank.

Bama, P. (2005, May 16). *Financement de l' éducation: Plus de 800 millions de F CFA à recouvrer au FONER*. Retrieved July 26, 2006 from *http://www.lefaso.net/article.php3?idarticle*

Bourdieu, P. & Passeron, J.C. (1970). *La reproduction: Eléments pour une théorie du système d'enseignement*. Paris, France: Editions de Minuit.
Johnstone, D.B. (2001). Those 'out of control' costs. In P.G. Altbach, D.B. Johnstone & P.J. Gumport (Eds.), *In defense of the American public university* (pp. 144–179). Baltimore, MD: Johns Hopkins University Press.
Johnstone, D.B. (2003). Cost-sharing in higher education: Tuition, financial assistance, and accessibility in a comparative perspective. *Czech Sociological Review*, 39(3), 351–374.
Johnstone, D.B. (2004). Higher education finance and accessibility and student loans in SubSahara Africa. *Journal of Higher Education in Africa*, 2(2), 11–36.
Korbeogo, G. (1999). *Logiques sociales et participation à l'espace syndical étudiant: Cas des étudiants de la FLASHS et de la FSS* (Université de Ouagadougou). Mémoire de Maîtrise: University of Ouagadougou.
Oketch, O.M. (2003). Affording the unaffordable: Cost sharing in higher education in Sub-Saharan Africa. *Peabody Journal of Education*, 78(3), 88–106.
Okuwa, O.B. (2004). *Private returns to higher education in Nigeria*. AERC Research Paper 139. Nairobi: African Economic Research Consortium.
Otieno, W. (2004). Student loans in Kenya: Past experiences, current hurdles, and opportunities for the future. *JHEA/RESA*, 2(2), 75–99.
Takyiwaa, M., Gariba, S. & Budu, J. (2007). *Change and transformation in Ghana's publicly funded universities*. Oxford: James Currey.
Taylor, S.J. & Bogdan, R. (1984). *Introduction to qualitative research methods: The search for meanings*. New York: John Weily and Sons.
Woodhall, M. (2004). Student loans: Potentials, problems and lessons from international experience. *JHEA/RESA*, 2(2), 37–51.
World Bank. (1994). *Higher Education: The lessons of experience*. Washington, DC: The World Bank.

Part III

Politics and Development

10 International Corporate Politics and the Hubris of Development Discourses

Desmond Ikenna Odugu

INTRODUCTION

In early summer of 2009, a prominent Nigerian education policymaker in the Federal Ministry of Education (FME) in Abuja made two striking admissions to me: first, that his office relies heavily on international organizations (IOs), (especially the UN Education Science and Cultural Organization, [UNESCO]) for most policymaking ideas and standards; and second, that any policy initiative from donor agencies passes much faster than those generated domestically. Earlier that year in New Delhi, a major player in the *Sarva Shiksha Abhiyan* (SSA) scheme, India's version of *Education for All* (EFA), gleefully informed me that his grassroots affiliates worked with UNESCO and UNICEF to push the government to adopt a pro-multilingual education policy. In five countries throughout that field research, public policy actors within and outside governments unequivocally resounded the convictions that intellectual and financial resources from IOs drive most domestic policies (Odugu, 2011).

Remarkably, many governments take for granted the role of IOs in creating and sharing ideas, resources and norms across cultures. Not only is their legitimacy assumed from the onset, but they also serve as legitimating bodies for entities seeking international recognition. This legitimacy is founded on three overlapping mandates: IOs (a) provide forums for negotiation among countries; (b) set norms for multilateral and international engagements; and (c) provide assistance, when possible, in several domains, including security and development (Coicaud, 2001). Not until the recent globalization discourse (in which nearly anything "international" is cast in serious doubt) did scholars begin to seriously reexamine the legitimacy of international regimes broadly (Breitmeier, 2008), and in specific domains such as international law (Wolfrum & Röben, 2008), education and development (Jones & Coleman, 2005) and security (Hurd, 2007). Insofar as these critiques of legitimacy offer loose architectonics for interventions in politics, economy and culture, their engagement in the discourses and processes of 'development' needs to clarify the grounds on which IOs' development visions are anchored.

Starting with the post-World War II reconstruction and meliorist interventionism in emerging states, this chapter briefly outlines contested histories of IOs and the forces responsible for their current 'legitimacy'. Contrary to the popularized 'glorifying' account, forces less benign and ominous in outcome underlie the philosophical foundations and operational dynamics of most IOs. Implicit in this process were assumptions of neutrality and objectivity about IOs' capacity to articulate, modulate and stimulate social *change* along definitive (West-centric) paths. While corroborating this more critical account, this chapter outlines a convergence of ideas between mainstream historiographers of IOs' legitimacy and their critics in that they assume a purely materialist conception of development and accept the primacy of the state as a viable agent of positive social change. To demonstrate the inadequacy of these ideas (and the intellectual hubris of ascribing IOs with objectivity and neutrality), I emphasize the neo-liberal ideological underpinnings of IOs' governance structures.

CONTESTED LEGACIES AND DUAL HISTORIOGRAPHIES

Understanding the sources of IOs' legitimacy entails grappling with two discordant historiographies of politico-economic ideologies imbricated in globalization discourses. In his penetrating analysis, *Bad Samaritans: The Myth of Free Trade and the Secret History of Capitalism,* Ha-Joon Chang (2008) offers two narratives of the history of globalization. The 'official' history involves the economic success of Britain's 18th-century free-market and free-trade policies that triggered worldwide trade liberalization and domestic economic deregulation. As the champion of liberal economics around 1870, the British hegemony epitomized the liberal world order embodied by domestic *laissez-faire* industrial policies, limited barriers to international flows of goods, capital and labor and macroeconomic stability. However, the economic instability heralded by World War I pressured countries to retreat imprudently to *dirigisme*, such that by 1932, even Britain had abandoned the free-trade logic for stiff tariffs. Exacerbated by World War II, this contraction and instability finally annihilated any remnants of the first liberal world order (Chang, 2008).

Whereas early General Agreement on Trade and Tariffs (GATTs) negotiations in the mid-century saw growing momentum around trade liberalization among wealthy countries, 'developing' and communist countries continued to adhere strictly to protectionism and state intervention. The failures of *dirigisme* in the 1970s gave impetus to the rise of neo-liberalism. Jolted by the 1982 Third World debt crisis and the free-trade oriented economic miracle of East Asia, developing countries quickly abandoned protectionism and interventionism for neo-liberalism. This shift was hastened by transformations in transport and communications technologies, which in turn strengthened the structures of global economic governance. In 1995, GATT was transformed into the World Trade Organization (WTO) to advance liberalization in trade, foreign investment regulation and intellectual property rights. Together with the International Monetary Fund (IMF) overseeing short-term financing and the World Bank (WB) in charge of long-term investments, WTO became the central global economic governance system. Under its leadership, a new global economy came to offer unprecedented opportunities for prosperity and boosted the potential for eradicating global poverty. This widely accepted account represents the 'route map' for economic planners to steer their countries towards prosperity (Chang, 2008).

The problem here is that this official account is also the history of colonialism, neo-colonialism and by historical extrapolation, the trans-Atlantic slave commerce. Thus, Chang (2008) views this official account as a misleading distortion. A more accurate account suggests that "the free movement of goods, people and money that developed under British hegemony between 1870 and 1913—the first episode of globalization—was made possible . . . by military might, rather than market forces" (Chang, 2008, p. 24). Rather than voluntary adoption of the free-market ideology, most free-market actors were weaker societies compelled by colonial forces and unequal treaties, such as the Nanking Treaty that resulted from the infamous Opium War. Such treaties, emboldened by centuries of slave traffic and subsequently the apportionment of Africa among European powers at the 1884 Berlin conference, represent more accurately the forces of economic shifts ignored in popularized historiographies of a benign global integration. Although the histories of trans-Atlantic slavery, colonialism and their concomitant economic machineries are well-documented, including them in this discussion is necessary precisely because of efforts to mute their significance in the official historiography. Indeed, apologists of the 'official' history reckon colonial plunders as unfortunate but ultimately positive economic exercises beneficial to all (D'Souza, 2002). As Chang (2008) demonstrates, "[t]he outcome for countries under colonialism and unequal treaties was dismal. Whereas *per capita* income between 1870 and 1913 in Western Europe (1.3%) and the US (1.8%) suggested significant growth, the figures for Africa (0.6%) and Asia, excluding Japan, (0.4%) indicate bleaker outcomes" (p. 25).

During this period in which rich countries imposed free trade on weaker ones, they typically maintained stiff tariffs and strong protectionist postures. Even Britain's earlier attempts at free trade gradually imploded in the face of competition from countries, such as the United States, which deployed protectionist policies in developing domestic industries. According to the official history, economic integration among wealthy nations accelerated after World War II but witnessed weaker participation from poorer countries to their detriment. Protectionism was bad business in the globalizing market. Although rich countries yielded to 'global market forces' and lowered tariffs, they pursued nationalist socio-economic policies (such as government investment in research and development and regulated subsidized public enterprises), which produced significant gains that were reversed as they adopted neo-liberal policies (Chang, 2008).

The corresponding economic disasters of poorer countries, the official history claimed, were primarily outcomes of their 'wrong' choice of economic ideologies (protectionism). In the euphoria of post-colonial independence, nationalist leaders assumed that their nationalist interests could defy ontologically superior global economic principles. Popular opinion about the supremacy of neo-liberalism was so strong that Gustavo Franco, former president of the Brazilian Central Bank (1997–1999), argued that the only choice of economic ideology was "to be neo-liberal or neo-idiotic" (Palma, 2003, as cited in Chang, 2008, p. 27). Yet, economic growth in so-called developing countries during the 1960s and 1970s, when they pursued these 'wrong' policies, was relatively high (3.0%). Like their Western counterparts, this growth only slowed to 1.7% after they implemented the 'superior' neo-liberal ideologies (Chang, 2008). What is often left out here is that these poorer countries were trying to 'develop' using insitutionalized economic tools contrived to expropriate their local resources. Their dismal performance under the strict control of the IMF/WB, champions of the free-market regime, is a scathing commentary on neo-liberalism.

Nobel laureate and former World Bank vice-president Joseph Stiglitz (see Diaz, 2008) argues that not only are these economic 'theories' flawed because they did not lead to economic growth, they also highlight the important role of IOs' *interests* in shaping ideological options in economic development. A dramatic example is the logic of capital market liberalization, which recommends opening up capital markets to the free flow of short-term capital. The IMF attempted to change its charter in September 1997 to force countries to liberalize and open up their capital markets when there was no evidence that it would promote economic growth but that it would actually lead to more instability. Because the Washington Consensus out of which these theories were born was not a consensus among the world nations but between the U.S. Treasury and the WB/IMF, Stiglitz draws the inference that they pursued this capital market liberalization only because "Wall Street wanted it" (Diaz, 2008). The trickle-down economic model, which suggests that more wealth must be created before it is distributed, even if it entails exacerbating inequalities, poverty and economic instability, was never evidentially justified. Given this unethical economic profligacy and corresponding dismal performance, it is doubly striking that IOs continue to dominate global socio-economic discourses and processes. To understand IOs' enduring influence calls for an appreciation of the evolution of development discourse within the competing historiographies outlined earlier.

GLOBAL INTEGRATION AND FABRICATIONS OF DEVELOPMENT

Development *ab ovo* is about processes of change. Human history is rife with transformations resulting from deliberate attempts to adjust to shifting natural conditions. Planned social change prior to the 20th century occurred mostly within particular societies and across relatively small-scale trans-cultural networks. This is true even without rejecting the notion that globalization has 'archaic' (not 'modern') origins (Bayly, 2004)—as captured in what was typologically stylized 'thick' vs. 'thin' globalization (Held, McGrew, Goldblatt & Perraton, 1999)—in attempts to capture primeval transnational networks of earlier empires. However, earlier patterns of small-scale planned social change gave way to highly intensive and more impactful global order due partly to the emergence of IOs. Development, under the nascent global order overseen by IOs, took on a definitively econometric character. Development discourse also assumed a purely Western genealogy out of which IOs emerged as a rational aspiration for a more democratic and internationally integrated world order after the two world wars. Philosophical foundations of international relations that undergird this integration were supposedly outlined in Hobbes, Locke, Rousseau, and other European philosophers of the Enlightenment (Burchill, et al., 2009).

Contrary to this Eurocentric ancestry, recent accounts suggest that global integration emerged due to contending and converging forces that sought universal categorizations of human realities. Amrith and Sluga (2008) argue that this contention and convergence of competing universalisms extend beyond Western traditions and include the influence of anti-colonial nationalists in Asia, Africa and Latin America, who embodied similar universal idealism as the popular Western Enlightenment and humanist traditions in which they were schooled, and who adapted their views to exigent socio-political contingencies of their respective non-Western societies. Indeed, Anderson (2006) provocatively argues that without these anti-colonial thinkers who appropriated elements of European Enlightenment thoughts but transcended their inherent racial exclusivity, the existence of IOs such as the UN would be unthinkable (see Amrith & Sluga, 2008). The result of these amalgam 'universalisms' is the creation and declaration of universal rights *nominally* protected under international charters and conventions.

It is not surprising, therefore, that while still in their formative years, most IOs shifted emphasis from post-war reconstruction to 'development' in less-industrialized societies. By extending international conventions to a universal humanity, the principle of human rights (hypocritically) ensconced in earlier national politico-philosophic discourses, such as found in Abraham Lincoln and Thomas Jefferson (Slaughter, 2005) took on a widened scope that both required and legitimated international regulation of social norms. To be sure, this unification and universalization was possible, not because of the supremacy of the principles of universal human rights—many slavery operatives were schooled in the cannons of Enlightenment—but due to the strategic integration of *decoupling* in IOs' operational principles. Human rights conventions lacked enforceability (and, therefore, became non-threatening) within domestic jurisdictions. Member states may adopt them on the international level but effectively abandon them under the dicta of domestic interests (Mazower, 2004).

Decoupling is a strategic product and *raison d'etre* of the primacy of nation-states in IOs' circles. For instance, reacting to violations of individual and community rights, IOs previously focused significant attention on individual rights as inviolable, not even by a benevolent state. Human rights could not be subject to the calculi of collective interests. Indeed, this 'rights' ethical awakening resulted partly from widespread anti-colonial and civil rights campaigns against competing European ascendancies for which economic development entailed the impoverishment of societies through colonial expropriations and exploitations, enslavement and racial oppression that left millions decimated through genocides and holocausts. By the 1960s, however, IOs had shifted their focus from individual rights to economic development and national self-determination. Pressured by civil rights movements worldwide to respond to continued waves of racial and economic oppression, the UN and other IOs paradoxically reaffirmed the primacy of the state, the prime detractor of human rights, as the ultimate safeguard of human rights. The implicit legitimation of Syria's Assad regime by the international community (in the 2013 chemical weapon deal) on occasion of mass killings of civilians emphasizes this tendentious prioritization of state over individual rights. Earlier, the UN emphasized individual rights due partly to lessons from the interwar period and state abuses of minority rights. But the shift to economic development supplanted individual rights with state sovereignty. When IOs intervened in peacekeeping and security, the overriding interest continued to be that of protecting and perpetuating state sovereignty (Amrith & Sluga, 2008). Amitav Ghosh (2002) captures this in an insightful commentary on the 1993 UN's peacekeeping intervention in Cambodia, under the United Nations Transitional Authority in Cambodia (UNTAC):

> [T]he UN represents the totality of the world's recognized nation-states, and the fundamental logic of its functioning is to recreate the image of its members wherever it goes, so wherever the demands of democracy or humanitarianism run contrary to the exigencies of the nation-state, it is the latter that will always win out. (p. 265)

If the existence of IOs dictates asserting state supremacy, thus providing space for meretricious ethical discourse that lack structures for domestic enforcements, regulating social behavior and enforcing compliance required more ideological apparatuses. It is here that IOs have wielded enormous influence in defining norms and directions of development. By shifting from military conquest to ideological control, this cultural hegemony (*à la* Gramsci) exploits systems of knowledge production, such as education and research, to 'engineer the consent' of marginalized people (Edward Bernays, 1947, as cited in Niedzviecki, 2006). The symbiosis between the state and IOs heralded the establishment of a vast network of specialized agencies, programs and funds to develop, finance and execute programs intended to enhance living conditions worldwide. These organizations—IMF/WB, World Health Organization (WHO), UN Education Science and Cultural Organization (UNESCO), International Labor Organization (ILO), Food and Agriculture Organization (FAO), World Intellectual Property Organization (WIPO), UN Children's Emergency Fund (UNICEF), UN Development Programs (UNDP), UN Drug Control Program (UNDCP), World Food Program (WFP) and UN Population Fund (UNFPA)—work together through the UN to promote 'peace and prosperity' worldwide (UN, 2012). Yet, by obliging this commitment to promote human welfare worldwide, nation-states inadvertently concede the credibility of IOs in constructing benchmarks and pathways for legitimate development.

In a 1952 report revealingly entitled "Preliminary Report on the World Social Situation", the UN not only assumed this crucial responsibility of establishing development orthodoxy but more importantly, inscribed on it a Western inflection when it argued that "the general impoverishment of any area is a matter of concern to all; and that the technical experience and knowledge acquired in rapidly changing industrialized societies have somehow to be made available to those communities that are less advanced and less well equipped" (UN, 1952). With this socio-economic imagination of global (inter)dependence, the UN positioned its sundry agencies as the legitimate facilitator of these exchanges, and outlined guiding principles for its technical/development assistance through which it sought to transform the world along Western lines (Amrith & Sluga, 2008). Alternative social conditions were collectively dubbed 'underdevelopment'.

The binary portraits of development were already institutionalized and legitimated under colonialism. A category of 'underdeveloped' (later, 'developing' and 'Third World') societies became necessary not only as justification for 'developed' and 'First World' ones but also as a rationalization for melioristic interventions of IOs in non-Western societies. The scope of its justificatory value extended from WHO vaccination schemes to UNESCO's educational norms and a battery of WB loan packages. Although earlier neo-colonial critiques exposed the conceptual inadequacies of this dualism, the assumption that the project of modernity for non-Western societies is necessarily tethered to Western tutelage quickly outstripped the fledgling post-colonial optimisms about self-determination. New nations quickly learned that to be accepted into the emerging global banquet of nations and to gain credibility, strict adherence to the rubrics of Westernized fabrications of development was imperative. In accepting the corresponding loan aid packages, less-industrialized societies become unwittingly complicit in sealing the fate of their societies' development. Indeed, Western delineation of development has become so paradigmatic that critics who highlight other alternatives are treated as inconsequential cynical detractors. As evident in Sachs' (2005, 2008) works, mainstream economists continue to offer Western 'philanthropic' levers to lift the most impoverished onto the lowest rung of modernity's Eurocentric ladder. The crucial point here is that the *economic* calculations of aid acceptance require a concomitant *ideological* concession to this unilineal Western imagery of development.

The legacy of the economic control and ideological manipulation of IOs are at least threefold: first, that the escalation of interests in development (redefined as Westernization) took on a new worldwide dimension is almost platitudinous. Yet, the ways in which the existence of international structures gradually became the primary tool for its own legitimation require constant reexamination. Second, this emphasis took on a particularly analytic character in that it compartmentalized arenas of development along manageable indices with empirical measures. Development was no longer a holistic exercise, but to be sought under education, health and political economics. Recent evolutions of Millennium Development Goals (MDGs), Education for All (EFA) and International Development Targets (IDT) are few evidences of this trend. Third, the emergence of quantification of development indices, whether through the Human Development Index (HDI) or other crude development measures (e.g., knowledge and learning, holistic well-being and material wealth) have been reduced to narrow standardized algorithmic values for ranking societies. To rank societies, quantitative measures were necessary to create an illusion of objectivity and neutrality. Empirical data, not socially constructed ideologies, must determine which societies are developed and which need development assistance. Consequently, ascribing IOs with objectivity and neutrality, arguably, remains the most unfortunate legacy of current development discourse.

STRUCTURAL CONSTRAINT, NEO-LIBERAL OBLIGATION AND NEW DEVELOPMENT VISTAS

Two sets of arguments have been advanced so far: (1) that IOs have played a significant role in defining and disseminating current development norms largely as 'Westernization' through *intellectual* organizations (e.g., UNESCO) and *economic* institutions (WB/IMF); and (2) that despite the hype about fostering historicized development around the world, IOs' development profiles have so far been dismal and bore profound deleterious consequences in less industrialized societies. If IOs continue to be influential in defining development discourse and if current visions of development are narrow, one must examine their structural capabilities and ideological commitments to a new and integrative development vista. Must societies abide by prevailing materialist vision of development and its neo-liberal economic cocktails to gain equal status and legitimacy internationally? Or, can they effectively adopt development pathways fundamentally different from current consumerist monocultural materialism without attracting *ipso facto* the antagonism of dominant Western powers and their IOs' surrogates? Whereas mainstream scholarship offers a very optimistic outlook, even a cursory analysis suggests that IOs are structurally constrained and ideologically disinclined to accommodate alternative discourses on growth or development. To explore these structural and ideological barriers, I refer to two considerations that, although obvious, are often ignored in popular IOs analysis.

Structural Constraints in International Organizational Governance

One fundamental flaw of current development practices lies in an inherent paradox. Whereas *prima facie* IOs' development initiatives are founded on principles of universal rights and freedom and purportedly uphold dialogue, their structural logic inherently operates by producing winners and losers. The prime casualties are individuals and groups forced to the margins of social and economic activities, mostly in the global South. As articulated in recent 'Occupy Movement', the economic, political and cultural activities that generated the opulence of New York's Wall Street and London's Square Mile is also responsible for the slums, ghettos and barrios spread across Africa, the Americas, Asia and Europe. Contrary to dominant accounts, such economic and political polarization occurs precisely because of nation-states' and IOs' activities.

Besides ideological presuppositions of nation-state supremacy, IOs are structurally constrained because member states are represented by diplomats and politicians whose plenipotentiary powers are directly limitable only by state institutions. Consequently, their decisions reflect state priorities because policy decisions and normative positions are the prerogative of member state representatives. Whereas non-member state parties, such as intergovernmental or non-governmental organizations, may be invited as observers without voting rights, most internal strategic and operational decisions are made directly or shaped indirectly by the dominant nation-states. For instance, only the United States, the United Kingdom, Russia, France and China are permanent members of the UN Security Council with only 10 additional non-permanent members elected for two-year terms. Over 70 member countries have never sat in the Security Council (UN, 2012). Both UNESCO and the WB have an Executive Board and a Board of Directors, respectively, comprised of a fraction of member state representatives. Indeed, a member state's voting power in the WB is proportionate to its financial investment in the bank, leaving the United States, Japan, Germany, France and the UK as the most dominant countries with permanent Executive Director Appointees (World Bank, 2012).

Apologists of this hegemony invoke the Hegemonic Stability Theory (HST) developed by Krasner (1999, 1985) and Kindleberger (1996) and recently advanced by Keohane (2005). HST accepts as a given the problem of collective action. With large groups, collective interests do not necessarily conduce to rational choices and collective goal-directed action. Instead, collective interest, especially among large groups engenders a situation where poorer individuals abdicate their responsibility to contribute to the public good, leaving the burden to wealthier individuals (see Olson, 1965). By defining the regulation and institutionalization of trade and finance as a public good, HST rationalizes the inevitability of a *hegemon* who, despite being motivated by domestic national interests, is required to superintend over international political economic integration.

We do not need to unveil the flaws of this logic to note that speaking of objectivity and neutrality, borne out of dialogue, under such structural hegemony is facetious.

In addition to this organizational structure, decision making within particular IOs depend largely on the same operational strategies characteristic of nation-state governance. During field research at the UNESCO headquarters in Paris, my interview with a prominent UNESCO ambassador was interrupted by another delegation that was lobbying for an upcoming General Conference vote. As the ambassador later clarified, "this is how things are done here. Sometimes you have to support issues you disagree with so that others can vote in your support in areas of strategic interest" (Cabrone, 2009)[1]. The ensuing review of IO governance revealed, first, that IOs' governance is simply national politics writ large. Yet, national policymakers view normative positions and policy prescriptions of IOs as a product of an intellectually honest, economically sound and culturally responsive process. Second, whenever IOs enlist academics or professionals in constructing normative or policy packages, such expert recommendations are ultimately subject to the economic and political gerrymandering of IOs' governance. Even experts who win IOs' endorsements cannot guarantee the credibility of their 'expert opinion' within this highly politicized structure. Overall, any optimism about IOs' structural capabilities to accommodate alternate development discourses is naïve.

Neo-Liberal Obligations in International Organizations Development Vista

It is not accidental that IOs purport to function as impartial development actors but uphold social and economic policies that for decades have produced dismal outcomes for the majority of the world's marginalized population. IOs' leadership structures were configured to serve entrenched interests of dominant socio-economic societies/classes. The issue here is well articulated in the recent controversy over *The End of Poverty*, the main title of both Jeffrey Sachs' (2005) book and Philippe Diaz's (2008) documentary film. The famous economist Sachs recounts a familiar tale of classical social evolution in which all societies are destined to a common teleological path (and, therefore, end) by adopting economic and social models of Western civilization as the contemporary pinnacle of social evolution. His economic remedy for eradicating extreme poverty is anchored on the basic assumption of unilineal Western economic development. Poor societies, in Sachs' account, have to be assisted by wealthier nations to step onto the lowest rung of this predetermined economic ladder. Sachs explains the existence of extreme poverty due to lack of six kinds of capital: sufficient *human capital* (e.g., health, nutrition and skills required for economic productivity); *business capital* (machinery and transport for increased productivity); *infrastructure* that are critical inputs for business productivity; *natural capital* that provides the environmental services necessary for human society; *public institutional capital* that makes for peaceful and prosperous division of labor; and *knowledge capital* that elevates and promotes physical and natural capital.

To escape the poverty trap created by the dynamics of these exiguous capitals and to begin ascent to full humanity, extremely poor supplicants must depend on Western donor-based investment to boost their level of capital for economic productivity that meets their basic needs (Peet, 2006). According to Sachs, "[t]he key to ending extreme poverty is to enable the poorest of the poor to get their foot on the ladder of development" (2005, p. 244). To accomplish this by 2025, in keeping with visions contrived under the aegis of IOs (e.g., the UN MDGs), rich nations only need to fulfill their existing commitment to provide 0.7% of GDP as foreign aid. Indeed, Sachs argues, "*the Millennium Development Goals can be financed within the bounds of the official development assistance that the donor countries have already promised*" (2005, p. 299, emphasis in original). Once foreign aid fills this 'financing gap' between what a poor country needs and what it can actually produce on its own, an extremely poor society will "break out of the poverty trap and begin growing on its own" (Sachs, 2005, p. 250).

Sachs' arguments reiterate earlier 'Big Push' *contra* 'incremental reform' controversies of the past two decades, in which shock therapy was pitted against gradualism and piecemeal reform (Easterly & Sachs, 2006). In a more recent book, *Common Wealth: Economics for a Crowded Planet*, Sachs (2008) extends this argument by integrating concerns about how (a) global population growth (projected at 9.2 billion at mid-century); and (b) increased rates of consumption place unsustainable pressures on natural resources and global environment. His ternary recommendations of improved sustainable technologies, population control (especially in Sub-Saharan Africa) and ending poverty should be underwritten by rich nations in their own terms. Despite Sachs objection to the characterization of his arguments as a 'top-down' global planning prescription, the role he assigns IOs and countries are revealing. In his prescriptions for 'planning for success', Sachs (2005, pp. 269–270) argues as follows:

> The UN secretary-general, overseeing the UN agencies and the Bretton Woods Institutions (which are also part of the UN family), should oversee the entire effort. Working through the United Nations Development Program—the economic development arm of the UN system—the secretary-general, on behalf of the member nations, should ensure that the global compact is put into operation. . . . To organize country-level work, each low-income country should adopt a poverty reduction

strategy (PRS) [Structural Adjustment Programs (SAPs)] specifically designed to meet the Millennium Development Goals.

Thus, adopting the popularized narrative of poverty and development, Sachs places possibilities for complex social changes across divergent world societies on Western philanthropy under the supervision of IOs.

Whereas such narrow top-down economic prescriptivism appears very attractive under prevailing globalization Zeitgeist, critics consider Sachs ideas naïvely optimistic or ethically abhorrent. In his documentary film aptly entitle *The End of Poverty? Think Again*, Philippe Diaz (2008) highlights some significant historical inaccuracies and strategic flaws in Sachs' analysis. First, divergent outcomes in development and the corresponding escalation of extreme poverty are not the product of impartial processes of technological advancement as Sachs argues. Sachs (2005) absolves the West from centuries of exploitations of non-European societies, and insists that although 'the rich' may not be innocent, "the real story of modern economic growth has been the ability of some regions to achieve unprecedented long-term increases in total production . . . while other regions stagnated" (p. 31). Sachs appears to be aware of Europe's imperialist exploits, but the intentions behind his interpretations are questionable.

The primary lesson in Diaz's response to Sachs pertains to continuity in history; it is problematic to dissociate contemporary social conditions from previous ones and to render insignificant major historical events of the past half millennium (Gerschenkron, 1962). Diaz's arguments infuses the present with the past. First, earlier European expansionism, which Eric Toussaint calls "an extremely brutal intervention" (Peet, 2006, p. 451), involved the expropriation of natural resources from non-European societies, stripping such societies of essential natural capital that were moved to Europe to become a major source of economic growth. According to Toussaint, trade in these resources and the consequent economic growth accounts for a significant part of Europe's wealth. Resource expropriation occurred contemporaneously with exploitation of land and people (mostly as free labor), both in colonial frontiers and in the Occident. The brutal exploitation of African free labor under slavery in the entire Americas echoes the oppressive conditions under which colonized people labored and died in Asia and Africa.

Second, as the Euro-American (and later in the 19th century, Japanese) economies grew at the expense of their colonies, colonial powers more and more defined capitalist rules of international economic exchanges and imposed a monoculture in which each peripheral society was assigned the role of producing particular export resources, thus creating a state of dependency under colonial control. To date, the locked economies of colonial frontiers ensure that raw materials, exported at extremely low-cost, are imported as expensive finished products. Since 1960, the price of agricultural exports from less-industrialized societies has fallen 70% compared to imports. Paradoxically, the quest to boost manufacturing in these countries often led to massive debt and inefficient or logistically inoperable industrial plants.

Third, colonial expansion deployed both military and ideological tools to extract the consent of the colonized in their subjugation. Former European forts (e.g., Elmina Castle in Ghana and Fort Jesus in Kenya), which are among the surviving relics of European military force bear ample artillery evidence. Although military force was essential at the onset, complete control of the colonial structure required a change in mentality, religion and cultures of the colonized. To do this, European colonists rationalized an odd convergence of religion and economy by propagating a version of individualistic Christianity in association with an individualistic capitalist view of personal property, both of which had little recourse and obligation to or regard for reciprocal African indigenous communal responsibility. The resulting identity crises paved the way for external incursions into the economies and social spaces of Africa.

Fourth, as societies emerged from colonialism, their dependence extended beyond former colonial power to the emerging international economic order, which dictated conditions of 'development', and assigned resources and loans with strict conditionalities. The SAPs of the neo-liberal movement is emblematic of this neo-colonial economic and ideological control. During this period, IOs unleashed teams of Western 'experts' on emerging states, who ensured that all social policies and economic planning were aligned to this established hegemonic order. For Diaz, this new economic order birthed a structural violence that used economic 'hit men' (Perkins, 2004) to coax governments of less-industrialized societies to accede to the Western hegemonic development paradigm. The results are piling debt, loss of sovereignty and continued economic, cultural and political subjugation. When economic hitmen fail in areas of significant Western interests, a military intervention (often involving overthrow/assassination of a democratically elected leader) often follows, as was the case with Guatemala's Jacobo Arbenz, Chile's Salvador Allende, Ecuador's Jaime Roldós Aguilera and Congo's Patrice Lumumba.

Although Diaz does not highlight this sufficiently, a fifth expression of historical continuity lies in the adoption of nation-state as the 'natural' structure of society. Ontologically, nations are imagined communities (Anderson, 1991). But the adoption of national structures in ex-colonial societies took on a fundamentally problematic character due to the arbitrary splintering and amalgamation of first nations/'tribes' into new configurations that reflect little logic of internal cohesion. Even today, for a Western world whose colonial principle was *divide et impera,* persistent political disunity is auspicious for good business. Ultimately, the dominance of Western interests in current development vista and the ideological obligation to neo-liberal economic tools suggest that eliminating the aforesaid structural constraints hardly offers a more optimistic picture for expanding ideas about development.

CONCLUSION

Using Diaz's documentary film offers ample evidence for an alternate portraiture of how Western forces bear on discourses and practices of development but also represents a symbolic response to the narrowly defined criteria for academic scholarship (see Whitehead, 2005; Appadurai, 2000). IOs continue to play a significant role in defining the discourses and processes of social change worldwide partly due to their capacity to enlist or produce academic scholarship that ignores these bodies of evidence. For IOs to pretend that they possess a neutral and objective stance on development amounts to intellectual hubris. From a more critical standpoint, any development discourse that ignores indigenous perspectives and assigns a significant role to IOs without questioning their instrumentality in the systematic exploitation of global resources is morally questionable. Ascribing the rich-help-poor 'philanthropic' solutions to the global socio-economic inequality essentially undermines the moral *locus standi* of the poor to criticize the sources of the wealth through which they were impoverished (Peet, 2006). More importantly, grassroots actors who view IOs as strategic allies either against or in alliance with national governments ought to heed Diaz's advice to 'think again'. IOs cannot and should not purport to represent a diversity of voices besides pandering to their interest.

NOTES

1. Pseudonym used for confidentiality.

REFERENCES

Amrith, S. & Sluga, G. (2008). New histories of the United Nations. *Journal of World History*, 19(3), 251–274.
Anderson, B. (2006). *Under three flags: Anarchism and the anti-colonial imagination*. London: Verso.
Anderson, B.R. (1991). *Imagined communities: Reflections on the origin and spread of nationalism*. London: Verso.
Appadurai, A. (2000). Grassroots globalization and the research imagination. *Public Culture*, 12, 1–19.
Bayly, C.A. (2004). *The birth of the modern world*. Cambridge: Cambridge University Press.
Breitmeier, H. (2008). *The legitimacy of international regimes*. Surrey: Ashgate Publishing Ltd.
Burchill, S. et al. (Eds.). (2009). *Theories of international relations* (4th ed.). New York: Palgrave Macmillan.
Cabrone, A. (2009, June 10). *UNESCO Ambassador*. (D. Odugu, Interviewer)
Chang, H.-J. (2008). *Bad Samaritans: The myth of free trade and the secret history of capitalism*. New York: Bloomsbury Press.

Coicaud, J.-M. (2001). Conclusion: International organizations, the evolution of international politics, and legitimacy. In J.-M. Coicaud & V. Heiskanen (Eds.), *The legitimacy of international organizations* (pp. 519–552). Tokyo: UN University Press.

Diaz, P. (Director). (2008). *End of poverty? Think again* [Motion Picture]. United States: Cinema Libre.

D'Souza, D. (2002, May 10). Two cheers for colonialism. *The Chronicle of Higher Education*, 48(35), B7.

Easterly, W. & Sachs, J.D. (2006). The big push déjà vu: A review of Jeffrey Sachs' "The end of poverty: Economic possibilities for our time". *Journal of Economic Literature*, 44(1), 96–105.

Gerschenkron, A. (1962). On the concept of continuity in history. *Proceedings of the American Philosophical Society*, 106(3), 195–209.

Ghosh, A. (2002). *The Imam and the Indian: Prose pieces*. New Delhi: Ravi Dayal Publisher.

Held, D., McGrew, A., Goldblatt, D. & Perraton, J. (1999). *Global transformations: Politics, economics and culture*. Stanford, CA: Stanford University Press.

Hurd, I. (2007). *After anarchy: Legitimacy and power in the United Nations Security Council*. Princeton, NJ: Princeton University Press.

Jones, P.W. & Coleman, D. (2005). *The United Nations and education: Multilateralism, development and globalization*. New York: Routledge Falmer.

Keohane, R.O. (2005). *After hegemony: Cooperation and discord in the world political economy*. Princeton, NJ: Princeton University Press.

Kindleberger, C.P. (1996). *World economic primacy: 1500–1990*. New York: Oxford University Press.

Krasner, S.D. (1985). *Structural conflict: The Third World against global liberalism*. Berkeley: University of California Press.

Krasner, S.D. (1999). *Sovereignty: Organized hypocrisy*. Princeton, NJ: Princeton University Press.

Mazower, M. (2004). The strange triumph of human rights, 1933–1950. *Historical Journal*, 47, 379–398.

Niedzviecki, H. (2006). *Hello, I'm special: How individuality became the new conformity*. San Francisco: City Lights.

Odugu, D.I. (2011). *Education language policy process in multilingual societies: Global visions and local agendas in India, Nigeria and UNESCO*. Chicago: Loyola eCommons.

Olson, M. (1965). *The Logic of Collective Action: Public Goods and the Theory of Groups*. Cambridge: Harvard University Press.

Peet, R. (2006). The end of poverty: Economic possibilities for our time by Jeffery D. Sachs. *Annals of the Association of American Geographers*, 96(2), 450–453.

Perkins, J. (2004). *Confessions of an economic hit man*. San Francisco: Berrett-Koehler.

Sachs, J. (2005). *The end of poverty: Economic possibilities for our time*. New York: Penguin.

Sachs, J. (2008). *Common wealth: Economics for a crowded planet*. New York: Penguin Group.

Slaughter, A.-M. (2005). Disaggregated sovereignty: Towards the public accountability of global government networks. In D. Held & M. Koenig-Archibugi (Eds.), *Global governance and public accountability*, (pp. 35–66). Oxford: Blackwell Publishing.

UN. (1952). *Preliminary Report on the World Social Situation*. New York: United Nations.

UN. (2012). *United Nations Security Council*. New York: United Nations Security Council. Retrieved October 13, 2012 from http://www.un.org/en/sc/members/
Whitehead, C. (2005). The historiography of British Imperial education policy, Part II: Africa and the rest of the colonial empire. *History of Education*, 34(4), 441–454.
Wolfrum, R. & Röben, V. (Eds.). (2008). *Legitimacy in international law*. New York: Springer.
World Bank. (2012). The World Bank: Board of Directors. Retrieved October 13, 2012 from http://web.worldbank.org/WBSITE/EXTERNAL/EXTABOUTUS/0,,contentMDK:22494475~menuPK:8336906~pagePK:51123644~piPK:329829~theSitePK:29708,00.html

11 The Dual Sources of Political Development in Ethiopia and the Emergence of Ethnic Federalism

Berhanu Demeke

INTRODUCTION

In a century of national state-building projects in Ethiopia, the latest phase has been the most ambitious. So observes the notable Ethiopianist John Markakis (2011) describing Ethiopia's primary 'political' preoccupation since the revolution that ousted the *Derg*, in 1991. From that fateful year, the current governing coalition, the Ethiopian People's Revolutionary Democratic Front (EPRDF), has been engaged in bold, potentially transformative, albeit risky, experiments intended to enhance the country's political and economic well-being (Abbink, 2009) that is grounded in the lynchpin of a new democratic program, which is a uniquely constituted federalism (Markakis, 2011; Turton, 2006; Kymlicka, 2006). This program is designed to decentralize political power to representative ethno-cultural and territorially contiguous regions. In the economic sphere, EPRDF has combined gradual economic liberalization with staunch pursuit of a development strategy that makes the agricultural sector the engine of growth and poverty reduction.

This chapter is intended to provide a historically informed account of Ethiopia's current state of affairs especially as it relates to political development. From a methodological point of view, it implicitly argues that only a properly balanced approach, one that takes both external (global) factors and internal (domestic) ones in right measure, can supply us with an analysis that is closer to an accurate picture of the country's current state of political development. In this sense, I caution against methodological nationalism that views the nation-state as the most important and independent unit of analysis. Instead, the chapter makes a case for the need to look both at formative experiences of the nation-state from within and from outside. Substantively, the chapter presents a description of what constitutes political development in Ethiopia. It argues that a sufficient understanding of Ethiopia's current development experience requires taking stock of the historical factors that have had formative influences on the country's history *vis-à-vis* democracy, particularly the political management of ethnic diversity.

Both the current historic venture into democracy and the ethnic federalist formula adopted in Ethiopia are due in part to external factors, like the end of the Cold War and global wave of democratic movements of the time and the role of foreign entities (especially the United States). This aspect of the history is the subject of the first part of the chapter. The second part describes the internal (domestic) political dynamic in which longstanding demands for rights, representation and autonomy by ethno-cultural entities made federalism, one that is based on ethnicity, a viable political option. The chapter highlights that ethnic federalism's emergence, in the form of political accommodation of ethnic diversity, is a controversial answer to a perennial political question, perhaps *the* albatross around Ethiopia's political neck since the emergence of the modern state of Ethiopia in the middle of the 19th century.

This chapter is theoretical in approach and discusses the issues based on considerations of the histories of the Cold War and its aftereffects, democratization in Africa and Ethiopia's record on the accommodation of ethnic diversity. And although it is historically grounded, it is not a strictly empirical work and does not seek to assess whether the theoretical insights implied here are in fact being put into practice in Ethiopia at the present moment. It does, however, aim at explaining the promise that lies in the country's political development and is inspired by the hope that ought to guide the survival of democracy in the country.

EXTERNAL FACTORS

The end of the Cold War and the beginning of the decline of Soviet Union's power is a global event that in part enabled the most 'ambitious' political transformation that Markakis (2011) is referring to at the outset. The 1974 revolution that toppled the *ancient regime,* which had become bankrupt and devoid of legitimacy, highlights the way in which global events have been intimately tied to major shifts that brought radical changes to Ethiopia. As Kinfe (2001, pp. 264–265) states:

> The regime had run out of steam and the ability to cope with the dynamics of a changing world. . . . Gradually, the aristocracy had lost its vision and assertiveness, so much so that its legitimacy was being called to question . . . the regime had lost the religious ethic on which it heavily banked for years as the providential basis of its legitimacy.

The nature of the imperial rule that preceded the revolution and the temper of the times, a bipolar world in which Marxism was one of the two reigning political alternatives, made Ethiopia one of many testing grounds for 'socialism'. Thus, "Ethiopians saw the class struggle as the only radical path open to them to the extent that alternatives to 'scientific Marxism' were not mentioned, let alone considered" (Markakis, 2011, p. 162). And as the United States, an ally under former Emperor Haile Selassie, maligned by Ethiopia's infatuation with 'scientific Marxism', distanced itself, the Soviet Union jumped in and filled the power vacuum 'to help' "a fraternal country in transition to socialism" (Markakis, 2011, p. 183). Thus, Ethiopia positioned itself on the eastern side of the Cold War and followed a radical Marxist path with the support of the Soviet Union and its allies. As noted by Kinfe (2001, p. 406):

> The ties between the Soviet Union (and other East European states) and Ethiopia [had] become close over a period of several years. Mengistu [Ethiopia's leader] visited Moscow in late 1976 and again in May 1977 not long after he had firmly established his power. A twenty year treaty of friendship was signed during his visit in November 1978.

After about 15 years of Ethiopia's experiment with 'socialism', a new era was at hand. At the end of 1980s, Mikhail Gorbachev's historic policies of *perestroika* and *glasnost* were poised to alter the Soviet Union's standing in global power relations (Zewde, 1991). Decalo (1992, p. 7) argues and concludes:

> Spurred by the spectacle of the fall of the titans in Bucharest and elsewhere, in 1990, a powerful backwash of popular demonstration for 're-democratization' flooded all corners of Africa. By 1991, the backwash was a veritable tidal wave, methodically transforming the political map of the continent.

As the 1990s began, with the exception of a few countries, Africa had started a journey towards democratic pluralism (Keller, 1999). The collapse of the Soviet Union, a staunch ally of the communist military regime in Ethiopia and the *de facto* leader of the 'communist' world, meant loss of material and more importantly ideological support. Amid such loss of external support, domestic economic crisis and assault from resilient ethno-cultural insurgencies, the communist regime fell and its leader, Mengistu Haile Mariam, fled the country to Zimbabwe, paving the way for the EPRDF, the umbrella organization of dissident rebel movements, to enter the capital Addis Ababa on May 28, 1991 and take the reins of power.

In this sense, upheavals in the global balance of power, itself a consequence of the struggle for ideological and political dominance between super powers, has had a profound effect in the domestic politics of Ethiopia. It was a catalyst for Ethiopia's revolution of 1991 that overthrew one of the most doctrinaire Marxist-Leninist regimes around. But the irony was that the revolution was made possible by a resistance movement that was, itself, heavily steeped in Marxism. A stark example of this was public expressions of admiration for ultra-communist Albania as an example to be followed by one of leaders of the EPRDF (Kinfe, 2001).

During the transition from Marxist rule to the current EPRDF regime, the global spreading of political and economic theory and practice of democracy and liberalization has had decisive effects as well. The prevalence of this spreading orientation was evident in most African countries' experience. A salient feature of the post-1989 democratic wave in Africa is a rejection of Marxist communism either as foundation for legitimate government or pragmatic formula for economic development. Thus, during this period "[a]ll the continent's People's Republics . . . renounced Marxism, moving to adopt a market economy" (Decalo, 1992, p. 7). By the same token, "the EPRDF at its fourth congress in January 1991 came out with a new program which was responsive to the new global ideological mood" (Kinfe, 2001, p. 434).

The shift in political discourses in the world towards democracy and liberalization altered the ideological orientation of the 'victorious' dissidents that took power in Ethiopia. Ottaway (1995, p. 69) argues that it was pragmatic that "the TPLF dropped its radical rhetoric and adopted the language of democracy". As soon as it was in a position to start the process of democratization, the EPRDF endeavored towards a smooth transition, spearheaded the creation of a transitional government in which various political voices were heard and oversaw a fairly inclusive process that helped create a democratic constitution. The liberalization agenda is evident in the new constitution ratified in 1995. It affirms the sovereignty of citizens, ensures government accountability and transparency, protects human rights along the lines of UN Declaration of Human Rights and other international human rights conventions and protects diversity up to ethnic self-determination (Government of Ethiopia, 1994). In other words, nudged in part by global democratic wave, Ethiopia like other numerous countries in Africa ushered in a historically unprecedented epoch of democratic constitutionalism.

In this connection, the role played by the West, particularly the United States during the transition period in 1990–1991 and afterwards is especially noteworthy. This marked a reversal of US-Ethiopia relationship. "From 1977 onwards US–Ethiopian relations gradually grew sour, entering a phase of cold-war hostility until the second half of the 1980s" (Kinfe, 2001, p. 415). The repatriation of the U.S. ambassador in 1980, the Ethio-Russian comprehensive agreement in 1981 and the Reagan administration's policy review that determined to isolate Ethiopia are examples of a progressively antagonistic relationship between Ethiopia and the United States (Kinfe, 2001). But this state of affairs was to change as the Cold War was coming to an end and Soviet Union's support of Ethiopia was waning.

By the end of the 1980s, the Russians had made it sufficiently clear to the United States that they wanted to withdraw from Ethiopia, giving, in effect, a green light to the United States to find peace and a state of equilibrium in Ethiopia (Woodward, 2006). Due to the winds of change, Woodward

(2006, pp. 50–51) observes, "By 1989 the Soviet Union had disengaged from the horn leaving Mengistu weak and isolated". This coincided with a series of astounding military triumphs by the Tigrean People's Liberation Front (TPLF), the rebel organization then, and now a sub-group of the EPRDF who fought against the Mengistu's military regime, thus delivering debilitating strikes on the military spirit and creating hope for an alternative government (Kinfe, 2001). The upsurge in military gains together with the rebels ideological repositioning towards a more 'liberal' political agenda brought about a reversal of fortunes for Ethiopia. And this created a point of entry for U.S. involvement in Ethiopia as noted by Zewde (1991, p. 267) who states:

> [EPRDF] not only enjoyed military superiority but also had a clear diplomatic edge. Having been more thorough and more convincing than the *Derg* in formally renouncing their Marxist-Leninist credentials, they had managed to win considerable sympathy in the US State Department, just as their military successes had impressed on the US officials that they should be taken seriously in any future political restructuring of the region.

With this, the London negotiations of the 1990s, which were integral for a peaceful transition and a democratic constitution, were mediated by the U.S. Assistant Secretary of State for African Affairs, Herman Cohen. It is worth noting that these external involvements nudged Ethiopia towards representative and pluralistic democracy. As Herman Cohen said in 1994, "Our goal was to replace war with peace and find a path forward to a more broadly based and democratic political system. We sought a transitional mechanism that could produce an interim government made up of all Ethiopian parties" (Farkas, 2003, p. 57). Democratic change was the necessary condition for U.S. support which was based on the cliché, "No democracy, no aid" (Markakis, 2011, p. 231) as the United States' policy.

Everything that was done in the Horn of Africa was meant "to encourage the adoption of democratic methods and the practice of democracy" (Kinfe, 2001, p. 437) as it was pronounced by Paul Henze, a U.S. spokesman in *The Horn of Africa Recover Act 1991*. The clear break from previous U.S. policy is palpable in this excerpt from the same document, "We should be careful to avoid transferring attitudes that were developed toward Mengistu's regime to the TPLF/EPRDF" (Kinfe, 2001, p. 437).

In this section, I have focused on external (global) factors that shaped Ethiopia's recent political development. The end of the Cold War and the Soviet Union's retrenchment, the democratic wave of the times and the particular role played by the United States are all extra-national factors that ought to be taken into account in understanding Ethiopia's development narrative. Ethiopia's path is one of many stories of democratization in Africa that were seen in the immediate aftermath of the 1989 transformations in

Eastern Europe and it is in part a by-product of the end of the Cold War. Despite these global factors, however, there were also important internal historical sources of political development. And it is these sources that the next part of the chapter turns to.

INTERNAL FACTORS

In this section, first I will situate Ethiopia within the larger African context by pointing out how the collapse of the communist military regime in Ethiopia in 1991 fits a pattern of change seen in Africa in the 1990s. From there, the chapter segues into a discussion of internal causes. Among these, the political accommodation of ethnic diversity in Africa, or lack thereof, is perhaps a most vexing and decisive political concern. Having located Ethiopia within broader African political experience, I will critically look at Ethiopia's history of managing ethnic diversity as perhaps a most critical internal socio-political variable. The current attempt at accommodating ethnic diversity in Ethiopia is rooted in the history and politics of ethnicity. Coming to terms with both the history and politics can help us understand the current political development project and one of its central features, ethnic federalism.

This chapter maintains that one has to take both external and internal factors in accounting for the state of affairs present in Ethiopia. As exemplified in the first section, Ethiopia has been affected by the end of the Cold War and the ensuing shift in the relative global power configurations and the wave of democratization post-1989. However, there have been internal socio-economic and political challenges that plagued the nation and deeply affected its current political spirit. As Clapham (1993, p. 423) states:

> The changes currently under way are . . . much more than the simple backwash into Africa of events in Eastern Europe and the former USSR. Even though the timing of events in Africa has been affected by the upheavals in Europe, and though the African scene is inevitably influenced by the transformation of the international order, the democratisation process reflects a crisis in the African state itself which was in any event becoming clear.

This is the other side of the equation that helps us to take into account the dual aspects of a dynamic Ethiopian political development. External factors have certainly had impact on how Ethiopia's political journey has been unfolding. In saying so, however, one has to be careful not to overestimate the global influences at the price of politico-historical dynamics of the country when explaining the current character of Ethiopia's political landscape.

For instance, the fall of Ethiopia's communist regime in 1991 was due in good measure to the government's total loss of domestic legitimacy and failure to address the persistent calls for ethno-cultural justice. In this, Ethiopia is quite typical of most African countries in which legitimacy crisis within formal institutions of government and the internal political realities had much to do with change in government. Christopher Clapham's description of the collapse of African governments here captures what was true of Ethiopia:

> The shift to democracy has taken place because Africa's battered states were incapable of hanging on in any other way. Their political institutions had lost the legitimacy that they initially gained in opposition to colonial rule. Their economies were almost everywhere in desperate straits and in many countries in virtual collapse. Their ability to maintain themselves by force had been removed by the disappearance of external military support, and in several countries by the inability of an overstretched and demoralised military to hold off growing levels of insurgency. (Clapham, 2003, p. 434)

Amid these causes of legitimacy crises, the ethnic aspect of politics is a cardinal one. As Ndulo and Grieco (2010, p. 9) have argued:

> [M]ost scholars of Africa agree that one issue that continues to plague African states is how to manage diversity in their respective nation states and build institutions that are inclusive, promote economic development, consolidate political harmony and stability, and avoid conflicts through enfranchisement.

Ethiopia typifies this challenge. Like most African countries, it is multiethnic, with over 80 ethnic groupings (Abbink, 2009). Ever since the earliest days of the modern state of Ethiopia, political leaders have been faced with the challenge of coming up with approaches to governance that might ameliorate the potential for ethnic conflict while at the same time addressing claims of ethnic self-determination (Keller, 1999).

It is in response to this issue of the need to accommodate ethnic diversity, the deeply trenchant challenge, that federalism became necessary. As Fiseha (2006) succinctly extrapolates, "The federal system of government which was introduced in Ethiopia following the fall of the Derg in 1991 was intended to decentralize power and resolve the 'nationalities question' by accommodating the country's various ethno-linguistic groups" (p. 131). A proper understanding of the source, logic and aim of this current political response in the form of ethnic federalism requires examining Ethiopia's peculiar historical experience *vis-à-vis* the ethnic question.

Ethiopia's history, with ethnicity as a political issue, is long, deeply cantankerous and replete with violent episodes. In its genesis, it certainly diverges from the typical experience of other African countries. One historian has described the country's experience thus:

> Ethiopia's singular experience of ethnic politics is linked to its history of state building, which differs fundamentally from the common African pattern. In general, on the African continent, multiethnic states were created almost arbitrarily by colonization. Nationalism, including a downgrading of separate ethnic identities, became the dominant ideology of the decolonization and independent struggles. The Ethiopian state, however, was built by incorporating peripheral peoples into a state which already possessed a strong identity and historical core. This resulted in processes of marginalization, exploitation, and alienation. Ethnicity in Ethiopia thus has a peculiar edge which is lacking to a degree in post-colonial states. (Aalen, 2011, p. 25)

It seems that the horrendous colonial experiences in Africa may have abated politically divisive ethnic tension and conflict, at least in some cases. Under colonialism, African countries had a common cause to rally around. Resistance to colonialism was waged on principles of solidarity of all who faced the brunt of the heinous oppression. Collier and Rohner (2008, p. 7) are of the opinion that "people [define] themselves in terms of common external enemies". Thus, colonial power structure was the clear target around which nationalist movements were created and freedom movements exercised. It provided the opportunity for diverse ethnic identities that make up a nation to stand together even when the creation of the colonial state was itself a problematic amalgamation of different bounded ethnic groups. Ethnic identities and solidarities have created many problems that have almost destroyed the nation-state viability of few post-colonial African countries.

In the African experience the circle of solidarity against colonialism expanded into the whole continent and found expression and common goals in the notion of pan-Africanism. Nyerere was poignant in articulating this ideal when he noted that for centuries, Africans had been oppressed and humiliated as Africans, hunted and enslaved as Africans and colonized as Africans, and because we were humiliated as Africans, we had to be liberated as Africans (Nyerere, cited in Glassman, 2011). Thus, a common external enemy has enabled some envisioning of nationalism that can transcend regional parochialism and a powerful unifying cause for a broad campaign in African decolonization discourse and action.

Ethiopia is somewhat anomalous to this history, as it did not have quite the same experience with colonization. Markakis (2011, p. 3) aptly describes Ethiopia's defense against colonialism, "In the battle of Adwa (1896) the Ethiopians mustered a force of more than 100,000 to annihilate an Italian invading force of some 20,000. . . . European imperialism met its match in this corner of Africa". (For historical accuracy, it is worth pointing out that Ethiopia was under Italian occupation between 1936–1941 after the second Italo-Abyssinian war, after which Italy was expelled by Britain). This non-colonial historical experience has allowed the functioning of domestic sources of government for a long and uninterrupted span of time. And this lengthy time of sovereignty has had paradoxical effects. On the one hand, it gave the Ethiopian psyche a strong sense of self-assurance and national pride, but on the other hand, it had the effect of providing the conditions that fomented domestic conflict and internal oppression. In the absence of a compelling external adversary, Ethiopia has seen much in the way of inter-regional and inter-ethnic conflict and violence. So, in a way, Ethiopia has had a lot to deal with in terms of ethno-cultural conflicts for a relatively longer span of time than most African countries.

Ethno-cultural diversity as a political issue, therefore, has been a long-standing feature of Ethiopia's historical narrative. However, throughout the country's history, there have been tensions between the national center and diverse regional and ethnic groups (Mor Barak & Levin, 2002). Since the emergence of the modern Ethiopian empire-state in the second half of the 20th century, successive governments have sought the elusive dream of forging one nation out of a widely diverse people. Gudina has made this observation:

> The process [of creating Ethiopian polity] was completed by the end of the century, through the expansion of the Shewan-Amhara under Menilek II [1889–1913]. But this came at the cost of entrenching deep ethnic and religious inequalities, leading in the 1960s and 1970s to the rise of nationalist movements which sought to reverse the unifying historical process of the late nineteenth century. (Gudina, 2006, p. 119)

Ethno-cultural movements that championed the politics of recognition came to prominence during the rule of Emperor Haile Selassie (Gudina, 2006). And, any prospect that the emperor would cede the kind of political recognition ethno-cultural movements were after was deeply suspect, given the fact that the emperor's principal project was crafting a unitary Ethiopian state. The goal of building a unified nation was one which had been desperately sought but left unfulfilled by the predecessors of the emperor (Zewde, 2001). Giving ethno-cultural recognition and autonomy, even a limited one, would have been tantamount to Balkanizing the country and therefore, antithetical to achieving the holy grail of the country's elusive political dream of 'creating' one unified and cohesive Ethiopia. For the imperial regime, recognition of the right of nations and nationalities to self-determination, including secession (as the current formula has it) represented national betrayal, a treasonous act against the holy cause of a united Ethiopia (Gudina, 2006).

Picking up the story with Haile Selassie's (1930–1974) treatment of ethno-cultural diversity may hopefully give us a perspective on the emergence of ethno-cultural demands for political justice and provide comparative terms of reference from the beginnings of organized ethno-cultural movements. Continuing with the comparative analysis, we will now look at the fervently nationalist approach to ethno-cultural diversity of the communist military regime of Mengistu Haile Mariam (1974–1991), in order to see the trajectory of the history and politics of managing ethnic diversity in Ethiopia. Habtu (2004) states that Haile Selassie's approach to managing ethnic diversity is an example of the first of three social engineering projects that was implemented since the creation of the modern state of Ethiopia. The approach, "attempted to create a unitary state on the basis of cultural assimilation, using Amharic as the sole language of instruction and public discourse and Abyssinian Orthodox Christian culture as the core culture of Ethiopian national identity" (Habtu, 2004, p. 99). By ushering in *Decree 1* of 1942, the Emperor "brought unprecedented levels of centralization in the history of the country" (Adegehe, 2009, p. 56). The nation-building project that sought to homogenize the country was built around the expansion of Amhara culture. The Amhara were deemed to be superior for having scripted language, and evolved religious tradition and etiquette (Markakis, 2011). Language was the primary means of homogenization which was used even in schools. A Ministry of Education report in 1955 declared:

> The promotion of Amharic at the various levels . . . is an important task that is fundamental to national integration. . . . [T]he regime sought to eradicate all other languages. . . . Amharigna [anglicized: Amharic] was named the official language of the state in 1955 Constitution but, long before that, no vernacular was allowed to be printed, broadcast, taught, or spoken on public occasions. No school could use an indigenous language. (Markakis, 2011, pp. 125–126)

Under imperial rule homogenization went as far as Christianizing the names of towns, cities and imposing mass conversions of people into Christianity. Furthermore, under Emperor Haile Selassie, political rule in the periphery transferred more and more into the hands of representatives of central power. Regions that had enjoyed a certain modicum of local authority were replaced by designates of central power, in some cases doing away with regional powers altogether (Fessha, 2010, p. 170). "The policy of assimilation into mainstream Amhara culture provoked some subordinated ethnic groups into initiating ethnic movements in various regions of the empire-state" (Habtu, 2004, p. 100). Hence, when the revolution that ousted imperial rule in Ethiopia in 1974 gathered steam, it had a very strong and decisive ethno-cultural thrust. According to Aalen (2006, p. 28), "The political, cultural and economic structures of the imperial regime produced a level of alienation and exploitation that favoured the outbreak of both class and ethnic confrontations". The effect was the rise of nationalities in arms for self-determination (Zewde, 1991). The Emperor's approach failed and the myth of a constitutional monarchy was shattered in large measure because the emperor had failed to effectively address the self-determination issue (Keller, 1999).

The communist regime that supplanted imperial rule in 1991 did not do much better at all. Despite many radical changes, "it nonetheless preserved the old notion of the state" (Aalen, 2011, p. 31). The opposition to imperial rule had two distinct currents, one of which saw the ethno-cultural calls for recognition and self-determination as *the* political issue to be addressed. The other sought to tackle the issue of class—the socio-economic imbalance and land ownership question—as the cardinal malaises that were plaguing the nation. The communist regime provided a radical answer to the first problem in the form of doing away with the whole edifice of monarchical rule and its exploitative economic conditions, by decrees including the nationalization of the economy. To the second problem of the nationalities, the government only gave a ceremonial answer, hardly commensurate with the demands being articulated by ethno-cultural groups. Despite encouraging steps, like the lifting of the unofficial but effective ban on languages in various educational and vernacular texts and having affirmed the right to self-determination of all nationalities, the *Derg* recoiled once it succeeded in consolidating power.

The *Derg* sought to address the long standing national political riddle of ethnic diversity through the implementation of a shallow cultural program. Markakis explains that:

> The different ethnic groups were regarded as no more than cultural artefacts that embellish the festivities of the annual Revolution Day. . . . The socialist revolution, argued the Derg, had brought national oppression to an end by guaranteeing the 'equality of all people and cultures' and the rest, including the 'legacy of cultural oppression', shall be overcome 'through the cultural emancipation of formerly subordinate groups and the promotion of their culture'. (As cited in Fessha, 2010, p. 173)

The constitution of the People's Democratic Republic of Ethiopia, which was officially proclaimed in 1987, swallowed the nationalities question into one of membership in ethnicity-neutral mass organizations. Keller (1999, pp. 73–74) captures this move succinctly:

> The rights of nationality groups were deemed not as important as those of citizens belonging to mass organizations (e.g. workers and peasants associations, women's associations, student associations, etc.). In other words, individuals were expected to owe their primary loyalty to these types of mass organizations, rather than to their ethnic kin.

The response of Mengistu Haile Mariam's regime to ethno-cultural demands was tantamount to turning a blind eye to a real, substantive aspect of the issue at stake. Where an in-depth political question was on the table, the regime only provided cosmetic answers. There was neither a real dispensation of purpose to the demands, nor formal recognition of the rights of ethno-cultural groups or legal provisions to that effect.

The regime paid lip service to multiculturalism and made superficial gestures in the direction of respecting ethnic diversity and celebrating all the cultures that make up Ethiopia but in the end, these were feeble and woefully inadequate attempts. As Aalen (2011, p. 31) summarizes, "Rhetorically, the Derg recognized the equality of all Ethiopian nationality groups. But a genuine recognition of national self-determination appeared to conflict with the strong pan-Ethiopian nationalism that the Derg put forth from the beginning". To make matters worse, the communist regime pitted ethnic groups against each other out of political expediency. However, this had the unintended consequence of emboldening the opposition forces. Thus, as Kinfe (2001, p. 328) notes:

> Mengistu had tried to exploit ethnic and national affinity by magnifying historical differences and playing down the common heritage which had historically bound Ethiopians together. Thus, the Amharas were warned against the menace of the Tigray hegemony, while the Oromos were encouraged to close ranks with Amharas to forestall alleged northern encroachment. Such propaganda was paraded via the official media and press.

Ethno-cultural opposition groups like the OLF, TPLF, EPLF and the Afar Liberation Front "stepped up their criticism and resistance against the regime . . . [recording] significant battlefield victories against the Ethiopian forces" (Keller, 1999, p. 76). Ethnic insurgency intensified and "through the activities of the TPLF (the prominent ethno-cultural party that make up the core of EPRDF) and other ethnically based liberation movements, ethnicity became the rallying point for opposition to the Derg" (Aalen, 2011, p. 33). Surely the legitimacy crisis, particularly typified by the abysmal mismanagement of the nation's economy, helped topple the communist military regime in 1991. However, the most important cause for the government's downfall was the demand for justice from the various ethnic groups in Ethiopia and insurgency (Zewde, 1991). In sum, "Mengistu's fatal error was that he fiddled with the shadow of the nationalities question but he never really addressed it" (Kinfe, 2001, p. 345). As Zewde puts it, "One of the most nationalist (some would say ultra-nationalist) regimes in modern Ethiopian history fell under a barrage of ethno-nationalist insurgency" (1991, p. 274).

In Ethiopia's political history, the need to accommodate ethnic diversity has been the elephant in the room that a succession of leaders has been avoiding. On the whole, the pursuit of unified Ethiopia and avoiding balkanization was the fundamental reason that the politics of ethnic recognition had not seen the light of day. Wishing ethnic diversity away had the palpable effect of strengthening ethno-cultural resistance movements, who in the end toppled the communist military government. It seemed that after all, a new approach involving resistance politics was unavoidable as the tool for liberation. This was most effective especially "after many years of war between the Derg-controlled central state and ethnic liberation movements . . ." (Aalen, 2011, p. 36).

Ethiopia's experiment with ethnic federalism is essentially a means of addressing *the* political problem that has been perennial in the country's modern history, particularly the political accommodation of ethnic diversity. During the imperial rule of Haile Selassie, the consciousness of political identity grew, giving in turn ethno-cultural insurgencies the kind of energy they evinced in organization and political articulation. As Fessha (2010, p. 157) asserts, "[Prior to the era of Haile Selassie] regionalism rather than ethnicity was the most relevant divide in the historic Ethiopia". Regionalism was the source of political association and the means for political engagement. Furthermore, the Ethiopian Student Movement (ESM), which incubated essentially the urban opposition to the imperial rule of Haile Selassie, has had great influence on recasting Ethiopian identity and the case for the politics of ethnic recognition. Habtu (2004, p. 101) notes:

> ESM attempted to legitimate ethno-nationalism within the ideological compass of Marxism-Leninism, marking a radical departure from the inherited pan-Ethiopianist ideology. The ESM saw its resolution within the framework of the Marxist-Leninist doctrine of 'the right of nations to self-determination', up to and including secession.

These are the episodes that paved the way for ethnic federalism. Now, various aspects of the ethnic federalist approach to politics and its practice occasion much contestation, critique and analysis. Needless to say doing justice to these discourses is beyond the scope of this chapter. It should be noted, however, that from a theoretical perspective, "since federalism allows the creation of regional political units . . . with substantial (constitutionally protected) powers of self-government" (Kymlicka, 2006, p. 34), it provides a substantive rejoinder to addressing the calls for ethno-cultural recognition, the Achilles heel of Ethiopian politics.

From an empirical point of view, the sense in which this chapter contends that ethnic federalism is a significant development marker is captured splendidly by Turton (2006, pp. 1–2) who declares:

> The restructuring of Ethiopia as an ethnic federation has been an undeniable success. It has not only prevented the violent dismemberment of the country, but also provided peace and security for the great majority of its population and laid down, for the first time in the history of Ethiopia, 'the legal foundation for a full fledged democracy'.

However, it should be noted that ethnic federalism in Ethiopia remains at an experimental stage and thus involves risks, one of which is the potential balkanization of the country.

CONCLUSION

Assessing Ethiopia's current political development experience requires understanding the significance of both the external and internal factors that shaped the country's present day governance contours. From its days as a hereditary monarchy during the imperial rule (1855–1974), to being thrown into and languishing in a Marxist-Leninist regime from 1974–1991, the country suppressed, ignored or failed to address the most contentious national political issue, namely, the political accommodation of ethnic diversity. Ethiopia has been plagued by the issue of regionalism since its founding as a modern state in the middle of the 20th century. Regionalism evolved into politics of ethno-cultural recognition as various quasi-regional groups fighting for autonomy came to prominence during the imperial rule of Haile Selassie and strengthened in the era of the *Derg*. The current federal formula in Ethiopia was enacted as a response to the growing ethno-cultural movements for recognition and to right the wrongs of history by giving autonomy to ethno-cultural subgroups within a federal system. Ethnic federalism is the specific facade that democracy has been showing itself in Ethiopia. For this reason the emergence of ethnic federalism is a watershed experience in the political development of Ethiopia and the account given earlier attempted to provide the logic of this development.

REFERENCES

Aalen, L. (2011). *The politics of ethnicity in Ethiopia*. Boston: Brill.

Abbink, J. (2009). The Ethiopian second republic and the fragile 'social contract'. *Africa Spectrum*, 44(2), 3–28.

Adegehe, A.K. (2009). *Federalism and ethnic conflict in Ethiopia: A comparative study of the Somali and Benishangul-Gumuz regions*. Unpublished Doctoral Thesis, Department of Political Science, Faculty of Social and Behavioural Sciences, Leiden University.

Clapham, C. (1993). Democratisation in Africa: obstacles and prospects. *Third World Quarterly*, 14(3), 423–438.

Clapham, C. (2003). The challenge to the state in a globalized world. *Development and Change*, 33(5), 775–795.

Collier, P. & Rohner, D. (2008). Democracy, development and conflict. *Journal of the European Economic Association*, 6(2–3), 531–540.

Decalo, S. (1992). The process, prospects and constraints of democratization in Africa. *African Affairs*, January, 7–35.

Farkas, E.N. (2003). *Fractured states and U.S. foreign policy: Iraq, Ethiopia, and Bosnia in the 1990s*. New York: Palgrave Macmillan

Fessha, Y.T. (2010). *Ethnic diversity and federalism constitution making in South Africa and Ethiopia*. London: Ashgate.

Fiseha, A. (2006). Theory versus practice in Ethiopia's ethnic federalism. In D. Turton (Ed.), *Ethnic federalism: The Ethiopian experience in comparative perspective* (pp. 131–164). Addis Ababa: James Currey Publishers/Addis Ababa University Press.

Glassman, J. (2011). *War of words, war of stones: Racial thought and violence in colonial Zanzibar.* Bloomington, IN: Indiana University Press.

Government of Ethiopia. (1994). *Constitution of Ethiopia, 1994.* Addis Ababa.

Gudina, M. (2006). Contradictory interpretations of Ethiopian history: The need for a new consensus. In D. Turton (Ed.), *Ethnic federalism: The Ethiopian experience in comparative perspective* (pp. 119–129). Addis Ababa: Addis Ababa University Press.

Habtu, A. (2004). *Ethnic pluralism as an organizing principle of the Ethiopian federation.* Amsterdam, Netherlands: Kluwer Academic.

Keller, E.J. (1999). Political institutions, agency and contingent compromise: Understanding democratic consolidation and reversal in Africa. *National Political Science Review*, 7, 96–115.

Kinfe, A. (2001). *Ethiopian from empire to federation.* Addis Ababa: EIIPD Press.

Kymlicka, W. (2006). Emerging Western models of multination federalism: Are they relevant to Africa?" In D. Turton (Ed.), *Ethnic federalism: The Ethiopian experience in comparative perspective* (pp. 32–64). Addis Ababa: Addis Ababa University Press.

Markakis, J. (2011). *Ethiopia: The last two frontiers.* New York: James Currey.

Mor Barak, M.E. & Levin, A. (2002). Outside of the corporate mainstream and excluded from the work community: A study of diversity, job satisfaction and well-being. *Community, Work and Family*, 5(2), 133–157.

Ndulo, M. & Grieco, M. (Eds.). (2010). *Failed and failing states: The challenges to African reconstruction.* Newcastle upon Tyne: Cambridge Scholars Publishing.

Ottaway, M. (1995). The Ethiopian transition: democratization or new authoritarianism? *Northeast Africa Studies*, 2(3), 67–87.

Turton, D. (Ed.). (2006). *Ethnic federalism: The Ethiopian experience in comparative perspective.* Addis Ababa: Addis Ababa University Press.

Woodward, P. (2006). *US foreign policy and the HOA.* London: Ashgate.

Zewde, B. (1991). *A history of modern Ethiopia.* Athens, OH: Ohio University Press.

12 Leadership and Governance in Sub-Saharan Africa

Conceptual and Historical Perspectives

Lamine Diallo and Ginette Lafrenière

INTRODUCTION

Since the 1990s, we have witnessed a growing interest in governance and leadership as a major challenge in development for Sub-Saharan Africa. Scholars, international institutions and civil society organizations have all shifted their focus on programs aiming to improve governance and leadership in the continent. After more than 60 years of independence, Sub-Saharan Africa, with all its wealth and potential, has not been able to create the conditions for political, social and economic development needed to lift its people out of poverty, violence and exploitation. After hundreds of billions of dollars in investments over the last 60 years, Africa is still the poorest continent in the world with 47.5% of its people living with less than $1.25 a day in 2008 (United Nations Development Program [UNDP], 2010). This slow progress compared to other continents is explained by many external and historical factors: the slave trade, colonization, political and economic neo-colonialism and external programs that have jeopardized the development of the continent. But as stated by Mkapa (2008, p. 1), "Africa cannot forever hold its history of slavery and colonialism responsible for its current poverty levels and economic woes". An analysis of Africa's reasons for lagging behind in development has led to an examination of the role of leadership and governance in the continent. Today, it is commonly accepted that the heart of the multifaceted crisis that affects and marginalizes Africa is the twin issue of leadership and governance (Commission for Africa, 2005).

This new interest in leadership and governance is of critical importance because, since the early 2000s, Africa has been described as a new economic frontier, with new discoveries of natural resources, growth in trade, foreign direct investment and foreign development assistance. The Africa Progress Panel (2010) states that the problems of Africa are not the lack of knowledge and shortage of plans, nor the lack of funds, given the continent's vast natural and human resources, but political will. What this means, therefore, is that African States and political leadership are the primary factors responsible for underdevelopment in Africa. The debate on governance and leadership in the African context has also contributed to the development of an important body of literature, research and programs. Unfortunately, most studies and programs approach these two concepts with very little integration. Through a review of literature, this chapter seeks to integrate the analysis of leadership and governance in Africa using a multidisciplinary perspective. We will demonstrate how in current leadership and governance discourses leadership is becoming a central variable of governance practice and evaluation. We will also analyze how leadership has become a key variable of governance strategies in the international development agenda.

This chapter further explores the debate, the discourse and the analytical frameworks used to understand both concepts in the development landscape. We will use a multidisciplinary approach to provide an overview of research frameworks in leadership, and the importance of contextual analysis in understanding leadership in Africa. Through a brief illustration of the African context, we will offer an analysis of how the recent contextual changes provide an opportunity for new leadership for development in the continent. The central hypothesis underlying this work is that political leaders play a critical role in establishing effective institutions and states, but knowledge and understanding about these processes are limited (Lyne de Ver, 2008). Moreover, we argue that the role of leadership and governance in the failure of Africa needs to be contextualized with both external and internal factors in a historical perspective. As well as, we will be using the 'situational theory' of leadership if we want to better understand the challenges for which African leaders must prepare for in this 21st century.

THE CONCEPTS OF LEADERSHIP AND GOVERNANCE IN THE DEVELOPMENT DISCOURSE

Understanding governance and leadership in development and political discourses requires first some general considerations of substantive issues affecting both concepts. Whereas both have been central to international development policies, since the 1990s they have been approached from so many perspectives that they are losing the precision necessary for understanding the value systems and contexts they are supposed to articulate. The two concepts are approached separately, with research in governance dominated by studies in the public and political fields, whereas research in political leadership is dominated by the development studies field. Research in both fields is attempting to identify universal principles, conditions and practices, but the dominant models are still rooted in Western or Euro-centric approaches that can be difficult to translate into African realities.

The Concept of Governance in Developmental Studies

Although the relationship between governance and development is now central to the international policy agenda, there is not yet a clear consensus around a single definition. Different definitions are used in different academic sub-fields, from political science, public administration to development studies. Kjaer (2004, p. 133) remarks, "Governance theory is very influenced by the 'structuralist' school of the 1950s and 1960s and is mainly preoccupied with institutional change". The emergence of the governance concept in the development agenda can be linked to the period following the failure of structural adjustment programs (SAPs). According to Moore (1993), good governance was a new recipe from the World Bank (WB) and the International Monetary Fund (IMF) to respond to the failure of the neo-liberal adjustment policies they had imposed on the less-developed world in the 1980s. The Bank defines governance as "the institutional capacity of public organizations to provide the public and other goods demanded by a country's citizens or their representatives in effective, transparent, impartial, and accountable manner, subject to resource constraints" (World Bank, 2011, p. 48). The WB has proposed 'Worldwide Governance Indicators' that have been used to evaluate governance in all countries. These governance indicators are: (1) rule of law; (2) political stability; (3) democratic participation; (4) government and market efficiency; (5) government transparency and accountability; and (6) human rights (Kaufmann & Kraay, 2008).

Governance principles are mainly articulated around a strong democratic form of government and institutional arrangement (Ruscio, 2004; Ake, 1991). Democracy is believed to be a pillar of good governance, and most scholars, policymakers, aid donors and aid recipients recognize that good governance is a fundamental ingredient of sustained economic development (Skinner, 1998; Besancon, 2003). Good governance is today used as part of the new 'conditionalities' of international aid and cooperation. A recent survey from the Organization for Economic Cooperation and Development (OECD; 2009) revealed the existence of 45 general methodologies and good governance assessment tools from different organizations and governments. Critics accuse the donor community of imposing a concept of governance that is ideologically and politically driven and based on the dominant Anglo-American/liberal socio-political doctrine (Moore, 1993). Although conditions for good governance have been identified, and are more and more used to encourage democratization and to evaluate the success and progress of African countries, the concept and practice of leadership is still more difficult to articulate and operationalize.

Leadership Research in Development Policies

The literature on leadership is found across all main disciplines and suffers from disciplinary spread (Lyne de Ver, 2008). As a new and still emerging academic discipline, a great deal of what has been written about leadership in recent years has been produced by business schools, and focuses on leadership in an organizational context. But, according to Elcock (2001), of all forms of leadership, political leadership occupies a special position because it is vastly more visible. The role of political leaders has received considerable attention from imperial times to modern society, but, as argued by Hartley and Benington (2011, p. 204), "The academic literature on leadership has largely ignored the complex world of political leadership". The concept of political leadership is still difficult to define because it is dependent on institutional and cultural contexts and situations (Blondel, 1987; Klenke, 1996). As well, political leadership implies capacity of innovative adaptation in a specific situation and institutional cultural contexts (Nye, 1999). In the voluminous and growing social science literature on political leadership, there is very little agreement on what reliable knowledge exists (Grint, 2005; Yukl, 2009).

Because of its complexity and spread across disciplines, it is unsurprising that there is a range of perspectives that can be used to study, analyze and understand political leadership. In general, the research on leadership embodies theoretical as well as strong experiential components. In the literature survey of the role of leadership in the promotion of economic and social development, Lyne de Ver (2008, p. 6) found that, "because of a lack of interdisciplinary integration and collaboration, there appears to be little cross fertilization" of ideas and conceptual theories. This lack of a single theory to analyze political leadership has led to many analytical and conceptual frameworks that define, categorize and explore the leadership phenomena, and try to link theories to each other (Lowndes & Leach, 2004). Most analytical frameworks focus on the qualities, capabilities and styles of leaders. But, because of their isolation from the challenges or contexts, these approaches are limited in their capacity to understand political leadership and its motivations.

The Integration of Leadership and Governance: Inextricably Linked Concepts

Although governance and leadership are mostly analyzed separately, more recent literature integrating the two concepts is flourishing. Although governance involves an important institutional component, the individual aspect is no less important. Le Vine (1967) sees political leadership as being critical to the establishment, consolidation and survival of democracy. It is increasingly recognized that good governance requires principle-centered leadership that will encourage, promote, support and implement governance principles. The two concepts point to the same direction. Whereas there can be no progress without good governance, leadership is the pivot around which good governance revolves. In 2008, the President of the United States of America, Barack Obama, was correct when he declared while visiting Ghana, that Africa needs good institutions. It is true that Africa needs to go beyond personalities to the rule of law and to functional institutions. Unfortunately, most African institutions are in their formative stages, hence visionary and audacious leadership is critical to institutional development as well as adopting and sustaining policies and structural changes that will accelerate economic growth (Gray & McPherson, 2001).

In recent years, we have seen more institutions linking leadership and governance at the center of their strategies and programs (Cammack, Menocal & Christiansen, 2006). This is the case with the New Partnership for Africa's Development (NEPAD) through its 'Charter on Democracy, Elections and Governance' adopted in 2007, or the 'African Leadership Council' with the 'Code of Leadership' (The Mombasa Declaration, 2004). According to the Mombasa Declaration:

> Good leaders globally guide governments of nation-states to perform effectively for their citizens. They deliver high security for the state and the person a functioning rule of law education health and a framework conducive to economic growth. They ensure effective arteries of commerce and enshrine personal and human freedoms. They empower civil society and protect the environmental commons. Crucially good leaders also provide their citizens with a sense of belonging to a national enterprise of which everyone can be proud. They knit rather than unravel their nations and seek to be remembered for how they have bettered the real lives of the governed rather than the fortunes of the few. (2004, p. 1)

Intertwined in the previous statements and the recent consultation for an 'Africa Strategy' of the WB is the recognition that governance and leadership are the most important factors that should drive Africa's future development. This greater articulation is another layer on the pressure to improve leadership in the continent.

HISTORICAL CONTEXT OF GOVERNANCE AND LEADERSHIP IN AFRICA

The issue of leadership in Africa is not new, but in the last two decades, the interest has increased with more studies exploring African leadership from different theoretical perspectives. Studies focus on the relationship between traditional leadership figures and modern democracy, former African presidents, indigenous African leadership, African elites, gender and leadership or leadership in different organizational settings (van Wyk, 2007). The review of the literature on political leadership shows a strong Western cultural and contextual bias. According to Lyne de Ver (2008, p. 15), "The literature assumes, implicitly or explicitly, a stable institutional context and that leaders play by the rules as found in the West". This makes an important body of the literature irrelevant. The imposition of Western values and the fact that African leadership research is not rooted in African cosmology and worldviews (religion, philosophy, family, ageism, kingship and tribalism) adds to the complexity of understanding the context (Gordon, 2002).

The recent trend in research is slowly asserting alternatives to a Western leadership paradigm. But, the effort to develop a theoretical framework and synthesize the various experiences into one theory of leadership suitable for wider application on the continent has been difficult. The most important efforts integrating a theoretical framework to the studies of leadership have used a mix of the 'great man theory' of leadership and a 'behavioral approach'. These approaches focus on personal characteristics of leaders, describing their behavior through their traits (Edinger, 2007). VonDoepp (2009) provides an interesting framework for studying leadership in Africa. He places leadership as an important variable in governance trajectories. He proposes five questions that can guide inquiry into leadership behavior. He suggests that "as we capture variances in leadership behavior we can more effectively address the key issue of why leaders undertake development and governance enabling behaviors in some contexts while in others they do not" (p. 1). The questions draw attention to both the circumstances in which leaders find themselves as well as their personal characteristics.

It is clear that to understand the practices of governance and leadership in Africa we need to contextualize both in light of the historical, political and social contexts of the continent. As Mkapa (2008, p. 4) puts it, "Analyzing leadership and governance in Africa without putting them in their proper cultural and sociological contexts will be deficient and will not inform us of many aspects of their behaviors". To understand leadership and governance across a heterogeneous continent, we need an analytical framework for understanding the opportunities and challenges posed by the contexts. Many leadership theories were developed and studied during the last century, but no single approach to leadership has been identified as the best method for all situations (Northouse, 2010). The fundamentals of leadership, motivating and directing a group to achieve a common goal, have changed very little over time. However, the context of leadership and the complexity of and diversity within organizations and societal values have each evolved greatly over the last 100 years. The 'situational approach' in leadership research has been a very important analytical framework for studying leadership in organizational contexts and can be adapted and useful in this regard. Masciulli, Molchanov and Knight (2008, p. 11) suggest, "Individual approaches in conjunction with contextual and situational approaches are indispensable for understanding causality in international relations and comparative politics today". This approach helps determine the numerous contextual factors that influence leadership styles and behaviors.

The following historical overview by decades is only indicative, but each period since the 1960s has had strong impacts on expectations, styles and constraints to leadership in Africa. Each period can offer a specific understanding of the challenges and may help understand future perspectives for leadership in the continent.

The 1960s and the Early Independence Years

The independence process in Sub-Saharan Africa was marked by several internal and external contextual factors that had important impacts on both leadership and governance practices in the continent. The liberation movement in Africa carried its seed of instability in a context of fragile states and political structures, and the difficult transition from colonial rule to self-rule (Rotberg, 2007). African leaders had little time to prepare for independence, and most leaders found themselves for the first time in a position of public office with very little experience. The wave of independence also happened in the midst of the Cold War. Major dominant powers supported various regimes and dictatorships, and some promising leaders were overthrown or eliminated (e.g., Kwame Nkrumah, Patrice Lumumba). This, in some cases, led to deep internal tensions and conflicts and led the leadership to reorganize governance institutions to conserve, defend and sustain their powers.

African leaders inherited artificial states created by Western colonial powers. In many countries, building national unity led to the justification of single-party systems. Regarding its capacity, the continent, although rich in mineral resources, was weak in human, institutional and infrastructural resources needed to build viable economies. The rate of illiteracy was extremely high. Transportation and communication systems across the continent or within a country, to bring people closer, or to facilitate the circulation of goods and services, were almost inexistent. And finally, the economic infrastructures that the leaders inherited were extraverted, fueling the needs of the colonial powers rather than the African people. The post-colonial African state of the 1960s was a relay of colonial ideology and economic system. Political leaders of this period were mostly seen as puppets of the dominant powers.

The 1970s and the Beginning of Multiple Crises

In the early 1970s, the continent was marked by deep political, economic and social transformations. The struggle for national unity and pan-Africanism of the 1960s led to many conflicts, political instability and power struggles. The period was also marked by the increase in struggle for leadership and the multiplication of military coups. State institutions were weakened by armed conflict and the intensification of the Cold War, which led to open civil war in some corners of the continent. Governance institutions were more and more tailored to the needs of leaders, who were more concerned with maintaining their prerogatives over their sovereign states than regional integration. The little economic growth of the continent did not spread and led to an increased gap between the elite and the masses. This increased the dependency of the countries on external partners and external aid.

The development models used by the political leadership, which in many countries favored urban investments and development, created huge and inefficient public administration disconnects with the masses and led to rapid rural to urban migration. Large-scale infrastructure and prestige investment projects of the 1960s and 1970s led to an unsustainable debt made worse by the oil crisis. The results from this decade show poor economic performance across the continent, widening of poverty and situations of famine in some regions of the continent. In this decade, the role of international institutions was limited to providing aid and supporting large infrastructure projects with very little overseeing of results and impacts. The failure became emblematic of inappropriate development strategies.

The 1980s and Structural Adjustment Programs (SAPs)

The 1980s were particularly hard for Sub-Saharan Africa, due to the widespread economic recession and the debt crisis. After the recognition of the failure of the post-independence development model, the international community through the IMF and the WB came to the rescue with SAPs. These programs suggested institutional and economic changes based on the liberal models of Western countries as a solution. Policies included the privatization of public services, the reduction of the size of public administration, the opening of borders through tariff reduction for trade, the cut of social expenditures and the elimination of public deficits. The programs were very difficult and unpopular but most African leaders had no choice if they wanted to access development funds. The harsh nature of the programs strengthened opposition movements and civil society organizations and contributed to more pressures on the leadership who were caught in between applying these drastic economic measures and a greater demand from their people to lift them out of poverty.

By the end of the 1980s, it had become clear that the SAPs were not working. The African leadership had no choice but to recognize and give more voices to opposing forces and civil rights movements. The one-party system started to give way to multi-party systems. The period corresponded also with the end of the Cold War and a changing landscape in international relations. This created a new context because the Cold War rivalries that had supported African leaders as clients of both the West and the East started to vanish, and led to more demands for democracy. The end of this decade corresponded with a greater appreciation of democratic values and a fuller understanding within and outside of Africa that economic, social and political development of the continent depended almost entirely on strengthening governance and democracy.

The 1990s and the Acceleration of Globalization: From SAPs to 'Good Governance'

The failure of SAPs of the 1980s and the spread of the economic crisis and poverty across the continent led the international community to explore new ways to help Africa. The new response to the problem of the continent in place of SAPs was poverty reduction and good governance programs to create the conditions for institutional stability that could lead to economic growth. Africa was subjected to the democratization of the state and society, and the return of full multi-party systems across the continent. This led to the strengthening of civil society movements, an increased role of international institutions regarding the internal affairs of African countries, more demand for respect of human rights and the arrival in the political scene of a new generation of leaders. Unlike the SAPs, the democratization process and good governance principles had the support of both international organizations, national opposition political parties and civil society organizations.

The 1990s were also marked by the acceleration of economic globalization and the rapid development of communication across the globe (radio, newspaper, internet, cellphones, etc.). These changes contributed to strengthening the African urban population and youth in their demands for political and economic justice. In many countries, the transition to democracy derailed and escalated into civil wars and chaos. The refusal to leave power and the continual abuse of power, rigging of elections and manipulation of institutions became the main aspect of the political context. By the end of the 1990s, Africa was a "mosaic of effective democracy and desperate despotism, immense wealth and abysmal poverty" (Rotberg, 2007, p. 7).

The 2000s and the Economic Surge: From 'Good Governance' to Leadership

Since the beginning of the new millennium, Sub-Saharan Africa has been faced with new sets of circumstances. Both the external and internal contexts are favorable for economic, political and social development. Between 2001 and 2008, Africa was among the fastest growing regions in the world economy (United Nations Conference on Trade and Development [UNCTAD], 2010). According to the Africa Progress Panel Report (2010), the continent experienced a strong growth of 6% average in the five years leading to the 2008 economic crisis, underpinned by a spectacular increase in trade and value of exports that increased four-fold between 1998 and 2008. After the 2008 economic crisis, Africa's recovery has been very strong with growth reaching 5.9% (South Africa excluded), making it one of the fastest growing developing regions, and this is poised for acceleration (World Bank, 2012).

The World Bank (2012) also states that Africa's agriculture holds enormous potential for companies across the value chain with 60% of the world's uncultivated arable land and low crop yields. The McKinsey Institute Report (2010) estimates Africa's potential to increase the value of its annual agricultural output to be from $280 billion today to around $500 billion by 2020. Urban population has also grown very rapidly. According to the McKinsey Report, the urban population increased from just 20% in 1980, to 40% in 2010. There is a long tradition of scholarship explaining the role of urbanization in economic growth, social transformation and the growth of the middle class (Kessides, 2005; Venables, 2005). With almost 200 million people aged between 15 and 24, Africa also has the youngest population in the world, and the youth is getting better educated. Based on current trends, 59% of the 20–24-year-olds will have a secondary education by 2030, compared to 42% today (McKinsey Institute Report, 2010).

Although democratization has been a challenge in the continent, it has become increasingly prevalent across Africa over the last two decades. In 2011, 18 countries in Africa were considered electoral democracies, compared to only four in 1991. Electoral democracy is becoming institutionalized in several countries, acting as a powerful force for economic growth (African Development Bank, 2011). Electoral democracy pushes the boundaries of our current understanding of democratic politics and government and focuses on the nature of citizens' political beliefs and values and then considers the ways that those views connect with elite policymaking (MacKuen & Rabinowitz, 2003). Much of Africa fully appreciates today the overwhelming importance of good governance and accomplished democratic leadership. Nevertheless, the region remains prone to episodes of political instability and conflicts, as shown by the recent elections in the Ivory Coast or Kenya. There are many challenges to electoral integrity depending on the context in which elections take place, whether in poor countries, ethnically divided countries, countries in or emerging from civil war, authoritarian countries and consolidating democracies or mature democracies (Kofi Annan Foundation, 2010). Electoral-related violence and questions about quality of representation, especially for women, also pose particular challenges.

Other important new contextual factors have to do with the increased role played by civil society organizations in pushing for political reform and respect for human rights. As well, the creation in 1998 of the International Criminal Court (ICC) adds more pressure on African leaders who may be tempted to abuse the human rights of their citizens. Africa is also diversifying its partnerships with former colonial powers losing their grip on the continent whereas newer actors, especially India, Brazil, Korea, Turkey and China, are playing a larger role.

NEW CHALLENGES FOR SUB-SAHARAN AFRICA

Although the next several decades of the 21st century are one of promise for Africa, many challenges still need to be addressed by its emerging leadership. African leaders have failed to deliver national unity in most instances.

Many countries are still faced with very ethnically, religiously and regionally divided people that don't share a sense of citizenship. Corruption still poses a serious challenge. Political instability also continues to be a problem in many countries.

Although the continent has seen an extraordinary rebound in economic growth over the past decade, the UNCTAD 2012 Report (2012) shows that rapid progress has not brought food security for the substantial proportion of the population. The continent is also heavily dependent on non-renewable natural resources to drive economic growth. This growth is also accompanied by de-industrialization, as evidenced by the fact that the share of manufacturing in Africa's GDP fell from 15% in 1990 to 10% in 2008 (UNCTAD, 2012). Another concern is that the rapid urban growth (40% of total population and expected to rise to 60% by 2050) has not been driven by either industrialization or an agricultural revolution.

CONCLUDING COMMENTS: WHAT TYPE OF LEADERSHIP FOR AFRICA IN THE 21ST CENTURY?

In this new context, political leaders in the continent are more constrained than ever before. Although the process of change is still very slow, it is clear that Africans no longer accept to be governed by despotic leaders as in the first decades of independence. Increased demand for democracy, greater voice of civil society and external pressures from the international community are all contributing to a favorable emergence of new pro-active and visionary leadership in the continent. As defined by Rotberg (2009), African leaders are responsible for delivering specific political goods, namely, security, rule of law, citizen participation in political processes and an environment conducive to economic growth. This process will require more than just a leader who will implement policies or mimic Western models, but one who will inspire and empower people to tackle the daunting problems confronting the continent.

The contextual analysis offers a perspective to better identify the leadership type, style and behavior adapted to varying circumstances in Africa. The recent 'transformational leadership' approach provides an excellent analytical framework for these opportune times for the continent. The term emerged from the classic work of Burns (1978) and is defined by Northouse (2010, p. 172) as "a leadership process that changes and transforms people . . . [and] is concerned with emotions, values, ethics, standards and long-term goals". Transformational leaders go beyond exchange relationships and motivate others to achieve more than they thought was possible (Bass & Riggio, 2006). Africa needs 'transformational leadership' and leaders need to put their people at the center of their strategies.

The new African leadership needs to provide first a clear and coherent vision on how to lift its people out of poverty. This leadership needs to be able to protect and defend the interests of people even if this involves tensions with international institutions. In addition, the leaders should be inspirationally motivating in order to hold high expectations and encourage followers to achieve more than they thought possible, and they should also be intellectually stimulating to encourage citizens to challenge the status quo and to make the leaders accountable to their citizens (Arnold, Turner, Barling, Kelloway & Mckee, 2007). For example, by protecting their agriculture and their nascent industries and by defining how they want to integrate the globalization process. This will require imagining and proposing distinctive democratic practices and institutions that are appropriate for their own socio-historical and political contexts (for example, including traditional leaders in the institutional framework of governance).

The new African leadership needs to prioritize peace and nation-building, which have been the major failures of the previous generation of leaders. Without internal and regional peace and security, all other actions related to poverty reduction and improvement of services will be futile (Putzel & Di John, 2012). This means providing to their people a sense of belonging or citizenship to a national transformation and enterprise. Transformational leaders need to put citizenship ahead of ethnicity, religiosity and regionalism. At its core, citizenship holds that there is a "basic human equality associated with the concept of full membership of a community" and that it is the duty of government to ensure the civil and political as well as social and economic prerequisites for the realization of this equality (Liu, 2006, p. 336).

The message of the founding fathers of the Organization of African Unity of the 1960s is more relevant today than anytime before. Examples of successful regional integration around the world should serve African leaders. The African Union should lead this road to greater unity and solidarity between African countries and people. There should be a strong conviction that without unity the future will remain bleak for the continent. The new leadership of the continent should be informed by more audacity through the development of policies, strategies and vision rooted in local knowledge and perspectives. Only then, can the new dream created by the new economic growth be beneficial to the people of the continent. Africa should abandon the "great man" leadership style that has ruined the continent. Leaders are not born with leadership qualities but they are the products of their societies, and their actions would be impossible without the social conditions that make them leaders. Leaders should guarantee their citizens safety, rule of law, democracy, human rights and equitable development. It is hopeful that the new social, political and economic contexts in the continent will contribute to the emergence of new types of leaders capable of undertaking the implementation of new governance models and set the path for real development.

REFERENCES

African Development Bank. (2011). *Africa in 50 years' time—The road towards inclusive growth*. Tunis, Tunisia: African Development Bank.

Africa Progress Panel. (2010). *From agenda to action: Turning resources into results for people*. Africa Progress Report 2010. Geneva, Switzerland.

Ake, C. (1991). Rethinking African democracy. *Journal of Democracy*, 2(1), 32–44.

Arnold, A.A., Turner, N., Barling, J., Kelloway, E.K. & Mckee, M.C. (2007). Transformational leadership and psychological well-being: The mediating role of meaningful work. *Journal of Occupational Health Psychology*, 12(3), 193–203.

Bass, B.M. & Riggio, R.E. (2006). *Transformational leadership* (2nd ed.), Mahwah, NJ: Lawrence Erlbaum Associates.

Besancon, M. (2003). *Good governance ranking: The art of measurement*. WPF Report Number 36, World Peace Foundation, Program on Intrastate Conflict and Conflict Resolution, John F. Kennedy School of Government, Harvard University, Cambridge, MA.

Blondel, J. (1987). *Political leadership*. London: Sage.

Burns, J.M. (1978). *Leadership*. New York: Harper and Row.

Cammack, D., McLeod, D., Menocal, R.A. & Christiansen, K. (2006). *Donors and the 'fragile states' agenda: A survey of current thinking and practice*. Report submitted to JICA (May). London: Overseas Development Institute.

Commission for Africa. (2005, March). *Our common interest*. Report of the Commission for Africa.

Edinger, L.J. (2007). Approaches to the comparative analysis of political leadership. *The Review of Politics*, 52(4), 509–523.

Elcock, H.J. (2001). *Political leadership*. New Horizons in Public Series. Northampton, Massachusetts: Edward Elgar Publishing, Inc.

Gordon, R. (2002). Conceptualizing leadership with respect to its historical-contextual antecedents to power. *The Leadership Quarterly*, 13(2), 151–167.

Gray, C. & McPherson, M. (2001). The leadership factor in African policy reform. *Economic Development and Cultural Change*, 49, 707–740.

Grint, K. (2005). *Leadership: Limits and possibilities*. New York: Macmillan.

Hartley, J. & Bennington, J. (2011). Political leadership. In A. Bryman, D. Collinson, K. Grint, B. Jackson & M. Uhl-Bien, (Eds.), *The Sage handbook of leadership* (pp. 203–214). Los Angeles: Sage.

Kaufmann, D. & Kraay, A. (2008). Where are we? Where should we be going? *The World Bank*, 23(1, Spring), Washington, DC, 1–30.

Kessides, C. (2005). *The urban transition in Sub-Saharan Africa: Implications for economic growth and poverty reduction*. Africa Region Working Paper Series No. 97. Urban Development Unit. Transport and Urban Development. The World Bank, Washington, DC.

Kjaer, A.M. (2004). *Governance*. Cambridge: Polity Press.

Klenke, K. (1996). *Women in leadership: A contextual perspective*. New York: Springer.

Kofi Annan Foundation. (2010). *Global commission on elections, democracy and security*. Geneva.

Le Vine, V.T. (1967). *Political leadership in Africa: Post-independence generational conflict in Upper Volta, Senegal, Niger, Dahomey and Central Africa Republic*. Hoover Institution Studies Series; 18, The Hoover Institution on War, Revolution and Peace, Stanford University.

Liu, G. (2006). Education, equality, and national citizenship. *The Yale Law Journal*, 116(330), 330–441.

Lowndes, V. & Leach, S. (2004). Understanding local political leadership: Constitutions, contexts and capabilities. *Local Government Studies*, 30(4), 557–575.
Lyne de Ver, H. (2008). *Leadership politics and development: A literature survey, policy and practice for development, leaders, elites and coalition*. Background Paper 03, The Developmental Leadership Program.
MacKuen, B.M. & Rabinowitz, G. (Eds.). (2003). *Electoral democracy*. Ann Arbor, MI: University of Michigan.
Masciulli, J., Molchanov, M.A. & Knight, A. (2008). Political leadership in context. In J. Masciulli, M.A. Molchanov & A. Knight (Eds.), *Ashgate Research Companion to Political Leadership* (pp. 3–27). Burlington, USA: Ashgate Publishing Company.
McKinsey Institute Report. (2010). *Lions on the move: The progress and potential of African economies*. Washington: McKinsey and Company.
Mkapa, B.W. (2008). *Leadership for growth, development and poverty reduction: An African viewpoint and experience*. Working Paper #8, Washington, DC: Commission on Growth and Development. Retrieved October 12, 2012 from www.growthcommission.org
Moore, M. (1993). Declining to learn from the east? The World Bank on governance and development. *IDS-Bulletin*, 24(1), 39–51.
Northouse, P. (2010). *Leadership: Theory and practice* (5th ed.). London: Sage.
Nye, J., Jr. (1999). New models of public leadership. In F. Hesselbein, M. Goldsmith & L. Sommerville (Eds.), *Leading beyond the walls*. (pp. 279–288). San Francisco: Jossey-Bass.
Organization for Economic Cooperation and Development [OECD]. (2009). *Donors approaches to governance assessments: 2009 Source Book*. Retrieve August 20, 2012 from http://www.oecd.org/development/governanceanddevelopment/42472200.pdf
Putzel, J. & Di John, J. (2012). *Meeting the challenges of crisis states. The crisis states research center*. London: London School of Economics and Political Sciences.
Rotberg, R.I. (2007). *Africa: Progress and problems—Governance and leadership in Africa*. New York: Mason Crest Publishers.
Rotberg, R.I. (2009). Governance and leadership in Africa: Measures, methods and results. In *Journal of International Affairs*, 62(2), 113–126.
Ruscio, K. (2004). *The leadership dilemma in modern democracy*. Cheltenham: Edward Elgar.
Skinner, E.P. (1998). African political cultures and the problems of government. *African Studies Quarterly*, 2(3), 17–25.
The Mombasa Declaration. (2004). *Leadership in Africa*. World Peace Foundation, African Leadership Council.
United Nations Conference on Trade and Development [UNCTAD]. (2010). *Economic development in Africa: South–South cooperation: Africa and new forms of development partnerships*. New York: United Nations.
United Nations Conference on Trade and Development [UNCTAD]. (2012). *Trade and development report, 2012—Policies for inclusive and balanced growth*. New York: United Nations.
United Nations Development Program [UNDP]. (2010). *A guide to UNDP democratic governance practice*. Oslo: Bureau for Development Policy, Democratic Governance Group.
Van Wyk, J. (2007). Political leadership in Africa: Presidents, patrons or profiteers? *African Center for Constructive Resolution of Disputes: Occasional Paper Series*, 2(1), 3–38. Durban, South Africa. Retrieved November 24, 2012 from http://dspace.cigilibrary.org/jspui/bitstream/123456789/32018/1/op_2007_1.pdf?1

Venables, A.J. (2005). Spatial disparities in developing countries: Cities, regions and international trade. *Journal of Economic Geography*, 5, 3–21.
VonDoepp, P. (2009). *The leadership variable in Africa: Situating structure and agency in governance trajectories*. Paper prepared for the Annual Meeting of the American Political Science Association, September 4, Toronto, Canada.
World Bank. (2011). *Africa's future and the World Bank's support to it*. Washington, DC: The World Bank.
World Bank. (2012). *Africa pulse report: An analysis of issues shaping Africa's economic future*. Washington, DC: The World Bank.
Yukl, G. (2009). *Leadership in organizations* (7th ed.). New York: Pearson Education.

13 Revisiting the African Revolutionary Praxis in the Global Era

Siendou Konate

INTRODUCTION

Culture has ideological, scientific and historical manifestations, which, when detected and used by marginalized people, can result in retaking their right place in world history. Behind marginalization, it is European and/or Euro-American neo-imperialism that silence the expression of other voices and ways other than those of the so-called developed nations. For the world to be a true global village, those on the periphery of the global culture (Euro-American and European culture) need to be included, because a globalized world is one that is polycentric and has more than one voice.

Culture remains the right tool of resistance par excellence in a world which is in a process of becoming globalized under the terms of dominant cultures. There is an irreversible process by which the so-called developed world attempts to dominate the small and weak, thereby satisfying their will to homogenize the world. It is imperative that Africans revisit their revolutionary praxis in order to re-appropriate the potentialities of their people's comprehensive cultural, economic, political and social practices so as to counter the ever-growing notion of a global village. Thus, a series of questions needs to be addressed. For instance, questions on the role Africa plays in this 'global village' and the cultural stock Africans can tap into to become active participants in a truly globalized village. The question may be rephrased as follows: how can Africans contribute to defeating world monoculturalism or mono-voicedness as spearheaded by the Europeans and their American accomplices?

EUROPEAN INVASION AND CULTURAL IMPERIALISM

European invasion and the disruption of the life of the people they subjugated around the world were rationalized as a mission that God bestowed on the West *vis-à-vis* the rest of the world. Accordingly, the mission consisted of drawing the other parts of the world from darkness to civilization, and from underdevelopment and backwardness to the height of development. In carrying out this selfish and inhuman project of salvaging the non-Western, Western imperialist powers disrupted and demonized other cultures and histories. For instance, the French decided to make their African 'subjects' French citizens through the assimilation policy. In other words, the colonial subjects had to strip themselves of their African cultural identity. Contrary, British colonial rule was more subtle and allowed some space to the 'subjects' as long as this space did not endanger British hegemony in the domination of its colonial territories in Africa.

The '*mission civilisatrice*', as the French called their intrusion into the political, economic and social life and organization of African people, was not really a mission of civilization, or of taking Africans from darkness to modernity and development (concepts that are problematic) but a mission of domination, expropriation and dehumanization by attacking African cultural foundations. The imperialists were cognizant of the fact that the easiest way to subjugate a people was to alienate them from their identities. Thus, they homogenized their subjects through what they called 'civilization'. To civilize a people is to refine their culture that is, "the customary beliefs, social forms, the material traits characteristic of a racial, religious, or social group" (Merriam-Webster as cited in Clément & Kaufmann, 2007, p. 7). Civilization is a relatively high level of cultural and technological development, and it is the culture characteristic of a time or place. By culture, I mean social practices that unite members of a given community that differentiate them from others. Jan Vansina (1985, p. 124) says:

> Culture can be defined as what is common in the minds of a given group of people; it refers to a community of society. People in a community share many ideas, values, and images, in short, responsibilities which are collective to them and differ from others.

Culture can be re-appropriated to deal with the new configuration of colonialism in the same manner it was used by the nationalists of the era of independence and liberation struggle. This new configuration is what we call global capitalism or globalization. For, the same capital that animated the imperialist moves is what makes the backbone and foundation of the rhetoric of the world as a global village. The fallacy of such rhetoric is summarized in the word 'globalism', which Manfred Steger defines as "a political ideology that endows the concepts of globalization with market-oriented norms, values, and meanings" (2005, p. 12). Steger argues that the Anglo-Saxon-America's globalized market ideology is cloaked in pretentious and universalistic dressings, an attempt to Americanize the world order.

EUROPEANIZATION OF THE NON-EUROPEAN WORLD

Western imperialism has been the Europeanization of the non-European world. The imperial project is aimed at homogenizing those who have been 'otherized' by the colonial discourse. The homogenization makes those who are declared 'underdeveloped' desire to imitate, and hence fail to devise their own ways and means of advancement. Thus, the European model of social enhancement has been mirrored as the only viable way to get out of 'backwardness'. It confines the poor countries to the alternative that Samir Amin sums up as "either they accept Europeanization and internalize its demands or if they decide against it, they will lead themselves to an impasse that inevitably leads to their decline" (1989, p. 107). Amin posits an alternative consisting, on the one hand, in the disconnection of the marginalized and oppressed people from the centers of domination and power, and on the other, in remaining dependent on their oppressors. The latter alternative might be called adjustment to the standards of the center.

In Africa, the option of Europeanization was welcomed open-handedly to such a point that the rhetoric of African nationalists was replete with European worldviews of 'development' and 'modernity'. Besides, Europeanization denotes the inability of some nationalists to work out patterns of resistance to their subjugation. For, their allegiance to the Western paradigm shows that they were preaching freedom while they had no tangible clue in what it meant. In other words, they proposed theories of liberation without disconnecting/delinking from the instruments of their subjugation. The latter are the features of a capitalist society, the almost unbridgeable divide between the poor and rich and the centralization of political power in the hands of just a few people.

Cutting the umbilical cord that links the colonized with the colonizer requires the revitalization of the cultures of the colonized because these cultures have the capacity to frustrate or undermine the 'colonizing cultures'. Culture, as I stated earlier, is a whole, which is social, economic and political that translates the personality and configuration of a given society. Thus, it is what attests to the historicity of a people when the latter is denied such a process. The struggle for complete liberation should, therefore, first and foremost engage in rejecting the denial of the history and the culture of the dominated. As Amilcar Cabral used to say, the national liberation of a people is "the regaining of the historical personality of that people. It is the return to history through the destruction the imperialist domination to which they were subjugated" (1975, p. 294). According to Cabral, the real liberation of a subjugated people resides in that people's realization that they are under subjection and their determination to return to their history.

RESISTANCE TO CULTURAL DOMINATION

Because the lack of civilization was the motive of the invasion, and civilization was subsumed under culture, then, the latter is the last resort for the African people to carry out their political and socio-economic independence. Let me quote here from Cabral's definition of culture at work during the struggle of national liberation. "Culture has a material basis at the level of the forces of production and the mode of production. It is rooted in the milieu's material reality . . ." (as cited in Chilcote, 1975, p. 38). Elsewhere, he writes, "Culture is always the life of a society, the more or less conscious result of the economic and political activities of that society; the more or less dynamic expression of the kinds of relationships which prevail in that society . . . among individuals, group of individuals, social strata or class" (Cabral, 1974, p. 40). To end our references to Cabral, quoting extensively his final words on the resistance potential of culture will be of great avail in that it serves better the purpose of our discussion. According to Amilcar Cabral,

> The value of culture as an element of resistance to foreign domination lies in the fact that culture is the vigorous manifestations on the ideological or idealist plane of the physical or historical reality of the society that is dominated or to be dominated. Culture is simultaneously the fruit of a people's history and a determinant of history by positive or negative influence which it exerts on the evolution of relationships between man and his environment, among men or groups of men within a society as well as among different societies. *Ignorance of this fact may explain the failure of several attempts at foreign domination as well as the failure of some international liberation movements.* (1974, p. 41, emphasis added)

For Cabral, culture has some value that can be appropriated to overthrow external domination. In the process of colonization of Africa, the French, British and Portuguese imperialists were astutely aware of the fact that to harmonize the economic and political subjugation of Africa without marginalizing African cultures at the same time would be a doomed project. Thus, they denied the existence of 'indigenous' cultures. The attack on African cultures is what N'gugi wa Thiong'o terms as the 'cultural bomb' that prohibits Africans to learn and speak their mother tongues. Thus:

> The effects of the cultural bomb is to annihilate a people's belief in their names, in their environment, in their languages, in their heritage of struggle, in their unity, in their capacities and ultimately in themselves. It makes them see their past as one wasteland of non-achievements and it makes them want to distance themselves from the wasteland. (Ngugi wa Thiong'o, 1986, p. 12)

What wa Thiong'o denotes is the potentiality of culture to resist imperialism. Of course, the educated among the colonized were aware of the power of their cultural personality. And this explains the urgency of those intellectuals from Africa and the diaspora populations across the world to create a cultural awareness and celebrate their African personality, or what Senghor would call 'negritude'.

Negritude is defined by the former President of Senegal, Leopold Sedar Senghor, as "the whole complex of civilized values—cultural, economic, social and political—which characterize the black peoples or more precisely the Negro world" (Senghor, 1974, p. 230). Negritude had its counterpart in the English-speaking African colonies under the name of Pan-Africanism, which was principally animated by nationalists such as Kwame Nkrumah of Ghana. The negritude movement, unlike the cultural movements in Anglophone Africa, confined themselves in the romanticization, the glamorization of the African past, and the affirmation of the African culture and history whose existence was denied by the Europeans. Consequently, they had to represent themselves, thereby running counter to that famous quotation from Karl Marx's *The Eighteenth Brumaire of Napoleon Bonaparte*, "They cannot represent themselves, they must be represented" (Said, 1994, p. xiii).

The problem with Negritude was that it did not offer full self-representation by devising new patterns and new attitudes to the African situation as colonized peoples based on their indigenous teachings and mode of life. In other words, theirs was simply empty rhetoric because it had no practical dimension and no real political significance. These cultural movements were rather the things of those Africans who were assimilated by other cultures, and yet rejected by the cultures in question. It is in that respect that Ezekiel Mpahlele from South Africa wrote:

> It is rather the assimilated African, who has absorbed French culture who now passionately wants to recapture his past. In his poetry he extols his ancestors, ancestral masks, African wood carvings and bronze art and tries to recover moorings of his oral literature [. . .]. If there is any negritude in Black man's art in South Africa, it is because we are African. . . . We who grew up and were educated in Africa do not find anything new in them. (1974, pp. 236–237)

The charges that Mpahlele levies against the Negritude are absolute, but he overlooks the fact that the assimilation of the natives of the French colonies was part and parcel of the French imperialist agenda. The French were practicing direct rule and did not acknowledge the existence of African cultures, unlike the British who allowed room for these cultures to thrive. Therefore, the cultural 'revivalists' of the independence struggle era can have the benefit of the doubt. However, they ought to have gone past the glorification of the past by extracting from the past new patterns and modes of social advancement for their people.

The cultural defenders made a mistake that consisted in not only looking at culture as static, but also non-evolutionary. Culture in Africa is definitely not the same as it was before the encounter with the imperialist West. New elements got added to the existing components of culture and they need to be reckoned with. The environment has changed and new aspects are present in the economy, politics and our thought patterns. Put differently, culture is not to be viewed as the folklore or artistic expressions of a society. Such is what Fanon is warning against when he calls the attention of 'negroists' to a re-thinking of national culture. According to Fanon (1968, p. 233):

> A national culture is not folklore, nor an abstract populism that believes it can discover the true nature of people. . . . A national culture is a whole body of efforts made by a people in the sphere of thought to describe, justify and praise the action through which a people has created itself and keep itself in existence.

National culture, from Fanon's angle, is a dialectical process that builds on the mode of life, the relation of the individual in the community and his or her environment and the influence that they exert on each other. African culture, then, is not solely the old vestiges of Ancient Africa to be rescued from oblivion but that which takes into consideration the interaction of individuals and groups of individuals. It therefore includes the influence that the cultures and modes of thought of these different groups have on each other. The dialectics of culture is what deserves much attention and thought if culture is to be retained as a tool of social change and liberation. If culture is what we have described, then, how can African cultural heritage be de-homogenized, knowing that Euro-American neo-imperialism or globalization is speeding up?

INHERITED AND ADOPTED AFRICAN SOCIAL, ECONOMIC AND POLITICAL SYSTEMS

Culture, as a mode of political, economic and social thought and action can be explored by examining the social, political and economic institutions upon which traditional African societies were grounded in. In West Africa, for example, there were various empires and kingdoms that managed to keep themselves up to their apogee because of the visionary leadership of their kings. The empires of old Mali, Songhay and Ghana, the kingdoms in Nigeria, the Mossi kingdoms in Upper Volta or present-day Burkina-Faso, the Dahomey or Abomey and the Ashanti kingdom in present-day Ghana still remain the pride of Africans to the extent that at least they have historical references and facts to affirm that there was, and still is, a civilization in Sub-Saharan Africa. These states had strong political, administrative and military apparatuses, which during their days could be pointed at as proof of cultural development. Obviously, these vertically-structured societies were somewhat based on castes, class or social stratification and therefore on the exploitation of some members by others. However, their model of social, political and economic organization is still appealing. They did not depend on the outside to wield political power, but on their own capacities and creativity. Choosing this model offhand is not what is advised, however, the suggestion is that such models are worth exploring as alternative frameworks.

Aside from vertical-structured societies in Africa, there was another model that served as a source of inspiration for some African nationalists. It is communalism, which was practiced in some parts of Africa, especially in horizontally-structured communities. In these communal societies, different communities enjoyed some level of independence from one another. They managed their own affairs and self-governance with each member of the community taking part in running the affairs of the community directly or indirectly. The most important characteristics of these communal societies are the absence of classes, the absence of exploitative or antagonistic social relations, the existence of equal access to the land and other means of production, the equality at the level of distribution of products and ultimately the fact that family culture and kinship formed the foundation of social life. Because these societies were fundamentally agricultural and subsistence-based they were self-reliant and they would exchange the surpluses they produced through a barter system of trade. The political organization in communal societies was horizontal and characterized by a strong diffusion of power. Political leadership was built on the basis of family and kinship and exercised by the elders who in Africa are equated with wisdom and fair judgment. Elders presided over meetings and settled disputes but hardly showed any sense of superiority.

These examples of social, political and economic life may inspire contemporary Africans in dismantling European models forced on them. The communal mode has been explored by Julius Nyerere of Tanzania, who, like many other African leaders of the early post-independence era, blended European models with African realities in order to achieve socio-economic and political development via Africanized socialism. Here, it is worth giving reasons that actuated African leaders to adopt socialism. In *Negritude and African Socialism*, Leopold Senghor explains reasons for choosing African socialism:

> We decided to borrow from the socialist experiments—both theoretical and practical—only certain elements, certain scientific and technical values, which we have grafted like scions on to the wild stock of negritude. For the latter, as a complex of civilized values, is traditionally *socialist* in character. . . . Our Negro-African society is a classless society, which is not the same as saying that it has no hierarchy or division of labour. *It is a community-based society* in which hierarchy—and therefore power—is founded on spiritual and democratic values: on the law of primogeniture and election; in which decisions of all kind are deliberated in a *Palaver*, after the ancestral gods have been consulted; in which work is shared out among the sexes and among technico-professional groups based on religion. Thus in the working out of an

> African mode of socialism, the problem is not how to put an end to the exploitation of man by his fellow, but to prevent its ever happening, by bringing political and economic democracy back to life; our problem is not how to satisfy spiritual, that is cultural needs, but how to keep the fervour of the black soul alive. It is a question, once again, of modernizing our values by borrowing from European Socialism its science and technical skill, above all its spirit of Progress. (1974, pp. 232–233)

It is unfair to Senghor that his explications be generalized to the point of making them mean socialism in Africa. However, the Senegalese poet's reflection on socialism may well be construed as attempts to turn foreign concepts into an African reality. The worrisome part of Senghor's points is that whereas he pretends to be promoting African values, he denies them any potential for advancement. They are to be modernized with European science, technical skill and its spirit of Progress. In other words, the values he intends to use to Africanize socialism are obscurantist, reactionary and prove that African leaders cannot do away with externally imposed models. Why socialism at all?

In Tanzania, Nyerere explored the Africanization of socialism by laying a heavy emphasis on land, which is central to life among Africans. Nyerere tried his socialism through a program he called *ujamaa* villagization. *Ujamaa* was predicated on simplicity, freedom and egalitarianism, which used to be hallmarks of African traditional societies. The village, according to this program, is the laboratory of African socialism because in villages people live and work together for the good of the community. And the government in such a community is established and led by the working force. In the *ujamaa* villages, Nyerere (1967, p. 90) says:

> Most of our farming would be done by groups of people who live as a community and work as a community. They would live together in a village, farm together, market together and undertake the provision of local services and small local requirements as a community. Their community would be the traditional family group, or any other group of people living according the *ujamaa* principles, large enough to take into account modern methods and the needs of the twentieth century.

Conceptually, Nyerere's program is laudable in that it retrieves the values and achievements of African traditional societies for a practical purpose. However, the problem with the program stemmed from what it was aiming to eradicate, the features of capitalism: coercion and centralization of power in the hands of few people and bureaucracy. Whereas Nyerere says that in order to achieve the goal of *ujamaa*, no force was to be used but persuasion, peasants received orders from higher up to grow crops that the administration deemed necessary. Nyerere argued that the success of *ujamaa* "depends on willingness to cooperate, and an understanding of the different kind of life which can be obtained by participants if they work hard together" (1967, p. 91). This means that for the program to succeed, it had to be controlled by peasants, which was not the case. We also note that despite the good intentions of *ujamaa*, the program was overburdened and finally 'suffocated' by State control and bureaucracy. By reactivating the hallmarks of traditional African values and achievements, undoubtedly, Nyerere was stressing the *sine qua non* of delinking with Western patterns and models by introducing an African version of socialism. Thus, his example must be re-tried while taking into account the errors that were committed.

DELINKING AFRICAN DEVELOPMENT FROM FOREIGN MODELS

The main way to carry out the task of delinking is for Africans to first of all believe in their potentialities, their abilities and the achievements of their ancestors. To better carry out this 'disconnection' from models of Western domination, there is a need to build a strong unitary consciousness among Africans. Among the proponents of African unity was Kwame Nkrumah (1974, pp. 213–214) of Ghana who wrote:

> There is strength in the political unity of our continent and that is why the Convention People's Party, as the vanguard for African liberation, is always against any policy for the balkanization of Africa in small weak and unstable states. We believe that considerations of mutual security and prosperity of our people demand that all the independent states in Africa should work together to create a Union of African states. . . . So deep is our faith in African unity that we have declared our preparedness to surrender the sovereignty of Ghana, in whole or in part, in the interest of a Union of African States.

The idea of African unity was derided by the Organization of African Unity, which stated that the purpose of the organization was "to promote the unity and solidarity of African states, to coordinate and intensify their cooperation and efforts to achieve a better life for the peoples of Africa" (Davidson, 1967, p. 186). The statement does not include the defense of the sovereignty, the territorial integrity and the independence of the country members. This means that no one was ready to surrender their territory for the building of the unity Nkrumah was referring to. It is therefore, clear that the only integration that is possible in the whole of Africa seems to be an economic one. The revolution should have started from there rather from the political unity of Africa.

For Pan-Africanists, such as Sekou Toure of Guinea, the objective of political independence lies in delinking the African economy from the old structures of colonial power. Like Nkrumah, Sekou Toure believed in Africa forming its own economic zones without any political alignment with the West. For that purpose, he proposed African unity, the unitary consciousness he thought was the key to the African problem:

> To win and proclaim a nation's independence but keep its old structures is to plough a field but not sow it with grain for a harvest. Africa's political independence is a means to which must be used to create and develop the new African economy. Our continent possesses tremendous reserves of raw materials and they, together with its potential sources of power, give excellent conditions for the industrialization. That's why, though it would be unrealistic and irrational to think of associating African nations with European Common Market or any other form of economic monopoly, it is hoped that an African common market will be organized which eventually can cooperate on the basis of equality and solidarity with other economic zones. (Toure, 1974, p. 223)

The economic question articulated by Sekou Toure touches on the question that African states are still struggling to answer. The economic zones that were set up a few years after political independence failed because of a lack of good will and determination on the part of the leaders. For example, in West Africa, the Economic Community of West Africa was formed in 1975 and includes 15 countries: Ghana, Nigeria, Liberia, Burkina Faso, Côte d'Ivoire, Mali, Guinea-Conakry, Togo, Niger, Benin, Sierra Leone, Guinea-Bissau, Equatorial Guinea, Senegal, Gambia and Mauritania. The community is basically for the economic integration of countries that share the same cultures and languages across the artificially drawn borders. A similar community was set up in almost all the four corners of the continent. For example, in East Africa, there is the East African Community created in the early 1960s and used to pull together three countries, Uganda, Kenya and Tanzania. Like the West African community, the East African counterpart was set up for the integration of these countries. Notwithstanding the realization that sub-regional integration is necessary at this moment in African history, this integration has a long way to go because no state in Africa is ready to surrender their national sovereignty for political unification. Economic integration should be encouraged and reinforced by involving those who are laboring towards this togetherness, the masses of people.

INTEGRATION AND THE LANGUAGE PROBLEM

The biggest problem to integration in Africa seems to be that of language. The arbitrary partition of Africa among imperial powers included the imposition of their languages on Africans. Consequently, in West Africa, there is a plethora of foreign languages used as official languages. Nigeria, Ghana, Liberia and Sierra Leone are 'English-speaking' countries that are bordered by 'French-speaking' countries including Cote d'Ivoire, Togo, Benin, Mali,

Niger and Senegal. West Africa is also home to 'lusophone' countries such as Equatorial Guinea and Guinea-Bissau, which respectively use Spanish and Portuguese as official languages. The issue of language, chiefly our national languages, is one of the factors impeding the political unification of Africa. Yet the same languages represent the main tool in the development of Africa through the de-homogenization of the world.

As Ngugi wa Thiong'o says, the cultural rehabilitation of African countries is the way to say 'no' to the attempts of capitalist Europe and America to impose themselves on Africa. wa Thiong'o (1986) believes that the way out is through decolonization of the minds and the imagination of Africans by reaffirming their national languages. He sets the example for his fellow writers, for instance, by writing some novels in Gikiyu. *N'gahika Ndenda* was written in a national language aimed at the Kenyan peasantry and later translated as *I Will Marry When I Want*.

wa Thiong'o casts an appeal for the indigenization of literature which will recreate the atmosphere of democratic participation, which has always been an element of African societies if we take a retrospective look at those societies. He addresses the same issue in *The Allegory of the Cave: Language, Democracy and a New World Order* by saying that the working class is the basis of the economy in Africa and that they must be given back their voice and addressed in national languages, which have been denied by both colonization and Western-educated Africans. Because of the hegemony of European languages over their everyday life, the majority becomes voiceless. This state of affairs results in what wa Thiong'o calls "the rise of two nations in the same territory . . . a small minority speaking and conducting the affairs of the nation in European languages, [while] the majority [speaks] their own different African-nationality or communal languages" (1996, p. 12).

Giving back voice seems like one of the best propositions in carrying out decolonization, yet as discussed earlier, the multiplicity of languages in Africa raises problems that inhibit fighting against (neo)colonialism/globalization. For decolonization to succeed, Africans should accept one national language, a *lingua franca*, as the official language of the continent. As for whose language to use and the question of national unity/nationalism or national extremism, *Kiswahili* in Tanzania, Kenya and Uganda's experiment is the answer. But even so, can that experiment succeed, for instance, in some West African countries where there are more than 50 nationalities? Nigeria alone counts more than 80 national languages, and the Ivory Coast has 53.

Far from advocating for foreign languages, which we must acknowledge as part and parcel of our culture, these languages still function as a unifying factor for the African countries with multiple nationalities. Unless the national communities accept to go beyond nationalism, the question of language will be a thorny one. And yet, it is feasible to empower these languages by raising them to the status of official languages. An interesting and noteworthy anecdote confirms my belief in the use of local languages.

It all happened in the Guro market of Adjame where women sell vegetables. An old lady who spoke Mande came to buy some vegetables but did not speak French; neither did the seller who spoke Guro dialect. Because Dyula, a derivative language of Mandinka found in various parts of West Africa, is a commercial language, the old lady conducted the conversation in Dyula, the vernacular language in Cote d'Ivoire which the vegetable seller understood as well. Dyula acted as a *lingua franca* and was convenient for both of them to communicate.

The previous anecdote shows the potential of some national languages in easing inter-community communication and in contributing to the re-Africanization of Africa. A common national language can therefore be turned into a *lingua franca*. The solution to re-mapping Africa resides with the majority of the people as opposed to those political leaders, who instead of using this national and sociological diversity for good ends, use it to further widen the gap of difference. Unfortunately, the leaders capable of exploiting linguistic differences for unity, are certainly not those who run the affairs of African countries today, but a new breed of leadership that is willing to abandon personal interests on behalf of the well-being of Africa.

CONCLUSION

Culture, as discussed in this chapter, has the potential to subvert imperialism. It did it yesterday in Africa when people were subjugated, dehumanized by the West, and it can still do it today to destabilize Euro-American globalism. Political and economic power will continue being monopolized and consolidated by the West, thereby averting any chance of a polycentric world, if those who suffer exclusion, exploitation and oppression do nothing. In the African context, the actions to be undertaken are to be drawn from the achievements of our forebears, to set up "new patterns, new social customs, new attitudes to life so that while we seek the material, cultural and economic advancement of our people, while we raise their standard of life, we shall not sacrifice their fundamental happiness" (Ogboade, 1975, p. 2).

In keeping with the recommendations of Frantz Fanon, Africa and the oppressed world should take on the responsibility to re-humanize the world. For, as he says, "let us decide not to imitate Europe, let us try to create the whole man, [. . .] we do not want to catch up with anyone, what we want to do is go forward all the time, night and day, in the company of man, in the company of all man" (Fanon, 1968, pp. 253–255). In order to create the whole new man, as Fanon proposes, the oppressed in Africa and the victimized worldwide should react with either insidious or overt counter-violence to the violence of the capitalistic nations of the West against them. The subtle form of violence that Africa is capable of using in this situation is breaking up with the models of the West. To break up with the West means to call into question its models, which can only be appropriately done through the reaffirmation of the cultural identities of the oppressed (Amin, 1977). Local identities are what globalization seeks to deny through attempts of phagocytosis. Thus, one could not agree more with Samir Amin when he aptly says that "the people in the periphery, who are victims of this never ending imperialism, have no choice but to struggle to bring it to an end *by any means necessary*" (Amin, 1992, p. 100, emphasis in original). I must hasten to add that I am in no way endorsing acts of irresponsible violence but the logic used successfully by liberation movements around the world. One could not agree more with Albert Memmi when, back in 1957 in his book *The Colonizer and the Colonized*, he observed that the colonial context frustrated the colonized in such a way that the latter resolved to take action by rupture or explosion. According to Memmi (1965, p. 128), "the colonial situation, by its own internal inevitability, brings revolt. For the colonial condition cannot be adjusted to; like an iron collar, it can only be broken". Besides, he remarks that the less peaceful disconnection of the colonized from the standards of the colonizer is necessary for the recovery of the lost self of the colonized. The latter assimilated the values of the colonizer. The same perspective is shared by Frederick Douglass who aptly points out that when people long for freedom, they must not deprecate agitation and protest because if they do, they will look like "men who want crops without plowing up the ground, they want rain without thunder and lightening. They want the ocean without the awful roar of its many waters . . . power concedes nothing without demand. It never did and never will" (as cited in Toure & Hamilton, 1992, p. xviii).

For the world to be a global village, the process should break the hegemony of the West from the oppressed and exploited and become inclusive of different marginal cultural groups in the world. Thus, Samir Amin is right when he claims that "[T]he world polycentrism [. . .] is the only realistic basis for a new internationalism, and only the understanding that flows from its paradigm will equip us to recognize the objective diversity of our conditions and problems, to lay the foundations for reconstructing our world, and to acknowledge the common destiny of the peoples of our planet" (Amin, 1992, p. 30). In other words, to have a truly globalized world, the globalization project should be humane. To have a global village, one must first and foremost seek to establish an equal and plain field where all the members of the global family have a portion of the power to make decisions that concern them. That implies that they are recognized as different people with different perspectives on the issues that affect them as a whole.

REFERENCES

Amin, S. (1977). Self-reliance and the new international economic order. *Monthly Review*, 29(3), 1–21.

Amin, S. (1989). *Eurocentrism*. New York: Monthly Review.
Amin, S. (1992). *Empire of chaos*. (Trans. W.H. Locke Anderson). New York: Monthly Review.
Cabral, A. (1974). *Return to the source: Selected speeches*. New York: Monthly Review.
Cabral, A. (1975). *Unité et Lutte I: L'arme de la théorie, cahiers libres*. Paris: François Maspero.
Chilcote, R. (1975). *Amilcar Cabral's revolutionary theory and practice*. Boulder, CO: Lynne Rienner.
Clément, F. & Kaufmann, L. (2007). Paths towards a naturalistic approach of culture. *Intellectica*, 2(46), 7–24.
Davidson, B. (1967). *Which way Africa? The search for a new society*. Baltimore, MD: Penguin.
Fanon, F. (1968). *The wretched of the earth*. New York: Groove.
Memmi, A. (1965). *The colonizer and the colonized*. (Trans. H. Greenfeld). Boston: Beacon.
Mpahlele, E. (1974). Negritude and culture. In M. Minogue & J. Molloy (Eds.), *African aims and attitudes: Selected documents* (pp. 236–238). Oxford: Cambridge University Press.
Nkrumah, K. (1974). I speak of freedom. In M. Minogue & J. Molloy (Eds.), *African aims and attitudes: Selected documents* (pp. 212–216). Oxford: Cambridge University Press.
Nyerere, J. (1967). *Education for self-reliance*. Dar es Salaam: Government Printers.
Ogboade, F. (1975). *Nationalism in colonial and neocolonial Africa*. New York: Oxford University Press.
Said, E. (1994). *Orientalism*. New York: Random House.
Senghor, L.S. (1974). Negritude and African socialism. In M. Minogue & J. Molloy (Eds.), *African aims and attitudes: Selected documents* (pp. 230–234). Oxford: Cambridge University Press.
Steger, M.B. (2005). *Globalism: Market ideology meets terrorism* (2nd ed.). New York: Rowan and Littlefield.
Toure, K. & Hamilton, C.V. (1992). *Black power: The politics of liberation in America*. New York: Vintage.
Toure, S. (1974). Africa's future and the World. In M. Minogue & J. Molloy (Eds.), *African aims and attitudes: Selected documents* (pp. 221–225). Oxford: Cambridge University Press.
Vansina, J. (1985). *Oral tradition as history*. Madison, Wisconsin: University of Wisconsin Press.
wa Thiong'o, N. (1986). *Decolonising the mind: The politics of language in African literature*. London: James Carrey.
wa Thiong'o, N. (1996). The allegory of the cave: Language, democracy and new order! *Oxford: Black Renaissance/ Renaissance Noire*, 1(3), 1–21.

14 The Shifting Boundaries of the African State in Agricultural Institutions and Policies in an Era of Globalization

Korbla P. Puplampu

INTRODUCTION AND PROBLEM

The assumption that the African state, like its counterpart in other parts of the world, has an important role to play in establishing agricultural institutions and enacting relevant policies has persisted since the dawn of colonial rule. Colonial states and governments established Departments of Agriculture with the mandate to initiate and implement relevant policies. However, colonial agricultural institutions and policies were caught up in the contradictions of colonial rule and development. Hence, the expectation, at least from a theoretical perspective, was that the post-colonial African state would transcend the contradictions of its colonial predecessor and fulfill its mandate and promise as an authentic development partner. The enthusiasm that surrounded the development potential of the post-colonial African state in the early decade of political independence has been replaced by the sober realities of the agrarian crisis that engulfed the region in the 1980s and 1990s (Smith, 2003, 2006). Although the crisis led to a widespread condemnation of the state and policy interventions by multilateral financial institutions (for example, the World Bank and International Monetary Fund), the development trajectory of the region remains uncertain and an issue of immense intellectual interest (African Capacity Building Foundation [ACBF], 2012; World Bank, 2012, 1989, 1981; Seck & Busari, 2009; Taeb & Zakri, 2008).

This chapter examines the changing role of the African state in agricultural institutions and policies. The interest in agriculture stems from the continuing role and importance of the agricultural sector in many, if not all, African countries, even though the proportion of the sector's contribution also varies across the region (ACBF, 2012; Bates & Block, 2011; Chuhan-Pole & Angwafo, 2011; Rauch, 2011; Bruntrup, 2011; World Bank, 2007). In view of the pivotal role of the agricultural sector, the state is the sole entity in charge of the institutional and policy affairs in the sector. At the same time, the current reiterations of globalization require significant changes in the state's role in the economic and social spheres. Therefore, the question becomes the extent to which the state, in view of its changing role, can serve as an influential entity in the institutional and policy framework for the agricultural sector so that the sector can play its significant part in society. Understanding the nature of the African state through the performance of African agriculture has led to an examination of the policies in operation in the agricultural sector and an evaluation of the institutional capacity and support provided by the state for measures of governance (Bryceson, Sarkar, Fennell & Singh, 2010).

To answer this question, the chapter is divided into two sections. The first section will examine the role of the colonial and post-colonial African state in agricultural institutions and policies. The examination will lay bare the similarities and differences in the role of the African state in agricultural institutions and policies. The discussion in the second section will re-think the role of the contemporary African state in the institutional and policy aspects of agriculture.

THE AFRICAN STATE, AGRICULTURAL INSTITUTIONS AND POLICIES: BACK TO THE FUTURE?

The writings of Karl Marx and Friedrich Engels, as well as that of Max Weber, have informed the scholarly debate on the state. Marx and Engels highlight the state's role in mediating conflict between social groups, specifically the owners of capital and labor. Engels maintains that because "the state arose from the need to keep class antagonisms in check . . . the modern state is an instrument for exploiting wage labour by capital" (Engels, 1884/1986, p. 210). For Marxian-oriented writers, the state is an institution representing the interests of powerful sections of society. Max Weber conceptualized the state in terms of its institutional character, its rule making functions and the monopoly over the use of legitimate force (Gerth & Mills, 1946, p. 78). For Weberian authors, the state employs its bureaucratic machinery of specialized and graded hierarchy of officials, rational calculation of means and ends to attain a common good. The views of Karl Marx, Friedrich Engels and Max Weber have influenced the nature of theorizing of the post-colonial African state (Leys, 1975; Saul, 1974). With the state as the anchor in this chapter, the subsequent discussion is framed as follows: the state and development, the nature and structure of the state and the state and agricultural social groups.

Development, as Larrain (1989) reminded us years ago, must be placed in a historical perspective with an emphasis on the terms and conditions over resource allocations. The colonial state, taking its marching orders from the metropolitan mother country, viewed the colonies as a prized possession. Generally, colonial authorities presented colonial development as an obligation by metropolitan powers (Lugard, 1965). The obligation relied on economic and moral principles. The economic mandate presented development through trade in the export of agricultural raw materials (Hancock,

1942). Against this backdrop, colonial states pressed African cultivators to allocate and increase share of their productive resources to growing crops destined for Europe. Colonial states often relied on force "to subject cultivators to the demands and pressures of colonial markets" (Boone, 1994, p. 112). By incorporating local producers into a world economy, the colonies served as markets for imported industrial goods and food items from the metropolitan colonial countries. A vital component of the economic policy required the state to establish the infrastructure (railways, roads and harbors) as the conduit for the export and import trade. The moral imperative of colonial development was a belated recognition, because it assumed a tangible form when the decolonization process began in the 1940s. As part of this process, the colonial state became interested in using revenue generated through trade to establish public health projects, water systems, housing and schools (Havinden & Meredith, 1993).

For the colony to continue as a source of raw materials and a market for imported industrial goods, some conditions were necessary. Agricultural production systems had to perform at a maximum level and agricultural produce also had to fetch consistently high prices in overseas markets. Events during and after the two world wars (1914–1918 and 1939–1945), did not sustain these conditions. The war disrupted the external market for agricultural exports, upset transport links and reduced market prices and revenue. One major feature of colonial agricultural policy was to leave the systems of production intact and interfere in marketing arrangements, largely because production was in the hands of the local people and marketing was in the hands of the expatriate population. This was because the colonial order "was managed by extreme caution" (Kay, 1972, p. 9). Leaving production in local hands offered a workable arrangement because policymaking was the product of "tension between the demands that were voiced and the fears of the future and visions of political disruption were a continuing preoccupation" (Phillips, 1989, p. 160). Thus, the colonial state in many African countries established agricultural marketing boards which eventually became a mechanism for surplus extraction and enabled the colonies "to finance their own conquest" (Young, 1988, p. 45), albeit provided a powerful lesson for the post-colonial state.

An aspect of the moral imperative in the post-World War era was industrialization. The Colonial Development Corporation, established in 1947 under the 1940 Colonial Development Welfare Act, was to spotlight schemes for primary production, in partnership with colonial or other Commonwealth governments (Havinden & Meredith, 1993, p. 229). The development corporation was a major shift in colonial thinking to the extent that it provided the machinery "for the promotion of industrial capitalism within the colonies" (Phillips, 1989, p. 151). Killick (1978) argues that in the case of Ghana, and other African countries by extension, these processes were consistent with the prevailing theories of modernization that equated development with industrialization. This is the backdrop to the post-colonial state's involvement in the establishment of import-substitution industries and a host of public sector organizations in agriculture and other sectors of the economy (finance, transportation and utility companies).

Much of the development discourse and literature relies heavily on a historical characterization of African governments and cultural predispositions (Chabal & Daloz, 2006). It is necessary to trace the origins of development to understand the historical processes that have generated the present circumstances. The post-colonial state played a dominant role in development because of two historical factors (Sandbrook, 1993; Howard, 1978). First, the colonial state established the interventionist tradition and the post-colonial state simply followed that practice. The second factor, a by-product of colonial rule, was the absence of indigenous private investors. During the colonial era, administrators privileged expatriate firms over local or indigenous ones in policy formulation. Participation by indigenous entrepreneurs was limited in the formal institutions of state (legislature) and informal ones (social clubs). Many post-colonial governments also stifled the emergence of a business class for fear of a business elite competing with the state. Accordingly, the post-colonial state "assumed not only the tasks of all modern states: protector of public order and property rights, provider of social and physical infrastructure, and macro-economic manager. . . . It also appropriated the roles of economic regulator, planner, and, to varying degrees, entrepreneur" (Sandbrook, 1993, p. 22). The expanded role of the state in development called for institutional capacity and resources, raising questions about the nature and structure of the state as well as the relationship between the state and major social groups in the agricultural sector.

In terms of its nature, one relevant attribute of the colonial and post-colonial state is its 'softness'. 'Soft' states scarcely enforce their policies because of their inability to coerce their citizens and thus are unable to attain specific policy objectives (Myrdal, 1968). Berman (1984) presents two contrasting descriptions: the first view is that the colonial state is 'strong' in bringing colonized Africans into line for attaining the colonial development mandate and the post-colonial state is the pervasive institution and reliable ally for development. The second view depicts the colonial state as 'weak' and struggling to maintain a delicate balance among various social groups to attain the colonial mandate, while the post-colonial state fails as a development institution. The contrasting depictions demonstrate state and society relations and, by implication, limits on state power (Migdal, Kohli & Shue, 1994; Chazan, Lewis, Mortimer, Rothchild & Stedman, 1999).

The state bureaucracy had problems ranging from the paucity of staff, the caliber of colonial administrators, to the absence of any system of training for local staff (Tordoff, 1993; Davidson, 1992; Kulick, 1979). This state of affairs, in view of the frailty of colonial rule, implies that costly political decisions would not be taken even if there would be potential benefits for agriculture. For the colonial state it was difficult to enact or implement the relevant or required policies to address agricultural problems without the risk of a negative reaction from the farmers. One foremost concern of the post-colonial African state was to Africanize the civil service. Through this policy, 50% of Africans occupied the civil service in Ghana, Nigeria and Sierra Leone in the early decades of the post-colonial period (Chazan et al., 1999, p. 43). The program was not accompanied by any systematic training or careful transfer of power. Therefore, the post-colonial bureaucracy operated in an atmosphere where the "functional notion of government . . . did not distinguish between decision making and implementation roles" (Chazan et al., 1999, p. 42). Without any structural changes, the post-colonial administrative structures "and the concepts that guided their creation and operations, reflected the concerns of their colonial designers. These institutions, together with their underlying assumptions, were handed over virtually intact and constituted the organizational legacy of African states at independence" (Chazan et al., 1999, p. 45). In an apparent haste to respond to the demands of self-government, institutions under the post-colonial state 'overcentralized' and 'overdeveloped' (Alavi, 1972) their functions.

Centralized bureaucratic system of colonial administration proved to be inadequate to the many tasks of development facing the newly independent African countries, because of the lack of qualified personnel. The same bureaucrats initiated and implemented state policies, and "because of the incompetence of existing administrative agencies, political leadership respond[ed] by administrative shortcuts, and setting up new and hopefully more responsive administrative units" (Berg, 1971, p. 210). These bloated government bureaucracies were the focus of significant restructuring under structural adjustment programs (SAPs) in several African countries in the 1980s and 1990s (Djokoto-Asem, 2003). In the last decade, aspects of the restructuring of state institutions accompanied theories of globalization, explicit calls for a minimal role of the state in the economic sphere and the ascendancy of the private sector. However, Bryceson et al. (2010) argue that an institutional and historical examination of the structural adjustment programs in African countries suggest that African agriculture's poor performance is not necessarily due to the negative influence of African governments, but could also, in large part, be attributed to the policies advocated by the international financial institutions and donor countries. They suggest that the resolution of the problems associated with these policies to call for improving the ability of African farmers to benefit from new agrarian technologies that raise staple food productivity and thereby enhance food security and national stability.

Ever since commercial agriculture began in the colonial era, agricultural policies have had a differential impact and response from social groups within the agricultural sector, specifically producers and buyers or distributors. Historically, small-scale farmers were at the forefront of the production of agricultural export crops throughout the region (Williams, 1981;

Hill, 1963). The underlying reason, as mentioned earlier, was the inability of the colonial state to manage the implications of changing local production systems without risking the colonial order. Indeed, the strategy or policy on agricultural production was "to *modify*, rather than sweep aside . . . pre-colonial systems of agricultural production" (Boone, 1994, p. 112, italics in original).

In any case, the boom and bust cycle of agricultural produce markets had an impact on the profit margin of merchant firms and on the income of farmers and each took unilateral actions to protect its interests. Merchant firms formed a group, the 'Pool', and consolidated their activities, took to information-sharing, price fixing and other arrangements in the purchase of export of produce (Bauer, 1963; Miles, 1978; Simensen, 1990). Farmers, in response, first decided to form producers' associations and later embarked on a hold-up, refusing to sell to the merchant firms. The hold-up and the worsening relationship between the farmers and merchant firms threatened to dry up government revenue and the participation of other actors like brokers, drivers and women traders that "created a mood of discontent and disillusion graver than anything before" (Miles, 1978, p. 169). The response of the colonial state to the hold-up led directly to the institutionalization of agricultural marketing boards, which was a source of finance to the state after World War II until the 1980s (Beckman, 1976).

The agricultural aspects of SAPs and the subsequent calls for a changing role of the state, as the literature has shown, are consistent with the wider trends in the theoretical and policy aspects of globalization in general and globalization of agriculture in particular (Satgar, 2011; Yusuf, 2009; Baffes, 2009; Gibbon, 2007; Puplampu, 2006; Gross, 2006). One area of intense focus is agricultural marketing institutions and several African governments, which since the mid-1980s have restructured their agricultural marketing boards with varying outcomes (World Bank, 1994). The differential outcomes can be traced to several factors, including the political context of the restructuring exercise and the fact that the restructuring also had implications for the supply or access to relevant agricultural inputs (Banful, 2011). The recent assessments of restructured agricultural marketing and inputs supply institutions in Burkina Faso (cotton), Mali (mango), Rwanda (coffee), Ghana (cocoa and fertilizer), Kenya (fertilizer) and Malawi (fertilizer and credit subsidies, controlled prices) reinforce reasons for the differential outcomes: the inability to pursue a full-blown privatization of agricultural markets and the supply of inputs; the enduring relevance of the state; the need to pay a closer attention to the local context of the policy framework; human resource and institutional capacity considerations (Ariga & Jayne, 2011; Banful, 2011; Boudreaux, 2011; Cooksey, 2011; Dorward, Chirwa & Jayne, 2011; Kaminski, 2011; Kolavalli & Vigneri, 2011; Sangho, Labaste & Ravry, 2011).

RE-THINKING THE STATE IN AGRICULTURAL INSTITUTIONS AND POLICIES IN AFRICA AND CONCLUSION

The genesis of development theory and practice has been closely aligned with the state, not only with respect to development in general, but also agriculture in particular. Hence, the continuing significance of the state has been part of the development discourse. For example, the Keynesian model at the center of the development debate in the 1950s and 1960 favored a centralized presence of the African state in development planning, highlighting the state's role in addressing underdevelopment (Galli, 1992; Hettne, 1991). Both modernization and dependency/world-system theories privileged the role of the post-colonial African state and presented it as an effective ally in the development possibilities in the early post-colonial era. Contemporary globalization proceeds from the standpoint that a minimal role of the state in the economy will bring about the required benefits to society (Schuurman, 2001; Hoogvelt, 2001). However, analysis of agricultural globalization in Africa and other continents demonstrates a continuing presence of the state (Puplampu, 2003, 2006). The question thus is not whether or not the state plays or should play any role in the agricultural sector, but what role it should play, if at all.

The theoretical ambiguities of decentering the state in the development discourse and search for a viable option call for re-thinking state–society relations. The African state, like its global counterparts, continues to be at the center of agricultural policy and institutional issues, for example, the case of the global and continental development initiatives. The UNDP's (2003) Millennium Development Goals (MDGs) is first and foremost a call by and on states as well as a state-driven agenda. To be sure, global and other multilateral policy and institutional initiatives continue to implicate or suggest the presence of the state. It is therefore not surprising that at the continental level, the African Union's (AU) pronouncements also involve the state. For example, AU's major initiatives on agriculture, the New Partnership for African Development (NEPAD) and the Comprehensive Africa Agriculture Development Programme (CAADP) are also both state led and state-driven. So also are specific agricultural initiatives on research—the Forum for Agricultural Research in Africa (FARA) and in biotechnology like the 2003 African Model Law on Safety in Biotechnology, the Africa Science and Technology Consolidated Plan of Action as well as the Freedom to Innovate Policy Documents (Juma & Serageldin, 2007; FARA, 2006; NEPAD, 2001, 2003, 2006). The biotechnology initiatives have significant implications for an understanding of the broader issue of the state, institutional capacity and policies in agricultural research.

The history of funding regime in agricultural research in Africa, as in other parts of the world, also revolves around the state (Beintema & Stads, 2011; Cohen, 2005; Cohen & Pinstrup-Andersen, 2002). It is known that the level of public funding of agricultural research in Africa, with the exception of South Africa, has lagged behind that of other societies. According to FAO (2004), public agricultural research institutions have suffered from financial constrains in recent years, due to or in response to the changing role of the state under contemporary globalization. Nevertheless, there is also evidence to suggest that other developing countries, for example, China, India, Taiwan and Korea, continue to support their public agricultural research institutions (Beintema & Stads, 2011; FAO, 2004). That suggests that African states lack the political will to fund agricultural policy and institutions (Makinde, 2009).

The argument then is how the state and the broader civil society, working together, can bring about useful agricultural policy and institutions. One critical outcome of globalization is the emergence of a vibrant civil society, in this case, agricultural producers or associations that are able to and are in contestation with the state when it comes to agricultural policy and institutions. Halpin (2005) identifies three aspects of the relationship between agricultural producers and the state in a global era: decline, resilience and adaptation and/or transformation. The decline thesis suggests that the role of agricultural producers in policy and institutions is undermined in agricultural globalization because of the changing role of the state and the renewed importance of multilateral institutions. The resilience argument presents a central role for the state, notwithstanding the complexities of globalization, because of the need for partnerships and other forms of cooperation the state has to forge with agricultural producers. Finally, the adaptation and/or transformation thesis suggests that agricultural producers "may not merely adapt to new conditions, but fundamentally transform their existing structures, roll-over into new structures or be taken over or subsumed by new or existing groups" (Halpin, 2005, p. 22).

An analysis of cashew nut producers in Mozambique, poultry farmers in Ghana, reinstituted fertilizer subsidy programs in Malawi, Nigeria, Tanzania, Kenya and Ghana and the emergence of cooperatives in Ethiopia and Tanzania offer empirical cases on state–farmer relations in a global context and the value of Halpin's (2005) model (Banful, 2011; Francesconi & Heerink, 2011; Barham & Chitemi, 2009; Morris, Kelly, Kopicki & Byerlee, 2007; Christian Aid, 2005; Hanlon, 2001, 2000). First, the analysis shows the continuing role of the state in agricultural policy and institutions, even if in significantly different forms from the early post-colonial era. Second, the cases, particularly the cashew nut and poultry farmers, occurred in a context in which the state is focusing on the plight of farmers as citizens to contest the power of multilateral organizations and the farmers as citizens are contesting the state in terms of agricultural policymaking. The democratic context in addressing specific agricultural problems is clear evidence of resilience in Halpin's (2005) model. Hopefully, the resilience, over time, will lead to adaptation and/or transformation.

CONCLUSION

The primary interest in this chapter has been to analyze the changing role of the African state in the development possibilities of the region. Focusing on both the colonial and post-colonial state, the chapter showed significant areas of the state's role in agricultural institutions and policies. The state's role has persisted even in the current context of globalization, although in different forms. Both the colonial and post-colonial states were involved in establishing agricultural institutions and initiating policies. Both also had to pursue these activities with a keen eye on the broader society. The colonial state, cognizant of its precarious stand in terms of legitimacy, pursued or responded with half-hearted policies that would not undermine the colonial order.

Post-colonial states were also caught up in some of the contradictions of their colonial predecessors. Broader civil society activities continue to condition the post-colonial state's role in the institutional and policy context. A noteworthy and significant contemporary difference is how the broader civil society, within a context of democratic governance, seems to be asserting itself and thus is resilient in the policy and institutional terrain. Cooperatives, often seen as relics of a by-gone era, have survived and are serving as a veritable platform for the organization of farmers (Francesconi & Heerink, 2011; Wanyama, Develtere & Pollet, 2009). The question now is how both the state and society can devise novel ways to deal with and relate to each other in the institutional and policy requirements for optimum outcomes in Africa's agricultural development agenda.

REFERENCES

African Capacity Building Foundation (ACBF). (2012). *Africa capacity indicators 2012—Capacity development for agricultural transformation and food security*. Harare: Africa Capacity Building Foundation.

Alavi, H. (1972). The state in post-colonial societies: Pakistan and Bangladesh. *New Left Review*, 74(July–August), 59–81.

Ariga, J. & Jayne, T.S. (2011). Fertilizer in Kenya: Factors driving the increase in usage by smallholder farmers. In P. Chuhan-Pole & M. Angwafo (Eds.), *Yes Africa can: Success stories from a dynamic continent* (pp. 269–288). Washington, DC: World Bank.

Baffes, J. (2009). The 'full potential' of Uganda's cotton industry. *Development Policy Review*, 27(1), 67–85.

Banful, A.B. (2011). Old problems in the new solutions? Politically motivated allocation of program benefits and the 'new' fertilizer subsidies. *World Development*, 39(7), 1166–1176.

Barham, J. & Chitemi, C. (2009). Collective action initiatives to improve marketing performance: Lessons from farmer groups in Tanzania. *Food Policy*, 34, 53–59.

Bates, R.H. & Block, S. (2011). Political institutions and agricultural trade interventions in Africa. *American Journal of Agricultural Economics*, 93(2), 317–323.

Bauer, P.T. (1963). *West African trade: A study of competition, oligopoly, monopoly in a changing economy*. London: Routledge and Kegan Paul.

Beckman, B. (1976). *Organizing the farmers: Cocoa politics and national development in Ghana*. Uppsala: Scandinavian Institute of African Studies.

Beintema, N. & Stads, J. (2011). *African agricultural R&D in the new millennium: Progress for some, challenges for many*. Washington, DC: International Food Policy Research Institute.

Berg, E.J. (1971). Structural transformation versus gradualism: Recent economic development in Ghana and Ivory Coast. In P. Foster & A.R. Zolberg (Eds.), *Ghana and the Ivory Coast perspectives on modernization* (pp. 187–230). Chicago: University of California Press.

Berman, B. (1984). Structure and process in the bureaucratic states of Colonial Africa. *Development and Change*, 15, 161–202.

Boone, C. (1994). States and ruling classes in post-colonial Africa: The enduring contradictions of power. In J.S. Migdal, A. Kohli & V. Shue (Eds.), *State power and social forces: Domination and transformation in the Third World* (pp. 108–140). Cambridge: Cambridge University Press.

Boudreaux, K.C. (2011). Economic liberalization in Rwanda's coffee sector: A better brew for success. In P. Chuhan-Pole & M. Angwafo (Eds.), *Yes Africa can: Success stories from a dynamic continent* (pp. 185–199). Washington, DC: World Bank.

Bruntrup, M. (2011). The comprehensive Africa agriculture development—An assessment of a Pan-African attempt to revitalize agriculture. *Quarterly Journal of International Agriculture*, 50(1), 79–106.

Bryceson, D., Sarkar, P., Fennell, S. & Singh, A. (2010). *Globalisation, structural adjustment and African agriculture: Analysis and evidence*. Cambridge: Centre for Business Research, University of Cambridge, Working Paper No. 414.

Chabal, P. & Daloz, J.-P. (2006). *Culture troubles: Politics and the interpretation of meaning*. London: C. Hurst & Co.

Chazan, N., Lewis, P., Mortimer, R.A., Rothchild, D. & Stedman, S.J. (Eds.). (1999). *Politics and society in contemporary Africa* (3rd ed.). Boulder, CO: Lynne Rienner.

Christian Aid. (2005). *The damage done—Aid, death and dogma*. London: Christian Aid.

Chuhan-Pole, P. & Angwafo, M. (Eds.). (2011). *Yes Africa can: Success stories from a dynamic continent*. Washington, DC: World Bank.

Cohen, J.I. (2005). Poorer nations turn to publicly developed GM crops. *Nature Biotechnology*, 23(1), 27–33.

Cohen, J.I. & Pinstrup-Andersen, P. (2002). Biotechnology and the public good. *SciDev Net* Retrieved October 15, 2005 from http://www.scidev.net/en/opinions/biotechnology-and-the-public-good.html

Cooksey, B. (2011). Marketing reform? The rise and fall of agricultural liberalisation in Tanzania. *Development Policy Review*, 29(Supplement), S57–81.

Davidson, B. (1992). *The black man's burden: Africa and the curse of the nation-state*. New York: Random House.

Djokoto-Asem, E.D. (2003). 'A plurality of resistances' to economic reform: The case of state-owned enterprises. In W.J. Tettey, K.P. Puplampu & B.J. Berman (Eds.), *Critical perspectives on politics and socio-economic development in Ghana* (pp. 177–200). Leiden: Brill.

Dorward, A., Chirwa, E. & Jayne, T.S. (2011). Malawi's agricultural input subsidy program experience over 2005–09. In P. Chuhan-Pole & M. Angwafo (Eds.), *Yes Africa can: Success stories from a dynamic continent* (pp. 289–317). Washington, DC: World Bank.

Engels, F. (1884/1986). *The origin of the family, private property and the state*. Harmondsworth: Penguin Books.

Food and Agricultural Organization (FAO). (2004). *The state of food and agriculture, 2003–4: Agricultural biotechnology, meeting the needs of the poor?* Rome: FAO.

Forum for Agricultural Research in Africa (FARA). (2006). *Framework for African agricultural productivity.* Accra, Ghana: FARA.

Francesconi, G.N. & Heerink, N. (2011). Ethiopian agricultural cooperatives in an era of global commodity exchange: Does organizational form matter? *Journal of African Economies*, 20(1), 153–177.

Galli, R.E. (1992). Winners and losers in development and anti-development theory. In R.E. Galli (Ed.), *Rethinking the third world: Contributions towards a new conceptualization* (pp. 1–27). New York: Crane Russak.

Gerth, H.H. & Mills, C.W. (1946). *From Max Weber: Essays in sociology.* New York: Oxford University Press.

Gibbon, P. (2007). Africa, tropical commodity policy and the WTO Doha round. *Development Policy Review*, 25(1), 43–70.

Gross, A. (2006). Can Sub-Saharan African countries defend their trade and development interests effectively in the WTO? The case of cotton. *European Journal of Development Research*, 18(3), 368–386.

Halpin, D. (2005). Agricultural interest groups and global challenges: Decline and resilience. In D. Halpin, (Ed.), *Surviving global change? Agricultural interest groups in comparative perspective* (pp. 1–28). Aldershot: Ashgate.

Hancock, W.K. (1942). *Survey of British Commonwealth Affairs: Problems of economic policy 1918–1939.* London: Oxford University Press.

Hanlon, J. (2000). Power without responsibility: The World Bank and Mozambican cashew nuts. *Review of African Political Economy*, 83, 29–45.

Hanlon, J. (2001). Mozambique wins long battle over cashew nuts and sugar. *Review of African Political Economy*, 83, 111–112.

Havinden, M. & Meredith, D. (1993). *Colonialism and development: Britain and its tropical colonies, 1850–1960.* New York: Routledge.

Hettne, B. (1991). *Development theory and the three worlds.* New York: Wiley.

Hill, P. (1963). *The migrant cocoa farmer of Southern Ghana: A study in rural capitalism.* Cambridge: Cambridge University Press.

Hoogvelt, A.M.M. (2001). *Globalization and the post-colonial world—The new political economy of development* (2nd ed.). Baltimore, MD: The Johns Hopkins University Press.

Howard, R. (1978). *Colonialism and underdevelopment in Ghana.* London: Croom Helm.

Juma, C. & Serageldin, I. (2007). *Freedom to innovate: Biotechnology in Africa's development—A report of the high-level African panel on modern biotechnology.* Addis Ababa and Pretoria: African Union (AU) and New Partnership for Africa's Development (NEPAD).

Kaminski, J. (2011). Cotton dependence in Burkina Faso: Constraints and opportunities for balanced growth. In P. Chuhan-Pole & M. Angwafo (Eds.), *Yes Africa can: Success stories from a dynamic continent* (pp. 107–124). Washington, DC: World Bank.

Kay, G.B. (1972). *The political economy of colonialism in Ghana documents and statistics 1900–1960.* Cambridge: Cambridge University Press.

Killick, T. (1978). *Development economics in action: A study of economic policies in Ghana.* New York: St. Martin's Press.

Kolavalli, S. & Vigneri, M. (2011). Cocoa in Ghana: Shaping the success of an economy. In P. Chuhan-Pole & M. Angwafo (Eds.), *Yes Africa can: Success stories from a dynamic continent* (pp. 201–211). Washington, DC: World Bank.

Kulick, H. (1979). *The imperial bureaucrat: The colonial administrative service in the Gold Coast, 1920–1939.* Stanford, CA: Stanford University Press.

Larrain, J. (1989). *Theories of development.* Cambridge: Polity Press.

Leys, C. (1975). *Underdevelopment in Kenya: The political economy of neo-colonialism 1964–1971.* Berkeley: University of California Press.

Lugard, F.D.L. (1965). *The dual mandate in British Tropical Africa* (5th ed.). London: Frank Cass and Co.

Makinde, D. (2009). *NEPAD biosciences initiative: The African biosafety network of expertise.* Paper presented at the Delivering Agricultural Biotechnology to African Farmers: Linking Economic Research to Decision Making at Imperial Resort Beach Hotel, May 19–21, Entebbe, Uganda.

Migdal, J.S., Kohli, A. & Shue, V. (Eds.). (1994). *State power and social forces domination and transformation in the Third World.* Cambridge: Cambridge University Press.

Miles, J. (1978). Rural protest in the Gold Coast: The cocoa hold-ups, 1908–1938. In C. Dewey & A.G. Hopkins (Eds.), *The imperial impact: Studies in the economic history of Africa and India* (pp. 152–170). London: Athlon Press.

Morris, M., Kelly, A., Kopicki, R. & Byerlee, D. (2007). *Fertilizer use in African agriculture: Lessons learned and good practice guidelines.* Washington, DC: World Bank.

Myrdal, G. (1968). *Asian drama: An inquiry into the poverty of nations.* New York: Twentieth Century Fund.

New Partnership for African Development (NEPAD). (2001). *NEPAD policy document English version.* Midrand: NEPAD.

New Partnership for African Development (NEPAD). (2003). *Comprehensive Africa agriculture development programme.* Midrand: NEPAD.

New Partnership for African Development (NEPAD). (2006). *Africa's science and technology consolidated plan of action.* NEPAD, Pretoria: Lynnwood.

Phillips, A. (1989). *The enigma of colonialism: British policy in West Africa.* London: James Currey.

Puplampu, K.P. (2003). Globalization of Agriculture: Lessons from Ghana. In M.S. Smith (Ed.), *Globalizing Africa* (pp. 385–396). Trenton, NJ: Africa World Press.

Puplampu, K.P. (2006). The World Trade Organization, global trade and agriculture. In M.S. Smith (Ed.), *Beyond the 'African tragedy': Discourses on development and the global economy* (pp. 233–245). Aldershot: Ashgate Publishing.

Rauch, T. (2011). Fundamentals of African agriculture. *Quarterly Journal of International Agriculture*, 50(1), 9–27.

Sandbrook, R. (1993). *The politics of Africa's economic recovery.* Cambridge, UK: Cambridge University Press.

Sangho, Y., Labaste, P. & Ravry, C. (2011). Growing Mali's mango exports: Linking farmers to market through innovation in the value chain. In P. Chuhan-Pole & M. Angwafo (Eds.), *Yes Africa can: Success stories from a dynamic continent* (pp. 167–183). Washington, DC: World Bank.

Satgar, V. (2011). Challenging the globalized agro-food complex: Farming cooperatives and the emerging solidarity economy alternative in South Africa. *Working USA*, 14(2), 177–190.

Saul, J.S. (1974). The state in post-colonial societies: Tanzania. In R. Miliband, & J. Saville (Eds.), *Socialist register* (pp. 349–372). London: Merlin Press.

Schuurman, F. (Ed.). (2001). *Globalization and development studies—Challenges for the 21st century.* London: SAGE Publications.

Seck, D. & Busari, D.T. (Eds.). (2009). *Growth and development in Africa.* Trenton, NJ: Africa World Press.

Simensen, J. (1990). Farmers, chiefs and the world market the Gold Coast cocoa hold-ups of the 1930s. In M. Lundahl & T. Svensson (Eds.), *Agrarian society in history essays in honour of Magnus Morner* (pp. 239–260). New York: Routledge.

Smith, M.S. (Ed.). (2003). *Globalizing Africa*. Trenton, NJ: Africa World Press.
Smith, M.S. (Ed.). (2006). *Beyond the 'African tragedy': Discourses on development and the global economy*. Aldershot: Ashgate Publishing.
Taeb, M. & Zakri A.H. (Eds.). (2008). *Agriculture, human security, and peace: A crossroad in African development*. West Lafayette, IN: Purdue University Press.
Tordoff, W. (1993). *Government and politics in Africa* (2nd ed.). Bloomington, IN: Indiana University Press.
United Nations Development Program (UNDP). (2003). *Human Development Report 2003 Millennium Development Goals: A compact among nations to end human poverty*. New York: Oxford University Press.
Wanyama, F., Develtere, P. & Pollet, I. (2009). Reinventing the wheel? African cooperatives in a liberalized economic environment. *Annals of Public and Cooperative Economics*, 80(3), 361–392.
Williams, G. (1981). The World Bank and the peasant problem. In J. Heyer, P. Roberts & G. Williams (Eds.), *Rural development in Tropical Africa* (pp. 16–51). London: Macmillan.
World Bank. (1981). *Accelerated development in Sub-Saharan Africa: An agenda for action*. Washington, DC: World Bank.
World Bank. (1989). *Sub-Saharan Africa: From crisis to sustainable growth, a long-term perspective study*. Washington, DC: World Bank.
World Bank. (1994). *Adjustment in Africa reforms, results and the road ahead*. Washington, DC: World Bank.
World Bank. (2007). *World development report, 2008—Agriculture for development*. Washington, DC: World Bank.
World Bank. (2012). *Africa's pulse: An analysis of issues shaping Africa's economic future*. Washington, DC: The World Bank.
Young, C. (1988). The African colonial state and its political legacy. In D. Rothchild & N. Chazan (Eds.), *The precarious balance: State and society in Africa* (pp. 25–66). London: Westview Press.
Yusuf, G. (2009). The marginalization of African agricultural trade and development: A case study of the WTO's efforts to cater to African agricultural trading interests particularly cotton and sugar. *African Journal of International and Comparative Law*, 17(2), 213–239.

Contributors

Ali A. Abdi is Professor of International Education and Social Foundations of Education in the Department of Educational Policy Studies at the University of Alberta, Edmonton, Canada, where he is also Co-Director of the Centre for Global Citizenship Education and Research (CGCER). His areas of research include international studies in education, citizenship and human rights education and decolonizing philosophies and methodologies of education.

George J. Sefa Dei [Nana Sefa Atweneboah I] is Professor of Humanities, Social Sciences and Social Justice Education at the Ontario Institute for Studies in Education of the University of Toronto (OISE/UT). His teaching and research interests are in indigenous philosophies, anti-racism, minority schooling, international development and anti-colonial theory. Among his many books include *Anti-Racism Education: Theory and Practice* and *Teaching Africa: Towards Transgressive Pedagogy*. In June of 2007, George J. Sefa Dei was installed as a traditional chief, the Adumakwaahene of Asokore, near Koforidua in the New Juaben Traditional Area of Ghana. His stool name is Nana Sefa Atweneboah I.

Berhanu Demeke received a master's degree from the University of Alberta in Political Science and is currently pursuing Ph.D. in theoretical, cultural and international studies at the Department of Educational Policy Studies at the same university. His research interests include citizenship education, communitarianism and globalization. His academic interests draw on his work experience with immigrants, refugees and African diaspora in Edmonton, Alberta.

Lamine Diallo is an Associate Professor in the Leadership Program at Wilfrid Laurier University, Brantford, Canada. He is the co-founding member of the Tshepo Institute for the Study of Contemporary Africa, which is a research group interested in African issues using a multidisciplinary perspective. Lamine's research interests are in leadership and governance, development through co-operatives and integration and diversity among Africans in North America.

Gloria T. Emeagwali is a Professor of History and African Studies at Central Connecticut State University, New Britain, Connecticut. She is also the Chief Editor of *Africa Update* and the author of several websites, including the UNESCO award winning resource www.africanhistory.net. She has authored and edited seven books and 60 journal and book articles. Her teaching interests are in world history, African history, the African diaspora in the Caribbean and history of South Africa. Her current research is on the historical context of African indigenous technology and sustained economic growth.

Siendou Konate is a Fulbright alumnus with a Ph.D. in Comparative Literature from the State University of New York at Binghamton. He specialized in African and African American literatures and cultures. He is currently an Assistant Professor of American Studies and Comparative Literature at the University of Cocody, Abidjan, Cote d'Ivoire. His research focuses on violence in African American literature and in West African Anglophone and Francophone literatures. His publications are in protest and conflicts in African and Afro-American literatures and cultures.

Ginette Lafrenière is an Associate Professor at the Lyle S. Hallman Faculty of Social Work at Wilfrid Laurier University, Canada. She is the director of the Social Innovation Research Group (SIRG) comprised of graduate students and community partners dedicated to community-based research and university-community collaboration. Her research is on survivors of war, torture, organized violence and survivors of intimate partner violence.

Ngoni Makuvaza is a Senior Lecturer at the University of Zimbabwe, in the Department of Educational Foundations. He lectures Philosophy of Education to undergraduate and graduate students. His research interests are in applied philosophy and education in the post-colonial era. He has published extensively on philosophy, education, liberation and *hunhu/ubuntu* in post-colonial states.

Oliver Masakure is Assistant Professor at Wilfrid Laurier University, Brantford, Canada. He is a development economist with research interests in health and labor economics. He has publications on the economics of food nutrition and food safety, food trade and entrepreneurship in sub-Saharan Africa. He is a Research Fellow and Associate Director of the Tshepo Institute for the Study of Contemporary Africa housed at Wilfrid Laurier's Brantford campus.

Musembi Nungu is a Postdoctoral Research Fellow at the Centre for Global Citizenship Education and Research, Department of Educational Policy Studies, University of Alberta, Canada. He teaches comparative and international education in the Department of Educational Foundations,

University of Nairobi. His scholarly interests include teacher education, education for citizenship, rural education, teacher management and participatory policy processes.

Desmond Ikenna Odugu is Assistant Professor of Education at Lake Forest College. He received his Ph.D. in cultural and educational policy studies (with focus in comparative and international education) from Loyola University Chicago. His academic interests are in philosophy, educational psychology, mass communication, history and political economics. He researches on language in multilingual societies and the historiography of Western education in non-Western contexts. He is also Director of the Institute for Research and International Studies (IRIS), an international research, policy analysis and advocacy network.

Korbla P. Puplampu is Chair of the Department of Sociology at Grant MacEwan University, Edmonton, Canada. He has a Ph.D. in sociology as well as an M.Ed. in international and global education. His research interests are in the global restructuring of agriculture and higher education, global citizenship, diaspora and identity politics.

Grace John Rwiza is currently a Ph.D. student in the Department of Educational Policy Studies at the University of Alberta. She has a master's degree in education from the University of Dar-es-Salaam. Previously, she was assistant director, Primary Education Department, Ministry of Education and Vocational Training, Tanzania. She has also worked as a classroom teacher; head-teacher, district and regional adult education coordinator; regional academic officer; and regional education officer.

Edward Shizha is an Associate Professor in Contemporary Studies/Youth and Children's Studies and a Fellow of Tshepo Institute for the Study of Contemporary Africa at Wilfrid Laurier University, Brantford, Canada. He has a Ph.D. in sociology of education with academic interests in contemporary social problems and education including: globalization, development theories, post-colonialism and indigenous knowledges in Africa. He has published four books and a number of book chapters and articles in peer-reviewed journals.

Touorouzou Herve Some is a Fulbright scholar with a Ph.D. in educational policy from the University of Buffalo, New York. He has published several peer-reviewed book chapters and journal articles in educational reform and financing higher education in Africa. Other research interests include globalization, neoliberalism, alternative forms of education and gender bias in education. He is currently an Assistant Professor at Ripon College, Wisconsin, where he teaches social and philosophical foundations of education and issues on Africa and its diaspora.

Index